D2

D0699554

THE CENSORSHIP OF ENGLISH DRAMA
1824–1901

HOUSTON PUBLIC LIBRARY

THE CENSORSHIP OF ENGLISH DRAMA 1824–1901

JOHN RUSSELL STEPHENS

Lecturer in English
University College of Swansea

CAMBRIDGE UNIVERSITY PRESS

Cambridge

London   New York   New Rochelle

Melbourne   Sydney

HOUSTON PUBLIC LIBRARY   In *ech*³

Published by the Press Syndicate of the University of Cambridge
The Pitt Building, Trumpington Street, Cambridge CB2 1RP
32 East 57th Street, New York, NY 10022, USA
296 Beaconsfield Parade, Middle Park, Melbourne 3206, Australia

R0147208314
HUM

© Cambridge University Press 1980

First published 1980

Photoset and Printed in Malta by Interprint Limited

British Library Cataloguing in Publication Data
Stephens, John Russell
The censorship of English drama, 1824–1901.
1. Theater — Censorship — England — History —
19th century
1. Title
792   PN2044.G6   79–41601
ISBN 0 521 23021 7

To my Mother and Father

CONTENTS

ILLUSTRATIONS

ACKNOWLEDGEMENTS

To record my gratitude to those who have helped me in the writing of this book is a pleasing task. One of my earliest debts is to Professor Cecil Price of the Department of English, University College of Swansea, who first suggested to me the topic of Victorian dramatic censorship, who supervised most of my original research, and whose meticulous standards of scholarship have always been an inspiration. My debt to my friend and former colleague Professor Leonard Conolly, now of the University of Alberta, Edmonton, is almost equally long-standing. Without his initiative and encouragement this work might never have been published.

Draft versions of the MS. have been read at various times by Professor Peter Thomson (University of Exeter), Emeritus Professor James F. Arnott (University of Glasgow), and Dr David Mayer III (University of Manchester). Their advice and constructive criticism have been invaluable; but, needless to say, the responsibility for any 'wild blunders and risible absurdities' which remain is solely my own.

I express my thanks to Dr James A. Davies, the late Professor Alan S. Downer, Miss Mary Barham Johnson, Professor Martin Meisel, and Professor Peter Wearing for help in many ways. As ever, the staffs of such institutions as the Students' Room, Department of MSS., British Library, the Public Record Office, and the Library, University College of Swansea have been most courteous and long-suffering. I must record also the efficient, friendly, and conscientious way in which my type-script has been prepared for the printer by the staff of Cambridge University Press, notably by my editor, Sarah Stanton, and my sub-editor, Chris Lyall Grant. For much of the photographic work involved in the illustrations I am indebted to Mr Roger Davies.

The following individuals and institutions have kindly granted me permission for the use of copyright material: the Trustees of the Chatsworth Settlement and the Courtauld Institute of Art (plate 2); Messrs Methuen and Co. Ltd and Miss Mary Barham Johnson (plate 3); the Director, The Folger Shakespeare Library, Washington, D.C. (plate

4); the Controller, Her Majesty's Stationery Office and the British Library (plates 6 and 7); and Messrs Methuen and Co. Ltd (plate 9); Miss Mary Barham Johnson for the letters of J. M. Kemble and W. B. Donne which she has in her possession; and the British Library, the Public Record Office, and the Controller, Her Majesty's Stationery Office for quotation from the Lord Chamberlain's collection of MS. plays and the Lord Chamberlain's correspondence, all of which material is in Crown copyright.

My greatest debt is acknowledged in the dedication.

Swansea
December 1979   J.R.S.

A NOTE ON REFERENCES

Listed below are certain abbreviated forms of references used throughout the following study.

Manuscript sources

(1) References to Add. MSS. indicate the MS. collections of the British Library. (2) The Lord Chamberlain's Day Books (with entry dates) are cited as Add. MSS. 53,702—8. (3) L.C. refers to the Lord Chamberlain's papers and correspondence in the Public Record Office. This collection is further particularised by classification of the record, followed (after the colon) by the individual volume number. (4) Kemble's fee book (with entry dates) is classified as L.C. 7:19.

In quoting from MS. material I have generally retained the original spelling and punctuation but in a small number of cases I have silently edited for the sake of clarity. Ascription of authorship to MS. plays relies, unless otherwise stated, on the usual published sources.

Printed sources

(1) Allardyce Nicoll, *A History of English Drama 1660—1900* (6 vols., Cambridge, 1965—7) has been shortened to Nicoll. (2) Parliamentary reports on theatres and theatre licensing (1832—1909), printed in *British Sessional Papers: House of Commons 1731—1949*, ed. Edgar L. Erickson (Readex Microprint edition, New York), are referred to by date of publication (e.g. 1832 *Report*), followed by the question number (q.) in the minutes of evidence. Full titles will be found in the bibliography. (3) *DNB* indicates the *Dictionary of National Biography*.

Let the poets remember, when they appear before the licenser or his deputy, that they stand at the tribunal, from which there is no appeal permitted, and where nothing will so well become them as reverence and submission.

Samuel Johnson, 1739

INTRODUCTION

Ever since the enactment of Sir Robert Walpole's Stage Licensing Bill in 1737, dramatic censorship has been a decidedly contentious issue. In the early days it provoked the indignation and scathing irony of Lord Chesterfield and Samuel Johnson and, in its later history, of William Archer and Bernard Shaw. No less than that of their more illustrious predecessors, the work of the two main historians of stage censorship in the present century has originated from the authors' sense of the profound injustices for which it has been held responsible over the past two hundred years and more. Frank Fowell and Frank Palmer's pioneer study of the topic published in 1913 and Richard Findlater's survey in the late 1960s[1] are polemics arising out of the particular circumstances of their day (the aftermath of the Joint Select Committee's 1909 *Report* and the vigorous debate in post-war years which led to the complete abolition of the Lord Chamberlain's powers of censorship in 1968) and both works take up unequivocal stances on the intrinsically evil nature of censorship in all its forms. For this reason their stress lies purely on the alleged capriciousness, stupidity, small-mindedness, and pettiness which characterises its operation. The arguments for and against censorship have had a good airing in recent years and it is not my intention to rehearse them here. My purpose is different and, I hope, more dispassionate. It is to trace the changing faces of censorship and – just as important – of the censors in the years between 1824 and 1901 in the belief that, within a properly illuminated theatrical context, it will serve as a contribution to the history of nineteenth-century drama and to an understanding of the manners, attitudes, and preoccupations of its time.

Dramatic censorship has, of course, no natural limits and, though the period chosen for the present study has a certain integrity of its own, the defining dates have been governed by the availability of the primary source material. In January 1824 a new Examiner of Plays took office and from this date begins the Lord Chamberlain's collection of play scripts submitted for licensing, now housed in the British Library.[2] At

1

the other end of the period, I have opted for a compromise terminal date, the death of Queen Victoria in 1901, since the same collection does not yet extend beyond 1899 (the rest of the MSS. still await transfer from the Lord Chamberlain's Office at St James's Palace) and the theatrical papers and correspondence of the Lord Chamberlain after 1902 in the Public Record Office are not available to public inspection at present.[3]

These two sources have been surprisingly neglected in past discussions of nineteenth-century censorship. The collection in the care of the Public Record Office, comprising some 150 folio volumes relating exclusively to the theatre, offers an unique conspectus of the theatrical life of the period and is particularly rich in evidence of official censorship. The Lord Chamberlain's collection in the British Library contains many thousands of MS. plays, the bulk of them dating from 1843, when the Theatres Act forced all theatres to deposit their plays for official examination and licensing. Inevitably, some MSS. are missing for various reasons (such as the loan of a script to a theatre for copying); but much more unfortunate is the total absence from about 1855 of all plays refused a licence by the Lord Chamberlain. Presumably, plays of that class were returned to the theatre of origin and consigned to ignominy and darkness for evermore.

Neither of these important sources of theatrical material is adequately indexed up to the present. The vast official correspondence in the Public Record Office is classified by year but there are no indexes to the contents of individual volumes. While the first half of the Lord Chamberlain's plays in the British Library has the benefit of a published index,[4] the other half, from 1852 to 1899, relies on a contemporary index (somewhat impractical since it is not keyed to the volumes in which the plays are currently bound) in the shape of the Lord Chamberlain's Day Books.[5] These office books are of real value in another respect, however, because from about 1855 (rarely for earlier years), besides providing useful information on the date of licence, theatre, number of acts, and genre of the plays listed, they record in varying degrees of detail the passages which the Examiner of Plays directed for omission in performance.

In many respects the Victorian theatre — incidentally, the last time when England had a truly popular theatre — was the closest of all art forms to the mass of the public. As Johnson declared about a century earlier:

> The stage but echoes back the publick voice.

2

Plate 1   Specimen entries in the Lord Chamberlain's Day Book, vol. II

> The drama's laws the drama's patrons give,
> For we that live to please, must please to live.[6]

In the history of the institution of stage censorship many of the tensions and cross-currents of the age are thrown into focus: sometimes by way of the licensers' success in charting the public mood, sometimes by their failure. It is for this reason that the topic of censorship is of such enduring interest. The licensers cast themselves in the role of interpreters of the public conscience and tried to objectify the often deeply subjective currents of public opinion.

There are obvious dangers in the kind of study I have undertaken. The main one is of mis-emphasis, more especially as the discussion of censored plays has necessarily to be selective. It is only too easy to overstate the case against censorship or, equally, to underestimate its effects. My intention has been to strike a balance between the two extremes and to attempt an assessment of the effect of stage censorship on

3

the Victorian theatre in the light of the mass of official material now available. I have focused on an issue of great consequence for the theatre but it is one which in all fairness must always be set against the many thousands of dramas, comedies, tragedies, farces, burlesques, and operas performed on the stage unmolested by any form of official censorship.

1

LICENSING AND THE LAW

'Nothing on the stage is to be uttered without licence,' George Colman, the Lord Chamberlain's Examiner of Plays, grandly declared before the Select Committee on Dramatic Literature in 1832.[1] Until the abolition of dramatic censorship little less than a century and a half later, the theatre enjoyed the singular and dubious privilege of subjection to almost uninterrupted (though not necessarily always effective) government control. Censorship did not start in 1737 with Walpole's Stage Licensing Act; that was merely the first determined attempt to organise the random, arbitrary, and often indifferently exercised powers of the Lord Chamberlain into statute form. Remarkably, with that Act as pivotal point, the history of censorship in the theatre stretches very nearly as far back into Tudor times as it does forward into the twentieth century.[2]

Until 1737 the powers of the Lord Chamberlain (and, in earlier times, of the Master of the Revels) were enshrined in a variety of *ad hoc* injunctions and obscure statutes. A century before Walpole, regulation of the stage was working well enough, particularly during the long career of Sir Henry Herbert, who, as Master of the Revels, managed to wield an impressive and wide-ranging authority despite the vagueness of the legislative sanction.[3] As late as 1692 John Dryden recognised in the Lord Chamberlain such comprehensive powers as embraced 'all that belongs to the Decency and Good Manners of the Stage', enabling him to ban all scurrility and profanity and to 'restrain the licentious insolence of Poets and their Actors, in all things that shock the Publick Quiet, or the Reputation of Private Persons, under the notion of *Humour*'.[4] Yet within less than fifty years Robert Walpole, endlessly plagued by the insidious and damaging attacks made on his administration by the drama, had implemented —hurriedly and perhaps ill-considered — what is arguably the most radical and far-reaching piece of theatrical legislation ever written into the statute books.[5] The Stage Licensing Act (10 Geo. II, c. 28) regulated the theatre and its drama for over one hundred years until 1843; and even thereafter it formed the backbone of the law on play licensing and censorship — only certain details were changed by the Theatre Act of 1843 — for a further one hundred and twenty-five years. Under its terms, the Lord Chamberlain was empowered to demand (at least fourteen days before the projected date of performance) a 'true copy' of every new play to be acted 'for hire, gain, or reward' anywhere within Great Britain. The all-important clause relating to the censorship of plays was couched in broad terms granting unlimited power of veto to the Lord Chamberlain:

[I]t shall and may be lawful to and for the said lord chamberlain, for the time being, from time to time, and when, and as often as he shall think fit, to prohibit the acting, performing, or representing, any interlude, tragedy, comedy, opera, play, farce, or other entertainment of the stage, or any act, scene, or part thereof, or any prologue, or epilogue.[6]

Although the law was not usually applied retrospectively, it did enable him to prohibit, when occasion demanded, such 'politically dangerous' plays as Thomas Otway's *Venice Preserv'd* (1682) and even certain of Shakespeare's.[7]

One of the most troublesome results of the 1737 Act was the support it appeared to lend to the perpetuation of the notorious patent theatre monopoly, which by virtue of instruments granted by Charles II at the Restoration — the so-called Killigrew and Davenant patents — conferred upon the two Theatres Royal, Drury Lane and Covent Garden, exclusive rights (in perpetuity) to perform the 'legitimate' or 'regular' drama. The long, tortuous history of the monopoly, and of the ingenious schemes devised by the rival 'minor' theatres (whose repertoires were confined by the terms of their licences to entertainments accompanied by music, unassisted by spoken dialogue) in their heated antagonism against the exclusivity of the patentees, is outside the scope of the present study.[8] But the controversy is of more than peripheral interest for its bearing upon the practical extent of the Lord Chamberlain's authority as censor and for its having given birth to the radical revision of the law on theatrical licensing effected by the Theatre Regulation Act of 1843. By the beginning of our period the patent monopoly, though constantly under attack from the minors, still exercised a stranglehold on the other London theatres. At the same time, the accumulation of laws relating to the theatres produced a state of affairs in which, as Bradlee Watson observes, 'a more illogical and baffling array of legislation is hardly conceivable'.[9] In such circumstances, it might seem perilous to make any general comment on the relationship between this murky area of theatre licensing and that of censorship, but it is worth remarking that no small part of the confusion lay with the Lord Chamberlain's Office itself, where there seemed to be some uncertainty as to the precise extent of the Lord Chamberlain's authority. (Thomas Baucott Mash, Comptroller of the Lord Chamberlain's Office, with forty-three years' service behind him, confessed as much in evidence before the 1832 Committee.)[10] In one respect, the problem was grounded in the apparent inability to distinguish between his authority as licenser of theatres (which was limited) and his power as licenser of plays (which was, at least in theory, comprehensive); and, in another, it lay in his perplexity over the kinds of theatrical entertainment he was allowed to licence for those non-patent theatres which came under his secondary jurisdiction for theatre licensing.

Under the provisions of Walpole's Act, the Lord Chamberlain was permitted to licence in London only such theatres as existed inside the boundaries of 'the city of *Westminster*, and within the liberties thereof',[11] an area including, apart from Drury Lane and Covent Garden, the Haymarket (operating under a royal patent dating from 1766), and the King's Theatre (whose licence was restricted to opera and, on that account, tolerated on a more or less equal footing with the two main patent houses). But during the early nineteenth century the number of theatres within the city of Westminster had grown steadily, owing to the grace and favour of certain Lord Chamberlains (notably Lord Dartmouth and the Marquess Conyngham) who, hostile to the patent theatres, had granted restricted licences to the Adelphi, Olympic, English Opera House, and, later, to the St James's and the Strand.[12] All these theatres, as reference to the Lord Chamberlain's Day Books shows, submitted MSS. for official approval on a fairly regular basis; and this practice seems to have been a direct consequence of the Lord Chamberlain's separate authority as licenser of their premises. Outside the circle of Westminster matters operated rather differently. There the supplementary licensing statutes of 1752 (25 Geo. II) and 1755 (28 Geo. II)[13] provided suburban London magistrates with powers of licensing theatres for strictly limited periods (and on restricted terms) in areas appropriate to their jurisdiction. Such licences were given to theatres like the Surrey, Coburg, Grecian, and Pavilion. But in these cases the evidence of the Day Books suggests no consistent pattern of their submission to the authority of the Lord Chamberlain as licenser of plays. Nevertheless, there must have been some occasions when they did so, especially when they were under threat of possible prosecution for having strayed beyond the terms of their theatre licences. After all, possession of the Lord Chamberlain's licence for a play conferred not

7

only a form of prestige but a substantial degree of legal protection. Charles Matthews of the Adelphi told the 1832 Committee that his theatre had sent MSS. to the Examiner of Plays for many years past and that an official play licence was in itself a guarantee that he had not 'exceeded the terms of [his] annual licence' from the Lord Chamberlain. Similar kinds of guarantee must have applied with equal force to the suburban minor theatres licensed by the local magistrates. The case of the Coburg Theatre having paid occasional fees to the censor was mentioned to Thomas Mash during the deliberations of the same Committee; and, though he denied all knowledge of such transactions, there was probably more than a grain of truth in the accusation.[14] The Examiner, George Colman, had few scruples about the source of his fees.

In order to satisfy the terms of their licences, which forbade encroachment on the preserves of the patent houses in legitimate drama, the minor theatres, if they submitted MSS. for official approval at all, were obliged to describe them as 'burlettas'. The term was quite as tricky to define for contemporaries (including the Lord Chamberlain and the Examiner of Plays)[15] as it is for modern historians of the theatre. Joseph Donohue remarks that the burletta, defined in mid eighteenth century as a kind of burlesque of the Italian opera, 'had originally no taint of the illegitimate about it'.[16] Indeed, burlettas were often performed at the patent theatres. But in the nineteenth century the term rapidly became a device for satisfying the letter of the restricted licences of the minor theatres. The musical element was almost incidental and in practice reduced to just five songs per act in a maximum of three acts; but even then, as John Payne Collier (sometime Colman's deputy) pointed out, such songs were often sent to the licenser for form's sake and were afterwards silently dropped in performance.[17] With the music removed or played at a virtually inaudible level, there was little to distinguish burlettas from the regular drama. As Charles Matthews observed of his practice at the Adelphi, 'if the Lord Chamberlain chooses to allow us to play a piece infringing on the regular drama, we do not object of course'.[18] Across the Thames, beyond the Lord Chamberlain's jurisdiction for theatre licensing, the performance of plays classed as 'legitimate' was even easier and David Osbaldiston (Surrey Theatre) openly admitted to the 1832 Committee that Douglas Jerrold's *Black-Eyed Susan* (1829) and the same author's three-act historical tragedy *Thomas à Beckett* (1829) had been produced without interference either from the Lord Chamberlain or the licensing magistrates.[19] (Not everyone was, of course, quite as fortunate; but the

8

transpontine theatres did enjoy a relative freedom – to the extent, exceptionally, of providing refuges for plays which the Lord Chamberlain had actually refused to licence.)[20] The monopoly was not dead in 1832 but it was under extreme strain. At the basis of the attack was the burletta. Its remarkable serviceability, as Donohue reminds us, rested 'in the impossibility of defining it. For what cannot be defined cannot be prohibited.'[21]

In such a confused theatrical climate, and following a flood of petitions from both sides in the patent theatre dispute, the House of Commons Select Committee began its work in 1832 under the chairmanship of Edward Bulwer (later Lytton, which is the form used in this book). Its brief was to examine the laws on theatrical licensing, dramatic copyright, censorship, in fact anything which might bear upon or in some measure account for the widely acknowledged enervation of contemporary drama. For twelve days witnesses drawn from every branch of the theatrical profession gave evidence, including Edmund Kean, William Charles Macready, Charles Kemble, and James Robinson Planché, together with a number of theatre managers and the Examiner of Plays himself. No one could have been surprised at the Committee's final recommendation to abolish the patent monopoly – the chairman's fierce opposition to it had been known from the start – but the mass of evidence also confirmed Bulwer Lytton's view that dramatic censorship might profitably be abandoned into the bargain. On further reflection, however, he decided against tackling that delicate issue in the Bill being prepared for Parliament, fearing (quite rightly as it turned out) that enough controversy would be generated by the intention to abolish the monopoly alone. In the event, Bulwer Lytton's scheme was rejected by a small majority in the House of Lords in 1833 and a decade of continued theatrical frustration ensued before it was safe to reintroduce the Bill, in modified form, and restore long-awaited free trade to the London theatres.[22]

The framing of the Theatre Regulation Act (6 & 7 Vict. c. 68) in 1843, after passions had cooled sufficiently to allow the legislation a smooth passage through both Houses of Parliament, provided, on the face of it, a welcome opportunity to remove the imperfections of the 1737 Act in respect of the Lord Chamberlain's powers as licenser of plays. There were several important omissions to be repaired. According to the strict terms of the earlier Act, the Lord Chamberlain had no mandate to delegate his authority as censor to an Examiner of Plays (but the Lord Chamberlain of the day, the Duke of Grafton, had done so nonetheless and the office had been filled continuously ever since);

nor was there any reference in Walpole's Act to fees for licences or, indeed, to licences at all. Here again precedents had been created and eighteenth-century theatre managers had come to expect the issue of formal licences and had reconciled themselves to the idea of paying for the privilege.[23] Yet on these vital questions the 1843 Theatre Act is only marginally more explicit than its predecessor. The Lord Chamberlain was given the right to fix a graduated scale of charges for reading plays (subject to a maximum of two guineas) and, in the same context, the statute allows that such fees may be paid directly to the Lord Chamberlain 'or to some Officer deputed by him to receive the same',[24] which is the only reference in the whole Act to anything resembling an Examiner of Plays. The Act is similarly circumspect on the subject of play licences in its provision (clause XV) that penalties may be incurred in cases where 'any new Stage Play, or any Act, Scene, or Part thereof, or any new Prologue or Epilogue, or any Part thereof [is acted for hire], *until the same shall have been allowed by the Lord Chamberlain, or which shall have been disallowed by him*' (my italics). This does no more than imply sanction for the practice of issuing licences for plays. The conclusion must be that the 1843 Act was deliberately vague in these respects because of the fear that more explicit allusion to the office of Examiner or to the issue of formal play licences might suggest that the Lord Chamberlain's Office had acted illegally in the past. All in all, the Theatre Regulation Act, which retained much of the language as well as the provisions of its eighteenth-century ancestor, was a rather unsatisfactory attempt to embroider on the old.

In some respects, however, the new legislation was an improvement. The period of official examination was reduced from fourteen days to seven as a concession to theatres where programmes were determined at short notice. More importantly, the crucial clause XIV investing the Lord Chamberlain with powers to prohibit any stage play (new or old, in whole or in part) was qualified by the provision that such action was a discretionary right to be exercised only 'whenever he shall be of opinion that it is fitting for the Preservation of good Manners, Decorum, or of the Public Peace'. But Edward Bulwer Lytton must have contemplated with heavy irony the passing of a statute which, while achieving the laudable aim of abolishing the iniquitous patent theatre monopoly, far from removing the Lord Chamberlain's power as censor, actually reaffirmed its comprehensiveness by bringing all the previously exempted minor theatres in London securely under his paternalistic wing, together with every provincial theatre in Great Britain.[25]

II

During the years following Walpole's Act, the Lord Chamberlain's Office had tried to devise a workable system of play licensing out of the bare legal framework supplied. The code of practice that developed drew largely on the customs of the defunct office of Master of the Revels, from which the new Examinership of Plays was a more or less direct descendant. Although the 1843 Act extended the Lord Chamberlain's authority as licenser of theatres and clarified his power as censor, the system of licensing plays remained, in broad outline, remarkably consistent throughout the eighteenth and nineteenth centuries. There is, therefore, no need to make any real distinction between the practice adopted between 1824 and 1843 (under the terms of Walpole's Act) and that employed for the rest of the century under the new legislation.

The normal day-to-day routine of reading every play submitted for examination was undertaken by the Examiner of Plays, an official directly responsible to the Lord Chamberlain. Usually, the latter did no more than put his signature to the form of licence; but in doubtful cases referred by the Examiner he would read the play himself and come to his own judgement. Though nominally carrying relatively little power as mere adviser to the Lord Chamberlain, the Examiner was in fact very powerful indeed. His sole function was to deal with theatrical affairs, while the rest of the Lord Chamberlain's staff had to apportion their time between all the varied duties undertaken by their superior, who, as chief officer of the royal household, busied himself with matters ranging from appointments under royal warrant to vetting persons being presented at Court and arranging all ceremonial affairs, sometimes to the exclusion of theatrical business altogether. As a general rule, no Lord Chamberlain saw the MS. of any play unless specifically requested to by the Examiner.

Few contemporaries seem to have meditated very seriously on the possible dangers of the Examiner's considerable and largely unsupervised powers. When John Larpent was appointed to the post in 1778 he stayed in what amounted to a very comfortable sinecure (with the assumed additional privilege of regarding all MSS. submitted for licensing as his personal property)[26] for the next forty-six years until his death at the age of eighty-three, thus creating the dubious precedent that the job was for life. That certainly was how Larpent's successor, George Colman the Younger, regarded it. He stated pertly before the 1832 Committee that, as long as he did not misbehave, the Lord Chamberlain had no power to dismiss him.[27] Not a little alarmed by

11

Colman's disclosure, the Committee in their final report laid special stress on the Examiner's holding office 'at the discretion of the Lord Chamberlain, whose duty it would be to remove him should there be any just ground for dissatisfaction as to the exercise of his functions'.[28] The Earl of Jersey apparently tried to take advantage of the redefinition by forming plans in 1834 of removing the ageing Colman or at least of prevailing on him to resign — Theodore Hook, author of the infamous *Killing No Murder*, censored by Larpent in 1809, was reportedly Jersey's choice as replacement[29] — but nothing came of it and two years later Colman, like his predecessor, died in harness.

Though Colman denied it, the financial rewards of the Examinership were not inconsiderable. He revealed to the 1832 Committee that his annual gross salary, excluding fees, was £400 — apparently the same as that enjoyed by the first Examiner of Plays, William Chetwynd, in 1738[30] — but that as it suffered tax at the rate of £31.8s. per cent, allowing him a net income of £274.8s., it was 'a sum scarcely adequate, without the fees, to the labour of the business, as now executed, and the constant residence in or near London'.[31] But the fee system, with its indiscriminate charge of £2.2s for every MS. licensed — its length did not matter — became a subject of marked interest to the Committee. No witness seemed able to produce any firm evidence of its origin or even of its legality. John Payne Collier believed that the fee rested on 'prescription', Charles Kemble that it was paid voluntarily out of courtesy, and Colman himself could offer nothing more convincing than the alleged practice of the past ninety-five years and the fact that during his tenure of the Haymarket Theatre (between 1790 and 1819) he had consistently paid Larpent £2.2s for every licence.[32]

After Colman's death a commission investigated the whole matter and recommended a properly graduated scale of fees — £2 for plays of three acts or more, £1 for pieces of one or two acts, and five shillings for a 'Song, Address, Prologue, or Epilogue' — [33] which remained in force until the abolition of censorship in 1968. Colman's successors also received small salary increases (eventually fixed at £43) to compensate them, at least in part, for the estimated reduction in fee revenue.[34] In consequence, the Examiner's remuneration was much more closely linked to fluctuations in theatrical affairs. It meant that William Bodham Donne, for example, might receive as much as £367.7s. (in 1871) or as little as £213.5s. (in 1858), when he wrote dejectedly to his friend Fanny Kemble that he 'might be dead and buried for any trouble the Theatres give me, or any fees they pay for new pieces'. But there were sometimes other compensations: '[T]hough I get no money, I do get drink from the Theatres: for praise be blest, two of the Saloon-Managers are also vintners, and one sends me a case of red wine, and the other of white. For what cause the 'mighty knows, since I have been no more civil to them than to others.'[35]

Donne was in some ways rather more fortunate than some of his predecessors, who experienced occasional difficulties in collecting the fees that were due. Colman admitted that he could not force theatre managers to pay but that they nearly always did, apart, that is, from certain exceptions like Alfred Bunn of Drury Lane, who insisted that the 1737 Act 'arms with an authority to prohibit, but does not require [the Lord Chamberlain] to sanction. The "license" part of the business has been got up by the feelers of fees, and they have taken custom for right.'[36] In John Mitchell Kemble's fee book a comic extravaganza *A Turn Among the Knights of Chivalry* (licensed for the English Opera House in 1839) is marked in red ink with the note 'won't pay and don't'. At least three plays licensed for the Olympic in 1841 are also marked 'not paid', and the English Opera House was again a defaulter in the same year. Drury Lane again refused to pay in 1842. Generally, after the implementation of the 1843 Theatre Act fees were paid without demur; but, exceptionally, the Strand Theatre evaded payment on *The Birmingham Girl* in 1844 and Drury Lane neglected to pay for two further pieces in 1845. There was, too, some confusion whether the fee was payable on plays that were refused licences. John Kemble's practice in such an event was to return the fee —indeed, that is some- times the only way of identifying refused MSS. when they are not otherwise marked as such —and at the 1853 Committee it was plainly stated that fees were waived on plays which the Lord Chamberlain re- fused to licence.[37] However, some time between this date and 1866 the practice altered and William Donne, reverting to the procedure adopted in the eighteenth century, claimed that the fee had to be paid in all cases as it was a charge 'not for licensing, but for reading'.[38]

In the early days the Examiner's duties were light, never very time- consuming, and reasonably well paid. But after the 1843 Theatre Act brought all theatres under the Lord Chamberlain's wing the burden became progressively heavier. There were many more MSS. to read and the Examiners from John Kemble's time onwards were sometimes ordered to attend the theatres during performances of controversial plays to ensure strict adherence to the licensed text. (This was in sharp contrast to George Colman's notion that his function ceased immediately a MS. was approved and the fee pocketed.)[39] From 1857 a further responsibility was added when the Examiner, with the aid of a surveyor, was detailed to inspect the structural soundness, ventilation, and fire and safety precautions of every London theatre licensed by the Lord Chamberlain before the issue or renewal of the annual licence. It was a job for which William Donne had no relish, in spite of the humorous references to it in his letters. In 1867 he wrote to a friend:

If you ever accompany me in this quest of dirt and disorder, I shall be able, in some cases to say to you as the Angel said to Ezekiel —'I will yet show thee, son of man, greater abominations than these.' Reading pantomimes is pastime compared to raking out the foul places of Theatres — in one respect, far worse, for a Pantomime brings a sovereign with it, whereas though 'money be muck' as Lord Bacon says . . . *this* muck brings me no money. The only satisfaction is that in ten years, so long have I done this dirty work, I have abolished a large amount of danger and discomfort.[40]

Such inspections — they were later delegated to the Metropolitan Board of Works in 1878, though the Examiner was still expected to be present[41] — were vitally important in improving the general standards of the London theatres. The rules and regulations drawn up for the purpose by the Lord Chamberlain's Office provided the model for the provincial licensing authorities' exertions in the same cause.

By the later Victorian period the volume of plays to be examined demanded the full attention of the Examiner. Edward Pigott in the early 1880s was reading nearly 300 MSS. a year and, by the end of the century, George Redford was handling half as many again — 444 MSS. in 1899.[42] The usual method of reading and licensing plays, outlined to the 1866 Committee by William Bodham Donne, could have differed only in minor detail from the practice employed by other Examiners of the period:

If I find anything objectionable, I endorse on the license the objectionable passage, and then I recommend them to the Lord Chamberlain, or if I am doubtful about the whole bearing of a piece, it is then referred to the Lord Chamberlain to confirm or reject my opinion against it; if his opinion coincides with mine, the play is refused a license.[43]

It may be added that from Donne's time onwards all censored passages were usually transcribed into the office Day Books, where they became matters of permanent record. John Payne Collier told the 1832 Committee that it was usual for the Examiner to send out a separate notice of passages to which he conceived objection;[44] and much the same practice survived into the 1870s and later as an additional reminder of what had to be cut out. (The Day Book entries for scores of censored plays note that 'a copy of these excisions has been sent to the manager'.)

Normally, the function of the licenser ceased once the play licence had been dispatched to the theatre concerned, that is, unless attention was drawn subsequently to a production – often from press reports, which the Lord Chamberlain's staff habitually scrutinised – by an undesirable mode of representation, the speaking of unauthorised dialogue, or some kind of angry disturbance in the theatre, in which circumstances the authorities were entitled to interfere.

One of the most intractable problems faced by the licensing authorities during the nineteenth century, despite the rigorous provisions of the 1843 Act, was the performance of plays which were never submitted for official scrutiny. In London after 1846 it was relatively easy to keep a check because from that date, on the initiative of Earl Spencer, the Examiner of Plays was supplied weekly with playbills of all the Metropolitan theatres so that he could satisfy himself that nothing was announced contrary to the Lord Chamberlain's direction.[45] Even so, there were a few cases of unlicensed performances, either by producing a new play under an old title – a trick very hard to detect – or else by simply ignoring the rules in the hope that the authorities would not notice. Macready inadvertently allowed Browning's *A Blot on the 'Scutcheon* to be performed unlicensed at Drury Lane in 1843 and in consequence received a stiff warning from the Lord Chamberlain.[46] The blatant disregard of the regulations by Sadler's Wells Theatre in 1862 (reprimanded for performing four unlicensed plays within four months) was ascribed by the Lord Chamberlain's Office to an 'utterly ignorant' and 'incompetent Acting Manager'.[47] Later John Hollingshead of the Gaiety Theatre played Charles Reade's *Shilly-Shally* without official sanction in 1872. When Donne heard of it he wrote to the Comptroller, Spencer Ponsonby: 'I think if it recurs a letter from headquarters wd. be desirable. 'Tis not my business to "tout" for MSS.'[48] In cases of genuine oversight the authorities were usually prepared to deal mercifully with offenders, although under the terms of the 1737 and 1843 Acts the penalties for unlicensed performances were very serious and could include forfeiture of the theatre's licence.

In the provinces, of course, enforcement of the law was considerably more difficult. The notorious Newgate play *Jack Sheppard* (first performed in London in 1839) proved equally popular with provincial audiences, who enjoyed its performance long after the Lord Chamberlain had interdicted all variants on the subject.[49] And as late as 1890 an official circular had to be sent to all provincial theatres reminding managers of their obligations to the Lord Chamberlain in the matter of play licensing, with which they seemed 'to be imperfectly acquainted'.[50] Two years later the authorities showed their mettle when the manager of the Liverpool Adelphi rashly advertised a special Whit Monday attraction 'founded on facts from the life and Career of that most extraordinary Criminal, who so lately expiated his numerous offences with his life by the hands of the law at Melbourne'. The play was not licensed and, on the instructions of the Lord Chamberlain's Office 'with a view to the immediate cessation of a public scandal', the local authorities brought the case to court, with the result that the manager was fined £4 for each illegal performance and the licence of the theatre was 'voided'.[51]

As a piece of administrative machinery, despite its manifest imperfections and unresolved confusions, the licensing system during the Victorian period worked surprisingly well, especially after the appointment of William Donne, the first Examiner to take his responsibilities seriously and to administer his office on reasonably efficient business-like lines. To Donne must go much of the credit for the completeness of the records of the Lord Chamberlain's Office for the last forty years of the nineteenth century, including the preservation in the Day Books of passages marked for excision in licensed play scripts, the comprehensiveness of theatrical correspondence, and the indexing of many of the old volumes of bound plays deposited for licensing. He also suggested alterations in the way MSS. were kept at St James's Palace which helped prevent future losses in the official archives through loaning out scripts for copying. 'I am', Donne wrote to Spencer Ponsonby in 1870, 'always in favour of centralisation – that is, of systematic procedure in all matters of licensing.'[52]

Since it was the almost invariable practice of the Lord Chamberlain's Office to refuse all direct dealings with playwrights as such, its official relations were generally confined to the theatre managers, who looked after their own interests by cultivating an air of courtesy and respect towards officialdom. There must have been many Victorian theatre managers who had cause to be grateful for the guidance of the staff at St James's Palace,[53] and not least for the protection from outside interference implicit in the Lord Chamberlain's certificate that every licensed play did not 'in its general tendency contain any thing immoral or otherwise improper for the Stage'. As George Colman put it in 1832, 'every care is taken to facilitate the business of the theatres under the Lord Chamberlain's control; every possible accommodation is given'.[54] It may be safely assumed that seventy or so years later the majority of managers would still have endorsed such a claim.

2

THE CENSORS

However much censorship may be said to rely on some vaguely abstract standard of taste, it is in a quite fundamental sense a personal act influenced, consciously or not, by individual prejudices and predilections. Although the general principles of Victorian stage censorship are reasonably clear, the absence of any more precise rules on which that censorship might be conducted made it inevitable that the licensers should exercise a substantial degree of personal discretion. In other words, the personalities involved matter a great deal, whether the censor happened to be as unassuming as Charles Kemble or as forthright and colourful as George Colman. Yet, except in the latter's case (whose character forces its attention on every historian of nineteenth-century dramatic censorship), recent writers on the subject have been content to make their assessments without enquiring other than superficially into the kind of men behind its operation. They have tended to dismiss personal characteristics as unimportant or, worse, to deduce the personalities of the censors from the nature of the censorship they imposed.[1]

Because his powers were comparatively rarely wielded in person, the Lord Chamberlain's authority over the drama was of less practical significance than that of his Examiner of Plays: most decisions were taken at the lower level either by the Examiner alone or in consultation with his immediate superior, the Comptroller of the Lord Chamberlain's Office. Moreover, during the Victorian period the power of individual Lord Chamberlains was hardly ever prolonged beyond about five years, in contrast to some of their predecessors, who tended to remain in office for much longer terms. Between 1800 and 1900 there were thirty changes in the Lord Chamberlainship, no fewer than twenty of which took place in Victoria's reign.[2] Most were accounted for by the nature of the post, which was (and still is) a political appointment made by the government of the day. But some few, like Lord Dartmouth (1804—10) died in office, whilst others, like the Marquesses Wellesley and Conyngham (1835 and 1835—9), actually resigned. All were party men (though not necessarily active politicians) whose qualifications or even interest in theatrical matters were of little relevance to the appointment.

Even though the diversity of the office normally precluded the holder from anything more than a passing interest in the theatre, certain Lord Chamberlains did exert a significant influence at critical junctures on theatrical affairs. When George Colman was inducted into the Examinership of Plays in 1824, the Lord Chamberlain was the Duke of Montrose,[3] a Scots Tory who was determinedly antagonistic to plays on revolutionary themes. He fully endorsed Colman's action in suppressing such allegedly insidious plays as Shee's *Alasco* and Mary Mitford's *Charles the First*. For his part, Colman found his superior amenable to many of his eccentricities, including his schemes for increasing his personal revenue from licensing fees. The Duke of Devonshire, Montrose's successor during the Tory–Whig coalition of 1827–8, refused Colman permission to charge for foreign-language plays; but Montrose, on his return as Lord Chamberlain with Wellington's administration of 1828–30, promptly reversed the decision and the Examiner, interpreting the instruction as operating retrospectively, celebrated the event by licensing – in a single licence –some one hundred and fifty French pieces already performed at the English Opera House.[4] Thus the precedent became established for licensing at a reduced fee all foreign-language plays and operas. Again, it was Montrose who supported Colman's questionable proposal to licence lectures on astronomy to be given at a London theatre. When members of the 1832 Committee enquired whether the practice still continued, Colman replied drily: 'I do not believe anybody has been talking about the stars recently.'[5] Uncharacteristically, however, it seems that Montrose did countermand one of Colman's schemes: his plan to charge fees for licensing William Hawes' series of Lenten oratorios at Covent Garden. According to Peake, he accepted the argument that, since 'the words of the oratorios were selected entirely from the sacred volume', it could hardly be imagined that the Bible needed a licence from the Lord Chamberlain.[6]

In the Duke of Devonshire,[7] who succeeded Montrose for a second time in 1830, George Colman found a much less willing ally. The Whig Duke took a special interest in drama and was soon discovered to be a stalwart champion of the rights of the patent theatres and their monopoly, so much so that Alfred Bunn (as patentee of Drury Lane) was loud in praise of 'the acknowledged taste of that enlightened nobleman [who] was a guarantee for the due protection of vested rights, and for the countenance of all those embarked in the perilous task of

Plate 2   William George Spencer Cavendish, 6th Duke of Devonshire

maintaining them'.[8] Given his interference in such a sensitive area of theatrical politics, it is a little surprising that the Select Committee on Dramatic Literature (which sat during the Duke's second term as Lord Chamberlain) did not request his presence as a witness.

That 'liberal and princely Duke', as Samuel Arnold described him,[9]

19

was a popular figure in literary circles, where he was much respected for his intellectual powers, his patronage of the arts, and his fine library containing the dramatic collection of the late John Philip Kemble and a quantity of rare texts of the medieval drama. Long after he relinquished office, his love for the theatre was shown in a very practical way when he agreed, at the suggestion of Charles Dickens, to open his sumptuous London mansion — Devonshire House in Piccadilly — for the first performance of Bulwer Lytton's *Not So Bad As We Seem* (1851), which the author afterwards dedicated to him.[10]

In sharp contrast to the Duke of Devonshire, Lord Conyngham (who took office in 1835)[11] was no friend to the patent theatres. In the words of Alfred Bunn, he 'sanctioned alarming innovations' by granting extensions to the licences of the Haymarket, Adelphi, and Olympic theatres, as well as issuing entirely new licences to the Strand and to John Braham for the St James's. What was worse, Conyngham endeavoured to restrict the repertoire of the patent houses to English pieces only by refusing Bunn permission to stage Italian and German opera at Drury Lane. As Bunn put it, 'that noble lord set patent and precedent at defiance, disposed of petitioners in the most summary manner, and acted upon the dogma of *Ego et rex meus* on the most extensive scale'.[12] Conyngham was just as intractable over the delicate issue of performances on Wednesdays and Fridays in Lent. Only the patent theatres, not the minors, were prevented from opening on these days; and even after Parliament had recognised the injustice in 1839 the Lord Chamberlain refused to reverse his decision. It was in Bunn's jaundiced view the culmination of the Marquess Conyngham's prejudiced and unjustified persecution of his theatre.

When Conyngham resigned in 1839 and was replaced by the Earl of Uxbridge,[13] the ban on foreign-language opera at Drury Lane, much to Bunn's delight, was lifted. But Macready, as he recorded in his diary after an unsatisfactory interview, was much less impressed by the new Lord Chamberlain: 'His manners are merely average', he wrote, 'his understanding seems far below average; I fancy him a very proud man, which the deficiency of intellect, if I am right in that judgment, accounts for.'[14] Uxbridge, it is true, had really very little informed interest in the theatre; but it is mildly ironic that stage censorship in Victoria's reign should have begun under the charge of Lord Uxbridge and his predecessor the Marquess Conyngham, both of whom would have been much more at home under the relatively relaxed moral climate of the Regency. The latter continued in the dubious family tradition set by his mother, the notorious Lady Conyngham, who caused such a stir in aristocractic circles in the 1820s. (It was widely reported at the time that she was George IV's mistress — or, as John Wilson Croker put it, 'the Vice Queen'[15] —having supplanted Mrs Fitzherbert and Lady Hertford in the King's affections.) Within three years of his father's death and his succession to the title, Conyngham was Lord Chamberlain under William IV and had happily installed his own mistress as housekeeper at Buckingham Palace. Lord Uxbridge also kept a mistress on the staff of the royal household. While the private character of Conyngham and Uxbridge must have been known only to a very small circle, some hint of the latter's indiscretions did reach the ears of the strait-laced Prince Consort, whom Uxbridge quickly made an enemy of and 'always treated . . . with studied insolence'.[16] Such hostility, however, did not prevent Uxbridge from affording the Prince his protection as Lord Chamberlain when in 1840 the play *Mary Stuart* appeared to make improper allusions to Albert's forthcoming marriage with Queen Victoria.[17]

The special concern of the Marquess of Breadalbane (Lord Chamberlain twice between 1848–52 and 1853–8)[18] was the comfort and physical safety of theatre audiences. Under his direction new, stringent regulations were drawn up for every theatre under his jurisdiction as licenser. As the Comptroller of the Lord Chamberlain's Office commented in 1892, he 'was very strong on the subject of ventilation, and he went all round the theatres himself [in 1855] . . . and that was the beginning of the inspection',[19] which became a formal part of the duties of the Examiner of Plays in 1857.

By far the longest-serving Victorian Lord Chamberlain was Viscount Sydney, first appointed to the office in 1859.[20] Apart from a short interruption during the two years of Conservative government between 1866 and 1868, he continued as Lord Chamberlain for thirteen years until 1874. Almost the whole of William Bodham Donne's career as Examiner was spent under his generally enlightened authority and a *rapport* developed between them in the handling of theatrical matters. Lord Sydney had a great respect for Donne's talents as Examiner and for the kind of man he was. When the former was about to hand over to Lord Bradford in 1866, he wrote to Donne: 'the office, which I vacate on Tuesday, gave me the opportunity of making your acquaintance from which I derived much pleasure and satisfaction'.[21] The esteem was certainly reciprocated, for when Sydney finally retired in 1874 Donne wrote to Fanny Kemble: 'I have a new *chef*, Marquis of Hertford — *vice* Earl Sydney, and a very nice nobleman he is: though I am so used to the Earl that I always regret his loss.'[22]

As Donne was to discover, his new superior was a stickler for propriety on the stage, particularly in the matter of decorous costuming in ballets and pantomimes.

During the last twenty years of the nineteenth century, the Lord Chamberlain seems to have had less and less contact with theatrical policy. In contrast to the Donne–Lord Sydney period, neither Pigott nor Redford enjoyed direct access to the Lord Chamberlain and there were few occasions when the latter made his presence felt. It was a difficult period and, for the most part, successive Lord Chamberlains were content to let their Examiners follow their own inclinations, restrained only by the occasional interference of the Comptroller or by the press. But in 1888 Lord Lathom did venture to observe of his Examiner's censorship of *Francillon:* 'I think [Mr Pigott] has overdone it in one or two places.'[23]

II

When John Milton wrote his plea for the freedom of the press in 1644, he summarised the looked-for qualifications in an ideal censor. He argued that the occupant of such an office 'had need to be a man above the common measure, both studious, learned and judicious' but that, on the other hand, the 'tedious and unpleasing journey work' of being 'made the perpetuall reader of unchosen books and pamphlets, oftimes huge volumes' militated against the possibility of attracting men of the right quality. Yet in spite of Milton's forebodings, all the holders of the post of Examiner of Plays in the nineteenth century were men of some intellectual worth. None, not even Colman, if one is to be completely fair, could justly be branded, as Milton prophesied, 'ignorant, imperious, and remisse, or basely pecuniary'.[24]

Of all the nineteenth-century Examiners, there is perhaps today only one who is any more than just a name in the history of dramatic censorship, for George Colman the Younger (1762–1836),[25] who succeeded to the office through the influence of his friend the Duke of York in January 1824 on the death of the aged John Larpent, was never content with the cloak of anonymity on which most censors seem to thrive. As author of such famous plays as *The Iron Chest* (1796), *John Bull* (1803), and *The Heir at Law* (1808), together with some volumes of licentiously flavoured verse, he had already established a firm reputation with the theatre-going and reading public. Colman came from a family closely connected with the theatre. His mother was an actress and his father, the elder George Colman, was also a talented dramatist, his best-known work being *The Clandestine Marriage* (1766) written in collaboration with David Garrick. After his father's retirement from the management of the Haymarket Theatre, Colman took it over and stayed in charge until 1819, despite a variety of financial problems which at one point forced him to conduct the theatre's affairs from the King's Bench Prison, where he had been committed for debt.

Irregular though Colman's past had been, he was at least familiar with all aspects of the theatrical profession and, indeed, the first practising playwright and experienced theatre manager to occupy the office of Examiner. On the face of it Colman seemed an admirable choice for the post. Friends and contemporary dramatists had high hopes of a relaxation of the irksome, petty restrictions imposed by his predecessor. But in the event they were rudely disappointed. The eagerness with which the new Examiner fell to his task must have astonished all who knew him. His ruthless excision of oaths (including 'demme' and 'O, lud'), religious references, political 'subversion', and personal allusions of all kinds confounded associates long used to Colman's ready wit, *risqué* jokes, bluff manner, and talent for punning, especially when they brought to mind some of the bolder indecencies of the Examiner's own plays. But as Colman said: 'I was a careless immoral author, I am now examiner of plays. I did my business as an author at that time and I do my business as an examiner now.'[26]

The picture of George Colman which has survived to the present century tells of a greedy, prejudiced, almost fanatically puritanical censor appealing, as one modern commentator has put it, to 'the taste of the most conservative, most frightened, and most bigoted English minorities'.[27] That Colman did and said a great deal to deserve such a reputation is undeniable. His smug public pronouncements before the 1832 Committee on the impropriety of references to angels and any form of oath ('I think no body has gone away from the theatre the better for hearing a great deal of cursing and swearing') or, indeed, on the opportunities for indecent material in oratorios — he argued that they should be subject to the Lord Chamberlain's authority not for the fees but 'because I think they may be immoral things'[28] — were fairly common knowledge amongst playwrights of the period. Oddly, Colman claimed not to care whether his excisions were complied with or not since he baulked at the idea of becoming 'a spy as well as a censor on the theatre'.[29] It was certainly a situation convenient enough for the theatre managers. When Samuel Beazley complained to the Examiner that in one of his plays he had reduced 'all his full grown angels into cherubims, *id est,* cut them in half, and left them neither

Plate 3   George Colman the Younger

heaven nor cloud to rest upon' as well as removed 'some devilish
good jokes', Colman happily surrendered all his rights in the matter by
reminding the author that 'the play, you know, must be printed in
strict accordance with my obliterations; but if the parts be previously
given out, it will be difficult to make the actors preach from my text'.[30]
When the Examiner himself seemed to connive at such blatant dis-
obedience, the seriousness with which Colman carried out his work
as censor must be open to extreme doubt.

Colman's character had not changed in the slightest. Byron had met him on a number of occasions while he was a member of the Committee of Drury Lane and liked him to the extent of preferring him over Sheridan as a drinking companion: 'Sheridan for Claret or port; but Colman for every thing, from Madeira and Champaigne at dinner ... up to the Punch of the Night, and down to the Grog or Gin and water of day-break.'[31] Recalling their long friendship, the dramatist Theodore Hook described Colman as a man possessed of 'an inexhaustible fund of wit and humour ... the much-sought companion of every circle of society in which he chose to mix'.[32] But others were less charitable. Macready, who had no special cause for disliking Colman and who was often an astute observer of his fellow-men, referred to him in his diary as 'a man of some talent, much humour, and little principle'.[33]

George Colman was a strong individualist. He was sometimes driven to adopting extreme points of view — the result, as so many of his friends recognised, of his inability to accept defeat in an argument — but he seemed to enjoy enormously his role as interpreter of the public conscience. Despite all his eccentricities, his peculiarities, and his downright perversity, he is still the most colourful, if not the most responsible, character to fill the office of Examiner during the nineteenth century. It is easy to censure Colman but it is also worth remembering that in general his policies were supported by the theatre-going public and were by no means exaggeratedly out of tune with the prevailing temper of the times.

Two days after Colman's death, the *London Gazette* (28 October 1836) announced Lord Conyngham's appointment of Charles Kemble (1775–1854) as the new Examiner of Plays. In many ways it was a surprising choice, especially since Kemble was still under contract (and was to remain so for another two months) to Covent Garden Theatre. Macready, for one, received the news with characteristic cynicism and ill-humour:

Fortune seems to shower her benefits on those who certainly from their talents and virtues can make little claim to them. For character, look at C. Kemble — what he really *is* and what he *passes for*! I feel discontented (am I envious?) at seeing place and wealth conferred so unmeritedly; but thus it almost always has been, and I suppose ever will be.[34]

And for rather different reasons Kemble's unfitness for the task of censor was remarked upon by the *Age* newspaper, which disclosed that Kemble was a Roman Catholic and darkly hinted at corrupt and sinister motives behind the appointment of 'this cowardly Jesuit into office under a Protestant King, where he has thus the uncontrolled exercise of working Papist influences'.[35] But it was the Examiner's continued association with Covent Garden that provoked most anger, notably from Alfred Bunn, lessee of Drury Lane Theatre, who expressed to Lord Conyngham his apprehension at 'the selection of a performer and proprietor of the rival house deputed to sit in judgment upon the *productions* of *this*'.[36] It was a fair point; but the Lord Chamberlain refused to see any difficulty and Bunn was forced to endure subjection to Kemble's authority until the anomaly was resolved by the latter's nominal retirement from the stage at Christmas 1836, when he played Benedict in *Much Ado About Nothing* at the Haymarket.

Charles Kemble's career as an actor (which he resumed for a time by royal command after his retirement from the Lord Chamberlain's service in 1840) is sufficiently well known,[37] but his four years as Examiner of Plays between 27 October 1836 and 22 February 1840 are among the most obscure and least documented of all nineteenth-century terms of the office. The information that does survive is confined to a few chance remarks by friends and contemporary historians. Most agree that Kemble took very little interest in the work and that the major portion was delegated to his son John Mitchell Kemble. Percy Fitzgerald comments that he 'enjoyed the office of Examiner of Plays, which was for him a sort of sinecure, as he discharged it by a deputy'; and William Bodham Donne, giving evidence before the 1866 Committee, declared that Kemble 'did duty for little more than a year' and then went abroad, leaving his son in complete charge.[38] A member of the same Committee, Lord Ernest Bruce, added that 'John Kemble told me that his father said he did not think that he read five plays after he was appointed.'[39] During Kemble's first prolonged absence (from 15 July until 2 December 1837) John Kemble wrote to his friend Donne:

I have been making a few guineas by licensing modern nonsense; my father having named me his deputy during his absence; and managers pay pounds sterling for the liberty of inflicting tediousness upon the King's lieges: all which would be very satisfactory to the licenser, were he not in honour bound to read the tediousness he licenses; which is hard!

And a month later he wrote again with the news that 'the winter theatres are all opening, and the managers all anxious to have their stock of new pieces promptly read and licensed'.[40] By the end of January 1838, John Kemble was acting for his father again and continued to do so for most of the rest of that year. Charles Kemble went away again in early 1839 and for a third time nominated his son as deputy. The theatre managers became so confused over the identity of the Examiner of Plays that they began addressing their MSS. to '————— Kemble, Esq'. This highly unsatisfactory state of affairs was, however, shortly resolved when in January 1840 Charles Kemble wrote to the Lord Chamberlain requesting the formal transfer of his office. He pointed out to Lord Uxbridge that his own ill-health precluded him from permanent residence in England and, since 'the continued discharge of [my] duties by deputy is anomalous and in many respects inconvenient, I take the liberty of petitioning your Lordship to transfer to my son, Mr John Kemble, the office I now hold and of which he at present undergoes the labor without enjoying the advantages'. By such an arrangement, Kemble explained, 'my family will not be deprived of those benefits which it was the gracious desire of His Late Majesty, through your predecessor to confer upon them; benefits, for the attainment of which, I was call'd upon to make very great pecuniary sacrifices in the relinquishment of all my professional engagements'.[41]

Rumours of an imminent vacancy in the Examinership of Plays had been circulating since December of the previous year, at which time Bulwer Lytton unwisely encouraged William Charles Macready to apply for the post. Relating the episode in his diary, Macready describes an interview with Lord Uxbridge at St James's Palace, where he heard 'as indifferently as [he] could seem to do' the bitter news that the post was already filled.[42] The official announcement appeared in the *London Gazette* (25 February 1840):

The Lord Chamberlain of Her Majesty's Household has appointed John Mitchell Kemble, Esq., Examiner of all Plays, Tragedies, Comedies, Operas, Farces, Interludes, or any other entertainment of the stage, of what denomination soever, in the room of Charles Kemble, Esq., resigned.

John Kemble (1807–57) was a literary and philological scholar rather than a man of the theatre.[43] He was already widely respected in academic circles for his pioneer work in Anglo-Saxon studies, especially his edition of the *Anglo-Saxon Poems of Beowulf* (1833), and at the time of his appointment he was editor of the *British and Foreign Review*, a post which he retained until its closure in 1844.[44] As an undergraduate at Trinity College, Cambridge, he was an intimate of Tennyson, Hallam, Edward Fitzgerald, and William Bodham Donne — the two latter had been close friends since their school-days together at Bury St Edmund's Grammar School. When he left Cambridge, Kemble contemplated taking holy orders, but nothing ever came of this though Tennyson, amongst others, considered him well-suited to the Anglican ministry.

Most of his time thereafter Kemble devoted to philological and historical studies, which eventually took him to Germany, where he could be in touch with the latest scholarship. His intellectual reputation was finally confirmed with the publication in 1849 of his important historical study *The Saxons in England.*

For a man of Kemble's evident ability, the work of reading and licensing plays was neither mentally demanding nor very time-consuming, though there were occasional moments of interest in examining German, French, and Italian MSS. His domestic affairs, however, proved endlessly troublesome and in 1849 he began preparations for the dissolution of his marriage, contracted in about 1836, to the daughter of a Göttingen professor. The divorce entailed his presence in Germany and without any apparent difficulty he obtained unlimited leave of absence from the Lord Chamberlain, Lord Breadalbane, on condition that he find a suitable temporary replacement to continue his duties as Examiner. Kemble's life-long friend William Bodham Donne was the obvious choice and in June 1849 he put the proposition to him. 'My miserable affairs', Kemble began, 'which I shall not affect to suppose you ignorant of, call me, imperatively to Hanover.' Stressing that there were many precedents for a deputy to the Examiner, Kemble went on to spell out some of the attractions of the office:

To you, who read French, the duty would be a farce. There is no chance of any German or new Italian: and even if there were, you are master in them. This is the slack theatre season, and I really think that a dozen plays a month will be about the limit. Let me know what you think, *forthwith*, as I must arrange with the Lord Chamberlain. I want to start on the 5th of July.[45]

Donne good-naturedly agreed; but his services were not required until nearly a month later, when Kemble scribbled a hasty note indicating his immediate departure for the Continent: 'I shall direct the plays to be sent to you. I have also given a power of Attorney in your name at our Pay Office, to enable you to draw my salary for me in the commencement of October, and to do anything else that is needful. God help you!'[46] John Kemble's last entry in his fee book (15 July 1849) carries the comment: 'I went abroad.'

To begin with Donne acted as Kemble's unpaid deputy. The latter's monetary affairs were so precarious that soon after his arrival in Germany he began writing anxiously to Donne for the prompt transmission of his salary, which 'should amount to about 77 pounds, and if you could discover the proper means of sending me £60, to Hanover, that is what I should like done ... [but] be careful to send via *Ostend*: in this case a letter reaches me in 36 hours: via Bremen, it is four or even five days'.[47] Nine months later Kemble was still abroad, entangled in the German divorce laws, and complaining that the Lord Chamberlain's Office was sending him less money than was due —£110 instead of the expected £240 or £250.[48] In the event, Kemble's stay in Hanover was a protracted one and it was seven years before, disencumbered of his wife, he finally returned to England. In the interval, the anomalies of the Examiner's position — principally the fact that his duties were being discharged by an unpaid deputy — were not lost on the Lord Chamberlain, who felt uncomfortable at the demands he was having to make on Donne's time. When, in late 1851, Kemble applied for yet another extension of his leave of absence, the proposal was put by the Lord Chamberlain's Office that Donne should receive about one-third (approximately £110) of Kemble's net salary. As the matter was explained to him, Donne's 'very admirable & painstaking' performance of the duties required only made it 'more difficult for The Lord Chamberlain to exact from him those constant attendances which it is now found that the Examiner must be prepared to give'.[49] John Kemble was hardly in any position to quibble and so for the next four and a half years Donne, now paid though not very handsomely, continued with the business of the Examinership. When Kemble returned to England in the spring of 1856, he immediately resumed his duties and responsibilities; but within the year Kemble had fallen ill and Donne once more offered his services to the Lord Chamberlain.[50] Shortly afterwards, on 26 March 1857, Kemble died suddenly and the following day Donne was officially appointed Examiner of Plays.

William Bodham Donne (1807–1882)[51] dedicated himself as no other previous Examiner had to the efficient and, with very rare exceptions, scrupulously fair administration of his office. He was a Norfolk man, a relative of William Cowper and, so it was said, a descendant of John Donne. Educated at Bury St Edmund's Grammar School, where, apart from John Kemble, his friends included Fitzgerald and James Spedding, he went up to Gonville and Caius, Cambridge, in 1826 but was prevented from taking his degree by scruples over signing the Thirty-nine Articles, a step he was later much to regret.[52] At Cambridge he became a member, with John Kemble, of the famous Apostles Club and formed further lasting friendships which brought him firmly into the circle of Victorian letters. Donne was a great admirer of Tennyson's poetry and in 1831 Hallam sent him an advance copy of 'Southern Mariana', the poem published in

1833 as 'Mariana in the South'.[53] Other literary friends, like Richard Chenevix Trench and Bernard Barton, asked constantly for his guidance; he revised the proofs of Kemble's *Saxons in England*, of Charles Merivale's *History of Rome*, and contributed material to Southey's *Life of Cowper*. On his own account, Donne was an inveterate letter-writer and a frequent contributor of articles (on subjects ranging from Classical and English literature to the Hungarian Revolution of 1848) to most of the best-known contemporary periodicals such as the *Westminster Review*, the *Quarterly*, and *Fraser's Magazine*.[54] In 1852, on Carlyle's recommendation, he was elected Librarian of the prestigious London Library. He resigned on his appointment as Examiner in 1857.

Donne's early acquaintance with the Kemble family — Fanny was a regular and devoted correspondent for the whole of his life — stimulated his interest in the drama. He was a constant theatre-goer. He saw Fanny's début in her father's production of *Romeo and Juliet* at Covent Garden in 1829, was captivated by the Swedish opera singer Jenny Lind when she appeared in London in 1847, and full of praise for Dion Boucicault's *The Colleen Bawn* in 1860. Late in life, he saw Irving perform Hamlet at the Lyceum in 1876 but found him disappointing, especially in the soliloquies, in which 'he rants and puts himself in the strangest postures'. Donne resolved not to see him as Othello: 'I saw Salvini in that character last year, and E. Kean formerly, and that is enough for one mortal life.'[55] Indeed, Donne cared deeply for the fate of the theatre, which he believed under threat from the current demand for spectacle. 'Excess of decoration', he wrote, 'has ... been, in all ages and nations possessing a national drama, a symptom and accompaniment of decadence in the histrionic art.'[56] Yet in 1866, having had close contact with both the best and the worst of Victorian drama, he could view the trends with a certain optimism. English drama, as he reminded the 1866 Committee, was not necessarily inferior now to what it had been in the past century, since 'in looking back we see the top of the mountain only, the two or three good plays which have lived, but not the masses of rubbish that were acted in those days, and which have since sunk out of sight and mind'. Asked to name the plays which he thought might survive from the first two-thirds of the nineteenth century, he listed *Virginius, Ion, The Patrician's Daughter, Still Waters Run Deep, The Ticket-of-Leave Man, Arrah-na-Pogue*, and *The Colleen Bawn*. Some modern comedies, he thought, were 'very good; [but] of course I do not mean to say equal to *The School for Scandal*'. A few, however, were in his opinion the equal of Goldsmith's.[57]

Plate 4   William Bodham Donne

Through much of Donne's writing on the drama, there runs the
sense that he was somehow pleading the cause of a literary form which,
for most educated men, had lost what former attraction it possessed.
But again and again he stresses the centrality of the drama to human
experience: 'We cannot regard with apathy or aversion a branch of art
which delineates and appeals directly to some of the most earnest and
ennobling impulses of humanity; which, in the graver forms, is aux-
iliary to moral refinement, and in its lighter, a healthy implement of
satire or of mirth.'[58] The drama, he concludes, is integral to any notion
of civilisation. And, as one of the most recent writers on Donne justly
observes, 'these are not the words of a fool or of a Philistine or even of

a man with provincial views of the drama'.[59] These charitable principles Donne brought to his work as Examiner of Plays.

Including the period while he was acting for Kemble, William Donne was Examiner for twenty-five years and the longest-serving holder of the office during the nineteenth century. During that time he established a considerable presence at the Lord Chamberlain's Office. For two consecutive Christmas seasons in 1859 and 1860 he was even pressed into service at Windsor Castle to arrange a programme of theatrical entertainment, the Queen having conveyed to him 'such an unmistakable hint that I should manage her Theatre that there was no possibility of drawing back'.[60] (Donne's activities on behalf of the royal family gained him access to the Windsor archive of letters exchanged between Lord North and George III, the results of which he later published in 1867 as *The Correspondence of George III with Lord North*, one of Donne's most enduring pieces of scholarship.) His eventual departure from the Examinership in 1874, owing to continued ill-health, was a cause of genuine regret to most of the theatre managers and to his colleagues at St James's Palace. Spencer Ponsonby wrote to him at the time: 'Nothing has been pleasanter to me, in my whole official experience, than my relations with you — and I feel the breach of them deeply and sincerely.'[61]

Among the eager hopefuls who offered themselves for the vacant post of Examiner were several, including Alfred Wigan, Nelson Lee, Westland Marston, and Tom Taylor, who were actively engaged in one branch or another of the theatrical profession. But the choice fell on one who had no direct or obvious connexion with the theatre. Perhaps that was his primary recommendation. At fifty years of age, the new Examiner Edward Frederick Smyth Pigott (1824–95)[62] was the youngest of all the candidates. He came from a well-to-do Somerset family, was educated at Eton and Balliol College, Oxford, and in 1851 was called to the Bar, though he seems never to have practised. In the 1850s he was associated with George Henry Lewes and Thornton Leigh Hunt on the *Leader*, a weekly newspaper founded in 1850. According to William Archer, Pigott was said to have invested money in the venture and for a short time acted as editor. But certainly on 19 July 1851 'he adopted the pseudonym of "Le Chat Huant", under which designation he frequently acted as Lewes's deputy in dealing with theatrical and musical matters'.[63] Pigott stayed with the paper (later renamed *The Saturday Analyst and Leader*) until its closure on 24 November 1860. Thereafter his career is somewhat obscure. However, he was on the staff of the *Daily News* for a few years, at first it seems as one of the editors, though by the end of the decade he was contributing no more than the occasional leading article or review.[64] As a condition of his appointment as Examiner, Pigott was required to sever all remaining connexions with the press.

In consequence of his business association with Lewes, Pigott enjoyed the respect and friendship of George Eliot, in whose letters there are many references to 'our Mr Pigott'. He became a devoted family friend and an indispensable part of the Lewes's literary and musical circle. By the winter of 1861–2, together with Herbert Spencer and George Redford (the father of the next Examiner of Plays), he was a regular visitor to Blandford Square for their Saturday musical soirées. Pigott's intimacy with the family was an enduring one and in 1876 he was given the first of the presentation copies of *Daniel Deronda*.[65]

Edward Pigott was a well-known figure in other mid- and late-Victorian literary circles. He knew Trollope, William Holman Hunt, Wilkie Collins, and Mrs Oliphant. The last named affectionately recalled his presence at a certain Mrs Duncan Stewart's *salon* in Sloane Street, which was always filled 'with the most curious jumble of entertaining people and people who came to be entertained, the smartest (odious word!) of society, and all the luminaries of the moment, many writers, artists, &c., and a few mountebanks to make up'. Pigott, 'the kind, the gentle, the sympathetic "Censor of Plays"', was it seems, an habitual visitor. In Mrs Oliphant's sentimentalised view he was

always interested, always kind, — a sort of atmosphere of humanity and warm feeling and sympathy about him, his little round form and round head radiating warmth and kindliness. He is the only man I have ever met, I think, from whom I never heard an unkind word of any one … [H]e had the most extensive acquaintance with both people and things, and had many a happy turn of expression, and *mot* of social wisdom which preserved him from that worst of faults: he was never dull, though always kind, which is almost a paradox.[66]

Pigott's whole career is something of a paradox. As a public man, like Colman before him, he generated extremes of reaction. To some he was a tolerant, beneficent censor, actively encouraging high moral standards in the drama; to others he was a tyrannical bigot who retarded the progress of contemporary English drama. Modern historians of censorship have been content to accept Bernard Shaw's description of Pigott as 'a walking compendium of vulgar insular prejudice' and his somewhat hysterical assessment of the Examiner's career, which

in relation to the higher drama was one long folly and panic, in which the only thing definitely discernible in a welter of intellectual confusion was his conception of the English people rushing towards an abyss of national degeneration in morals and manners, and only held back on the edge of the precipice by the grasp of his strong hand.[67]

But Shaw was hardly a disinterested commentator and his remarks were as much directed against the institution of censorship as against the individual. At the opposite end of the spectrum Clement Scott (as fervent a supporter of censorship as Shaw was an opponent of it) wrote of 'the liberal sway of this amiable gentleman and scholar' which smoothed away all friction between the theatrical profession and the Lord Chamberlain's Office.[68] By the end of the century the issue provoked such strongly partisan feelings that contemporary estimates of Edward Pigott depended on one's stand on the principle of dramatic censorship.

Pigott was unlucky enough to be Examiner of Plays at one of the most troublesome periods in the history of stage censorship. But it should be remembered that the bulk of the criticism against him and on the issue of censorship itself came only in the last few years of his tenure of the office. For much of his term as censor, his conception of his duties was perhaps tolerable enough. As he explained to the 1892 Committee, the Examiner should always administer censorship

in the most liberal spirit, with the discernment and discrimination that belongs to a wide knowledge of the world, and that cultivated sympathy with literature and art, which is equally regardful of public morality and public decency, and of the freedom and dignity of a liberal profession and a noble art. He does not pretend to be an arbiter of taste or, as he is jestingly described, a *censor morum*. It is only at the point where public manners affect public morals that his responsibility begins.[69]

But 'that cultivated sympathy with literature and art' which Pigott claimed was not sufficiently flexible to accommodate the drama of the late 1880s and 90s. For instance, he had no capacity to make the intellectual leap necessary to appreciate Ibsen's worth; he believed that the playwright's characters were all 'morally deranged'.[70] His record in dealing with all advanced drama of the period mars his whole career as censor.

Much of Pigott's work in the early 1890s was shared with his friend George Redford, son of Redford the surgeon and art critic who had accompanied Pigott on the cello at the Lewes's musical evenings. Redford frequently represented the Examiner at theatrical performances and, as Pigott's health began to fail, took over much of the routine of reading and licensing plays. For some time before Pigott's death in March 1895 Redford was, for all practical purposes, the Examiner of

Plays and, much to his evident embarrassment, theatre managers began to direct their MSS. to him personally, under the impression that he had already supplanted Pigott.[71]

Despite the growing controversy surrounding the issue of dramatic censorship, the office of Examiner was much coveted in 1895. The vacancy caused by Pigott's demise attracted no fewer than seventy candidates — actors, editors, barristers, journalists, even a Member of Parliament and a professor of German. For the first time, the selection procedure was conducted on formal business lines: lists of candidates were drawn up with brief biographies and names of referees. Among the more notable applicants were Joseph Knight, John Hollingshead, Edmund Gosse, W. L. Courtney, Ernest Bendall, and Clement Scott. George Redford applied on 2 March 1895, pointing out that his 'long and intimate acquaintance with the late E. F. S. Pigott' had given him 'a considerable insight into the duties, and responsibilities of the Examiner of Plays'. As a bank manager, Redford went on,

I may perhaps be allowed to have judgment, tact, knowledge of the World, together with undoubted integrity and probably a fair amount of Common Sense. If I add that I possess an intimate acquaintance with the modern Stage both in France and England, that I read French with facility, I shall have enumerated most of my qualifications for the Post. I am not a Dramatic Critic, not a Dramatist, though I have written plays, and have only a very slight personal acquaintance with theatrical people. I am 48 years of age and married.[72]

After due deliberation, the only other candidate short-listed was Ernest Bendall, the editor of *The Observer*; but in the event the Lord Chamberlain's choice rested on George Redford, who was officially appointed Examiner on 12 March 1895. The announcement had been eagerly awaited by the newspapers, but when it came everyone was confounded at Redford's selection. Paragraph headlines appeared asking 'Who is Mr Redford?' or captioned 'The Mysterious Mr Redford' and 'The Great Unknown'. Some papers like *The Sunday Times* (17 March) called the appointment 'A Ghastly Joke'; but the *Stage* (21 March) welcomed the unknown figure as neither a party man nor 'Ibsen mad'.

The anonymity of George Alexander Redford (184[7?]—1916) has been carefully preserved. Ironically, although the latest in the succession of nineteenth-century Examiners of Plays, he is the one about whom less is known than any of his predecessors. Only the bare details survive: that he was the eldest son of George Redford, F.R.C.S., educated at Clewer House School in Windsor, employed as a bank manager, and formerly assistant to Edward Pigott.[73] Contemporary newspaper reports (the later ones were less speculative) add only that he was a manager in the London and Southwestern Bank, from which he resigned on accession to the Examinership. The fullest sketch appeared in the *Queen* (23 March 1895), but experience of Redford's regime gave the lie to its fulsome description of the new Examiner as 'a courteous and well-informed man of the world, with literary tastes, thoroughly in sympathy with the modern stage, possessing an intimate knowledge of dramatic literature, and distinctly broad-minded and liberal in his views'.

Redford was a man cast in the Pigott mould and his career as Examiner marks no perceptible change in policy or direction. Like his predecessor, he made worrying errors of judgment and was given to the occasional indiscreet remark. For instance, his claim that he was not a censor of morals (made in an interview with the *Daily Mail* in 1900) even provoked a question in the House of Commons.[74] He was a decidedly unimpressive witness at the 1909 Committee on censorship, especially when it tried to elicit some of the principles which he brought to bear on the licensing of plays.[75] His evidence, as one contemporary commentator observed, was 'occasionally quite ridiculous, but no Censor, were he as wise as Solomon and as harmless as "Punch", could avoid being ridiculous in the Censor's place'.[76] It was a hard task trying to defend the operation of an institution which, in the opinion of such notable victims as Bernard Shaw, Edward Garnett, and Harley Granville-Barker, had no rational means of defence left.

3

POLITICAL DRAMA AND THE ESTABLISHMENT

Because of its ancient associations with the Court and the central institutions of government, the English drama has behind it a long tradition of political censorship. From the Elizabethan period to Walpole's Stage Licensing Act of 1737 political allusion was one of the most frequent causes of friction in the authorities' relations with the theatre. According to the office books of Sir Henry Herbert, Master of the Revels for most of the Stuart era, such prohibitions as Massinger's *Believe As Ye List* (1630–1) 'because itt did contain dangerous matter' are by no means uncommon.[1] During the eighteenth century the licensers, fortified by Walpole's Act, armed themselves with wide powers and demonstrated their efficacy by suppressing such plays as Henry Brooke's *Gustavus Vasa* (1739) and Charles Macklin's *Man of the World* (1770, 1779) for what seemed their overtly political character, while towards the end of the century John Larpent was exercising an authority which embraced all improper political allusions, sedition, and hits or lampoons against the government.[2] While Larpent's comprehensive controls did not secure the complete exclusion of politics from the late eighteenth-century stage, they were a convenient starting-point for the activities of George Colman, who, in his own career as Examiner of Plays, eclipsed even Larpent in his assiduous devotion to the unearthing of potentially dangerous political references.

Much to Colman's advantage was the widespread middle-class belief that politics were inappropriate in the theatre. He observed in 1832 that 'it was but the other day that the word "reform" was mentioned, and I understand there was a hubbub';[3] while Macready (certainly no theatrical greenhorn) declared in his lively defence of Bulwer Lytton's *The Lady of Lyons* in 1838 that modern audiences and playwrights were mature enough to abrogate all political allusions.[4] On the other hand, for Robert Southey (whose article attacking the excesses of contemporary French drama appeared in the *Quarterly Review* in 1834) dramatic censorship still had a vital role to perform in securing both 'domestic peace' and 'public tranquility' —as evidenced by the 'alarming disregard of [political] delicacy' which was rife upon the unfettered stages of London's minor theatres. An uncontrolled stage, he warned his readers, might act as 'an instrument of popular excitement'; and he argued that the example of the disreputable French theatre only reinforced his view that

[a]gainst the libels and seditious provocations of the stage there can be no other than antecedent preservative, as there can be no subsequent redress: the line that dishonours a private character or excites a public tumult, when once uttered cannot be recalled —*fugit irrevocabile verbum* —and punishment is out of the question, for the offensive expression often is really, and may always be alleged to be innocent in itself: the danger is in the *application* which a heated audience may make of it.[5]

Similar, if usually less extreme, support for the principle of political censorship was voiced at the 1832 Committee by a variety of witnesses, among them John Payne Collier, who maintained that experience had taught him that, even if other forms of dramatic censorship were eventually to be abolished, the authorities' retention of political control was crucial to the well-being of the theatre and society.[6]

George Colman was never hoodwinked into believing that political drama had departed from the stage. He considered it one of his most important duties as censor to purge every MS. submitted of both deliberate political allusion and anything else which, by force of circumstance, seemed to have gained a political connotation beyond the author's intention or purpose. In this respect Colman defined his criterion as 'anything that might be so allusive to the times as to be applied to the existing moment, and which is likely to be inflammatory'.[7] In other words, the emphasis of political censorship centred not so much on the removal of allusions to the individual policies of governments (though that was certainly included) but on the larger issues that affected the well-being of society as a whole. The questions at stake in the early nineteenth century were generally of such universal importance that most transcended the usual bounds of party politics. There was, in an age nervous of great social upheaval, an identity of interest in the protection of the established order of things. The censorship of drama was one instrument which helped to shield the public from confrontation with any of the great divisive issues of the period. Included in the licensing authorities' mental list of prohibited areas of discussion were the Irish problem, the Reform Bill, Chartism, and the royal family. At least that was the ideal aimed at by Colman and his immediate successors. But momentary inattention on the part of the Examiner or bravado from certain playwrights and theatre managers meant that the drama did not always live up fully to that ideal.

Colman's first act of censorship after taking office in late January 1824 was a political one. It seemed to set the tone of his new career and contemporaries might have been forgiven for wondering whether they were witnessing the inauguration of a rigorous and inflexible regime such that they had not experienced even under Larpent. Preparations were already afoot at Covent Garden early in 1824 for the production of Martin Archer Shee's new historical tragedy *Alasco*, when word arrived from St James's Palace that it was to be refused a licence unless certain substantial cuts were agreed upon. Annoyed by the Examiner's unlooked-for interference and presumption, Shee (acting as Genest put it 'with more spirit than prudence')[8] withdrew his play from the stage. Following a direct appeal to the Lord Chamberlain, the Duke of Montrose, which only secured confirmation of Colman's decision, Shee decided to publish *Alasco* from the MS. returned by the licenser and with all the passages to which Colman had objected printed in italics. In a long preface of some fifty pages Shee set out his case, arguing that *Alasco* had never been intended (as Colman had alleged) as an attack on Church or State, class or politics. On the contrary, his hero, a Polish patriot, was a man of 'high spirit and honourable feelings', who was indignant at the subjection of his country and willing to become a martyr in her defence. To all appearances, Shee continued, 'the hero, and the patriot are to be interdicted on our stage, as characters of fearful influence, and dangerous example'.[9] Colman's principal objection to the play was that, in his opinion, it preached 'the doctrine that government is tyranny, that revolt is virtue, and that rebels are righteous', and he found evidence for such a view in a number of speeches, including the following:

> What little skill the patriot sword requires,
> Our zeal may boast, in midnight vigils schooled.
> Those deeper tactics, well contrived to work
> The mere machine of mercenary war,
> We shall not need, whose hearts are in the fray, —
> Who for ourselves, our homes, our country, fight,
> And feel in every blow, we strike for freedom

and Alasco's appeal to fellow rebels in the name of liberty that

> 'Tis not rebellion to resist oppression:
> 'Tis virtue to avenge our country's wrongs,
> And self-defence to strike at an usurper.

Possibly Colman may have detected some sly personal reference in another speech which he required cut:

> Why, if there were *some sland'rous tool of state* —
> *Some taunting, dull, unmanner'd deputy* —
> Some district *despot* prompt to play the Tarquin,
> *And make his power the pander to his lust,*
> By Heaven! I well could act the Roman part,
> And strike the brutal tyrant to the earth.[10]

Similar expressions of violence and revolutionary fervour Colman excised throughout the text. As he later explained, 'although the ferment of the times has greatly subsided, still plays which are built on conspiracies, and attempts to revolutionise a state, stand upon ticklish ground'.[11]

Alasco's plan is to liberate that part of the kingdom of Poland which had fallen under the domination and tyranny of Prussia. But Colman could not dismiss from his mind that the play attacked the established order of things and celebrated a rather dangerous form of patriotism analogous with the situation of the contemporary Irish under their British overlords. However, most of the reviews following the hasty publication of *Alasco* were unhesitatingly on the author's side. The one exception was *Blackwood's Magazine,* which congratulated the Examiner on having uncovered and successfully thwarted a devilish conspiracy for inciting Irish revolution. What other construction, enquired the reviewer, could be put on such inflammatory speeches as that of Conrad, the leader of the insurgents in the first Act? In order that his readers did not miss the point, the offending words were printed in large capitals:

> Though your wrongs are now throbbing at your hearts,
> Repress the impatient spirit, and AWAIT
> THE HOUR OF VENGEANCE NOW SO NEAR AT HAND.

He argued further that indisputable parallels could be drawn between certain characters in the play and sentiments retailed by such strenuous supporters of the Irish cause as Daniel O'Connell and Tom Moore. To cap it all, Shee was described as a Catholic and a Whig, whose play reeked of Irish republicanism and of thinly disguised Papist propaganda.[12] Whether Colman was himself so foolish as to believe that Shee had such insidious intent is not really the point. What is important is that the review was exactly the kind of justification he and the Duke of Montrose needed for their joint action in refusing *Alasco* a licence. Although the tragedy was performed soon afterwards at the Surrey

Theatre (a minor theatre where it was safe from the Lord Chamberlain's interference), it ran for only a short time and then fell into complete neglect. But *Alasco* was not forgotten at St James's Palace, where it served as the precedent for future objections to what Shee had called 'the energetic expression of any patriotic sentiment'.[13]

From the time of Shakespeare historical tragedy has readily provided a medium for the exploration of political ideas. In the early nineteenth century the form afforded the opportunity for displaying what one modern critic has referred to as 'the vaguely democratic devotion to liberalism'.[14] It is a point well illustrated in such plays as Sheridan Knowles's *Virginius* (1820) — itself the victim of censorship under Colman's predecessor[15] — in the same author's *William Tell* (1825), and in Thomas Noon Talfourd's *Ion* (1836), each of which is infused with this same spirit of defiance in their heroes' struggles against authoritarian oppression. For his part, Colman recognised the dangers and acted on the principle that theatre audiences were best not reminded about unpleasant or inconvenient facts of history and of political situations in other countries which could, by the process of analogy, be compared with either Britain or Ireland. The problem with Mary Russell Mitford's tragedy *Charles the First* (1825) was that it not only dealt with generally distasteful facts of history but that it was about regicide. Miss Mitford had already achieved some small success with her play *Julian* (1823) and she had been encouraged in her latest project by Macready and then by Charles Kemble, who agreed to read the MS. with a view to performance at Covent Garden. In Kemble's opinion her tragedy was 'admirable though somewhat dangerous'; and it was with some misgivings that he dispatched the copy for licensing.[16] His fears were confirmed when he heard nothing further about the play for three weeks. In the interval, Colman's suspicions had been aroused and within two days of receiving the MS. he had written to the Duke of Montrose recommending its suppression on religious and political grounds:

As a point of duty, I forward the enclosed Form of License; but it will surprise me if your Grace should think proper to sign it. It refers to a Play the very title of which, Charles the First (of England), — brings, instantly, to mind the violent commotions, & catastrophes of that unhappy Monarch's reign; — &, in following closely the historical facts previous to his Death, the *Dramatis Personae* (as far as Cromwell & his coherents are concerned) exhibit the fanatical manners & utter all the puritanical cant, peculiar to their times: — consequently, the Piece abounds (blasphemously, I think) with Scriptural allusions, & quotations, & the name of the Almighty is introduced, & invoked, over & over again, by hypocrites, & regicides.

If it be *in keeping* thus to delineate the morals & religion of the Cromwell party the political part of their dialogue is, by the same rule, democratical; most insulting to Charles, in particular, & to the Monarchy in general.[17]

On 13 October Montrose returned the MS., accompanied by a brusque note: 'I return the Play called *Charles the First*, & cannot think it is fit for representation on the Stage; more I think it is not necessary to say.' Two days later Kemble received a missive from Colman informing him of the decision and adding smugly: 'I have less regret in communicating this intelligence as I think you must have anticipated it; &, where there could have been little hope of permission, there can be little disappointment in a refusal.'[18] Kemble and Miss Mitford dutifully submitted to the decision and some time later the latter thanked Colman for his advice on another historical subject which she had been contemplating, namely his 'implied warning' not to meddle with the topic of Henry II, 'especially as I believe that I perceive the reason which induced you to think the subject a bad one'.[19]

Admittedly, there were reasons enough in Colman's letter to the Duke to secure the suppression of *Charles the First*, but there were probably other, more personal, grounds for the Lord Chamberlain's lack of sympathy with the play. The Montrose family had always been staunch Royalists. Indeed, during the Civil War the 1st Marquess had fought as Commander-in-Chief of the Scottish forces and later, after the King's execution, had led an abortive expedition against Cromwell, which resulted in his capture and execution at Edinburgh in 1650.[20] But the final seal on the rejection of the play was no doubt set by the fact that the date of Charles's martyrdom (30 January) was still observed in the Church of England's calendar and it was traditionally the practice of the Lord Chamberlain in office to order the closure of the theatres on that day. Miss Mitford observed in the preface to the published version of her play (after it had been produced at the Victoria Theatre, outside the Lord Chamberlain's authority), that she had understood that *Charles the First* had been banned because of objections 'to the title and the subject' and 'not to the details or the execution of the plot'.[21] But when Colman was called upon to justify his action against the play at the 1832 Committee, he confirmed that it had been interdicted 'because it amounted to everything but cutting off the King's head upon the stage'.[22] For at least the next quarter of a century Charles I, as far as most dramatists were concerned, was a prohibited subject.

Given Colman's manifest distrust of dramas founded on any kind of revolutionary theme, his approval of Thomas Doubleday's historical tragedy *Babington* (1825), based on the conspiracy of Antony Babington and his accomplices to assassinate Elizabeth I and restore Mary Queen of Scots to her alleged rightful position as Queen of England, must have struck even contemporaries as somewhat surprising. Admittedly, the Examiner did insist on some lengthy excisions touching on the controversy between the Protestant and Roman religions, but he seems to have had no misgivings about the general theme. Not so the Lord Chamberlain, who was startled by the import of the title and warned Colman that 'I fear I must see [the MS.] before I can sign my name.'[23] The memory of the recent Cato Street conspiracy and an awareness of the country's general mood of disquiet were certainly two of the reasons behind his uncertainty over the play; but what Montrose read was enough to convince him of his Examiner's sound judgment and Doubleday's tragedy was licensed without further difficulty. In all fairness to Colman it must be pointed out that, even in the early zealous days of his career, he was prepared to judge plays on their individual merits and did not hold doggedly to a set of inflexible rules.

On the other hand, Colman did make mistakes. Sometimes he censored the wrong things, as in Thomas Morton and James Kenney's *Peter the Great; or, the Battle of Pultowa* (1829), a semi-historical treatment of the rivalry between the Czar and Charles XII of Sweden, who was eventually defeated at the battle which forms the subtitle of the play. Colman's attention was caught by some of the political references, particularly in the first act, when Peter the Great enters with a sheaf of petitions from his subjects:

(reads) 'Your loyal Petitioners fearing your Majesty's new regulations may endanger our venerable and sacred institutions' —Menzikos! read that senseless scribble — does it not require the patience of an angel —these are the wilful blind, whose element is darkness, and who shrink from the light of day. I labour for my people. I sow the seeds of industry & I rouse them from the slumber that priests and place-men would keep them dreaming in and my harvest is blight and bitterness.

If Colman seriously believed that there was any possibility of an audience drawing parallels between the views here expressed and those of George IV, it is an indication of the lengths to which the Examiner sometimes went in his search for unwelcome political allusion. Some of the shorter cuts in the MS. —such passages as 'honest men at Court don't take up much room' and 'the monarch can do no wrong' — were perhaps more obviously tilted against the Court.[24] But when the play came to be performed the objections raised by the reviewers were not political at all. In his political zeal, Colman had completely overlooked the dubious nature of one of the female characters, a fact noticed

43

by *The Times* (23 February 1829), which described the part of Illo (a miller's daughter, with whom Peter takes refuge in disguise) as existing 'chiefly for the purpose of introducing a quantity of jokes, the indelicacy of which is much more remarkable than their wit'. Yet perhaps Colman had been right in focusing on the political allusions. As Thomas Morton himself remarked in 1832: 'There is a tendency in the audience to force passages never meant by the author into political meanings . . . and also we all know that a theatre is a place of peculiar excitement . . . I do not know anything more terrible than an enraged audience.'[25] Neither did the licensing authorities. That was Colman's justification for what in retrospect might seem to be over-severe political pruning.

George Colman's political regimen, though it became a little more relaxed towards the end of his career, did not escape protest from some of his later victims. In 1834 the ubiquitous Alfred Bunn was amazed to discover, as he announced to the world in the published version of the play, that his adaptation of Scribe's *Bertrand et Raton* (submitted under the title *The Minister and the Mercer*) had, despite the Examiner's verbal agreement to licence it (subject to 'a few casual words or passages'), suddenly fallen under official proscription. Bunn took the view that the objection must have lain in the fact that his play — set in late eighteenth-century Denmark in the period following the downfall and execution of the powerful Count Struensee, chief minister to the semi-idiot Christian VII, for alienating the affections of Queen Louisa, a sister of George III of England — contained a character representing Marie Julie (Queen Dowager and step-mother to Christian) who claimed kinship with the British royal family. With loud protests that 'a play more upholding ORDER, LAW, and CONSTITUTED AUTHORITY was never submitted to public opinion', Bunn appealed directly to the Lord Chamberlain for a reversal of the ban. The Earl of Belfast (acting temporarily for the Duke of Devonshire) gave him a sympathetic ear and, in Bunn's own words, 'a license was immediately granted, subject to certain alterations'.[26] But there was soon another political complication, for while *The Minister and the Mercer* (suitably purged of all offence to the Hanoverians) was running at Drury Lane news filtered through to the Lord Chamberlain's Office that the costume and make-up of the hero bore a distinct resemblance to the celebrated Prince Talleyrand, at that time ambassador to Britain from the court of Louis Philippe. The authorities' anger at this early attempt at political caricature swiftly cooled, however, after the Prime Minister and the Foreign Secretary attended a performance only to find Talleyrand himself occupying the box opposite and apparently enjoying his self-portrait as a huge joke. Bunn, who had engineered the whole business, was noticeably reticent about this aspect in his published preface, preferring the argument that no reply was possible other than the old adage *qui capit ille facit*.[27]

Just how serviceable historical drama could be for political purposes is well illustrated in the dramatic career of Bulwer Lytton, a radically inclined Whig member of parliament and, as we have already seen, a vociferous opponent of censorship. Of his time he is the outstanding example of a determinedly political playwright. His three plays, *Richelieu, The Duchess de la Vallière*, and *The Lady of Lyons*, constitute a political trilogy, designed to show the gradual shift of power from despotism to republican democracy;[28] but it was only the last-named that suffered contemporary criticism on political grounds, and none of the three encountered official censorship. The arch-Tory newspaper the *Age* (18 February 1838) described *The Lady of Lyons* as 'much more remarkable for its politics than its poetry'; and all the Tory press expressed deep concern over its scarcely disguised republican sentiments. The vituperation (led by the *Times* review, 16 February) was so bitter that Macready, who played the male lead, Claude Melnotte, was forced into a public *apologia* in the play's defence. A few nights after its first performance at Covent Garden he addressed the audience, begging to assure them that 'upon the strictest investigation, there are no political allusions that do not grow out of the piece, and are necessarily conducive to the working of the story'. 'Had it been otherwise,' he continued, 'I am certain that the author . . . would never have descended to such means to entrap your applause; the licenser would not have permitted it, nor, I believe, will you think that I should have had the bad taste to encourage it.'[29] Macready's remark about the licenser's refusal to permit political allusion – he must have been thinking about the censorship under George Colman rather than under his indifferent successor Charles Kemble – demonstrates how well-schooled theatre managers and actors had become in the principles operated by Colman. Yet, Macready to the contrary, *The Lady of Lyons* is a political play. As George Rowell suggests, its very success with the public, who rejected the lead of the newspapers, 'is perhaps best attributed to its appeal (discreetly dressed in period costume) to the radical sentiments of the decade of the Reform Bill'.[30]

But if, as Macready claimed, politics in the theatre were in such bad taste, it is nevertheless remarkable how alert audiences were for allusions which, whatever the author's intentions, could be twisted into political reference. James Haynes's historical tragedy *Mary Stuart* (1840) focuses some of the problems for the nineteenth-century dramatist in trying to accommodate both the sensibilities of his audience and the demands of the official censorship. Desperate to revive the theatre's fading glory by reintroducing the legitimate drama, the new manager of Drury Lane (W. J. Hammond) eagerly accepted the offer of Haynes's play and had no difficulty in persuading Macready to take the part of Ruthven, a dying Scots nobleman given new purpose by leading the conspiracy to rid his native country of 'foreign reptiles' like David Rizzio, who surround and counsel Mary Queen of Scots. The MS. was duly submitted to John Kemble and licensed within a week. During the interval, rehearsals for the tragedy went badly; but then Macready was enraged to discover that the censor had tampered with the text and cut out 'some important passages . . . that destroy its power and interest!' Always ready to sense sinister motives behind anything which adversely affected his own interests, Macready surmised that 'this interference with the play has either been the act of an unwise man, or a dishonest one, for the sake of Covent Garden Theatre. It looks very ugly, but my province is endurance, and to "do nothing", or say nothing, "from *strife*".'[31] The accusation is hardly credible; Macready's frame of mind is probably sufficient explanation. But, in any case, the motives behind the censorship of *Mary Stuart* are those of pure political expediency.

On the day after the return of the licensed copy from St James's Palace, Macready received a letter from Kemble directing him by 'command of the Lord Chamberlain to omit certain other passages, which had not been erased in the copy which Mr Hammond had returned to his office'.[32] This quite exceptional procedure — that is, the making of further cuts in an already licensed MS. and not yet performed — indicates something of the importance which the authorities attached to the play and its sentiments. Two cuts only are listed in the Day Book: the omission of the line 'Is there no corner free from these foreign reptiles?' and of a speech by Ruthven hinting at corruption at Court and the pressing need to remove Rizzio from the Queen's favour. In the Lord Chamberlain's licensing copy the latter reads:

> Then 'tis plain
> We must be rid of him, I see the way —
> We must search out the guilty secrets of
> This Court and bare them to the public gaze —
> The hidden story of the Bayonne league
> Must be unravelled! and whatever tends

> To set the King and Queen at variance nursed
> And cherished into life.[33]

Although some of the other cuts in the MS., totalling more than seventy lines, may have been the work of the manager in tailoring the play for performance, their content indicates fairly conclusively official censorship.[34] One early speech in particular, darkly suggestive of threatening rebellion, could hardly have been allowed to stand in the licensed text:

> Throughout the track
> I've measured in my journey, discontent
> Was every where — the storm-cloud fills the sky: —
> From every pulpit loud anathemas
> Are thundered at the Queen: — her enmity
> To the true worship shakes the crown upon
> Her head: nor is her love of foreigners
> Forgotten, nor her deadly hatred of
> The banished lords: in short, some dire explosion
> Is ripening fast; we must direct it, or
> Be swept away by't.[35]

Such sentiments were dangerously close to the spirit of *Alasco*; and patriot heroes, dedicated to the overthrow of the established order, were still regarded with a good deal of suspicion.

But there was another much more immediate and pragmatic reason for the opposition *Mary Stuart* encountered from the licensing authorities. Quite fortuitously, the production coincided with preparations for the marriage between Queen Victoria and Prince Albert of Saxe-Coburg-Gotha. The betrothal had not passed without criticism and there must have been many who felt, as Ruthven did of Rizzio, that the Crown was about to fall under malign foreign domination.[36] Most disturbing of all was the fact that the first performance of the play was scheduled for the very day when Albert's request for naturalisation was before the House of Commons. In the play the excised line 'Is there no corner free from these foreign reptiles?' could have been pointedly applied to Albert and his large German retinue. Indeed, despite Kemble's numerous expurgations, audiences at Drury Lane did recognise the parallel positions of Albert and Rizzio. A reviewer in the *Literary Gazette* (25 January 1840) advised that 'a few lines which the audience chose to apply politically to present affairs ought to be omitted, as they are not essential to the piece, and can only tend to uproar and confusion'. The most notorious example, he reported, occurred when Ruthven, speaking of Rizzio, said: '"I hate aliens, as all our noble forefathers have"' — a line which 'led to a tumult of applause and hisses'. In the inevitable confusion over the licensed text of the play (in consequence of the censor's having required cuts on two separate occasions) Macready and his fellow actors may have had difficulty in keeping faith with the expurgated version. And given Macready's frustrated confidences to his diary he might have enjoyed forgetting that certain passages had been officially prohibited.[37]

That the Lord Chamberlain, as head of the royal household, should have taken such pains to shield the Queen from innuendo and embarrassment is hardly surprising. Implicit in the actions of the censor on political matters is the protection of the person of the sovereign and of the institution of monarchy. Such motives determined the suppression in 1825 of Mary Mitford's *Charles the First* at a time when, as John Payne Collier suggested, 'there was a disposition to think lightly of the authority of kings'.[38] At any rate, apart from the single exception of Browning's verse drama *Strafford* (1837), licensed by Charles Kemble,[39] the authorities effectively prohibited from the early-Victorian stage all treatment of the events of Charles I's reign because it was an unhappy reminder of the vulnerability of kingship in the face of determined republicanism. The attitude of the Lord Chamberlain's Office was known widely enough for W. J. Fox to comment on the unlikelihood, under 'the injurious restrictions of foolish Lord Chamberlains', of Bulwer Lytton's ever obtaining a licence for his unpublished play *Cromwell*,[40] intended as part of a trilogy enacting the political and constitutional struggles of the seventeenth century. Fox was almost certainly correct in his assumption. In John Kemble's fee book (10 November 1837) a play entitled *Cromwell* — very probably Bulwer Lytton's — is entered as 'withdrawn', which in the vocabulary of the Lord Chamberlain's Office usually meant that the subject-matter of the play concerned was so unfit for the stage as not to merit official examination.

The prohibition on the subject was further consolidated in 1844, when a new play *Richelieu in Love; or the Youth of Charles I* by Emma Robinson (already in rehearsal at the Haymarket Theatre) was suddenly interdicted on the order of the Lord Chamberlain. It was Miss Robinson's first play and she vented her annoyance at the authorities' interference by publishing the full text, along with a preface defending her work and denouncing the iniquities of censorship as 'the literary Star Chamber'. Her innocent drama, she continued, is pronounced by the invisible but oracular bar at which it was condemned and found guilty, (the peculiar form of trial at it), unfit to be represented, because it is calculated to bring 'church and state into contempt'. How this result was to be effected by delineating the brilliant vagaries of a court two hundred years gone into dust, in colours taken from the pallet of history; what church was to be damaged by any aberrations from the beau-ideal of the priestly character in Cardinal Richelieu; what advantage was to accrue to the author from the completion of this ungodly purpose of his, — the judges, or rather sentencers, have not had the generosity to explain.[41]

So deeply rooted were the authorities' objections, the author explained, that 'nothing but the total ruin of the drama could remove them'. Emma Robinson was no doubt unaware that she had been unlucky enough to select a topic which had been on the Lord Chamberlain's proscribed list since 1825 and that the interdiction of her play was but part of a continuing policy to keep Charles I off the stage. Not that there was anything particularly harmful to Charles in the play. Indeed, his youthful escapade with the Duke of Buckingham when the pair tra- velled incognito to Madrid for the arranged betrothal between Charles and the Spanish Infanta forms only the subplot of the drama. But the generally cynical account of court life perhaps provided, if any were needed, further grounds for the licensers' action.

Precedent so often seems to have had the force of law at the Lord Chamberlain's Office in the nineteenth century; but it was left to the next Examiner of Plays, William Bodham Donne, finally to overthrow the rule on this particular topic by his agreement to licence a much- revised version of *Richelieu in Love* (reduced from five acts to three) for the Haymarket in October 1852. Miss Robinson's new version was rath- er less critical of court life than the original text of 1844, though the reissued published play[42] contains a number of passages enclosed within inverted commas (indicating that they were to be omitted in performance) which are absent from the MS. licensed by Donne. One section of Richelieu's interview with the queen warns her that her con- duct is bringing discredit on the court:

You are gradually melting the frost-work of etiquette, which shields the throne from the prying gaze of the vulgar! And yet, shear sovereignty of its glittering ceremony, and what remains but poor humanity?

We may be sure that Donne would have deleted that speech if it had appeared in the MS. Some while later in the play, there is an exchange between the queen and her ladies-in-waiting on the subject of patience, a quality which the queen asserts should be distributed more widely among her gentlewomen, one of whom replies: 'I am a lady of the bed chamber to your Grace, and cannot spare any.' (Both passages appear without inverted commas in the suppressed 1844 text. At the time the latter may well have been construed as an allusion to the Bed Chamber crisis of 1839). But the licensing of *Richelieu in Love*, albeit in an expurgated version, says much for Donne's reiterated belief that the stage should enjoy all reasonable liberty in the choice of subject-matter. His courage in overturning precedent is all the more noteworthy since Donne was still acting only as deputy for John Kemble, the official Examiner.

During the 1840s and 50s both Kemble and Donne remained acutely conscious of their traditional obligations to protect the monarchy from adverse criticism on the stage. Historically speaking, the Crown was in a relatively strong position at the accession of Queen Victoria in 1837, following the disrepute it had suffered under George IV and the 'Sailor King' William IV, but the indulgence for the new Queen lasted only briefly. At intervals during the next fifteen to twenty years, the press launched a series of attacks on Victoria and on Albert, whose ever-increasing political influence aroused much suspicion. Two further plays — *The Queen's Necklace* and Margaret Mellon's *The Major Domo* — were prohibited by John Kemble in 1844 on the grounds that they might bring the monarchy into discredit.[43] As with *Richelieu in Love*, the former contained nothing that was directly offensive to the institution — it was based on a scandal already more than fifty years old in the French royal family, when one of Louis XVI's cardinals fell prey to the seductive allurements of an adventuress — but it did involve an equivocal impersonation of the French Queen. The latter struck a little nearer home. Miss Mellon's *Major Domo* (set in Germany) concerns a recently married princess who, having insisted on bringing with her the whole of her former entourage, succeeds in disrupting the calm of her new German husband's household. Although the situation was reversed, there was much to suggest analogy both with Prince Albert's uncertain constitutional position and his stubborn insistence in retaining so many favourites from his old German retinue. Whether, indeed, *The Major Domo* was ever consciously intended to reflect on the domestic problems of Buckingham Palace was hardly relevant to the work of censorship — the possibility that an audience might perceive the link was enough to secure the play's suppression.

As a conscientious theatre-goer in her early days, Queen Victoria did much to elevate the declined social status of the drama. But on at least one occasion the Queen was directly responsible, through her personal expression of distaste, for the prohibition of a play by one of France's most celebrated dramatists. Victor Hugo's *Ruy Blas* (Paris, 1838) was first refused licence in England (so an article in *All the Year Round* informs us) soon after the accession of Victoria, 'lest playgoers should perceive in it, allusions to the choice of a husband her Majesty was then about to make'.[44] The first official record of its interdiction occurs in Kemble's fee book, where an entry (1 February 1845) describes *Ruy Blas* as a five-act drama refused licence for the St James's Theatre. Subsequent efforts to stage the play met with resistance from the Lord Chamberlain's Office as late as 1860 and no one was permitted to present it in its original form.

William Donne, however, unaware of the earlier proscription on the play, having read the text and found nothing in the least objectionable, recommended its licence for the St James's Theatre in 1852. But, as he remarked in retrospect, within two days *Ruy Blas* was 'speedily withdrawn because it was understood that Her Majesty was displeased by the representation of a *Queen* in love with and finally marrying a *footman in livery*'.[45] Through the machinations of his master, the hero of Hugo's play is forced into disguise as a Spanish grandee, becomes accepted at court, and finds himself in love with the Queen, who returns his affection. Ruy Blas' master has his intended revenge on the Queen when he triumphantly reveals to her the true identity and social status of her lover. In the original (though clearly not in the version performed at the St James's Theatre, where a marriage takes place) Blas takes poison and falls dying at the feet of his sovereign.

Understandably, when Donne was confronted with an English translation of the same play (under the title *The Secret Passion*) in 1858 he acted more cautiously and consulted his superiors. He suggested that all possible grounds for offence might be eliminated 'by expunging the term *footman*, & dressing Alvar [i.e. Ruy Blas] as the retainer (*serviteur*) not as the footman (valet) of a Spanish noble',[46] and the play was licensed on that specific condition. Likewise, when the play was submitted under its original title for the Princess Theatre in 1860, the Examiner was again careful to ensure that Blas' social status was sufficiently improved for his intrigue with the queen and that he should be 'properly attired' in order to make clear the crucial 'distinction between *retainer* and *menial*'. The Lord Chamberlain, anxious that there should be no cause for complaint, insisted that his Examiner visit the theatre during rehearsals. It turned out to be a necessary precaution, for after one such visit Donne reported that he had had to require further textual deletions so 'that by no possibility the *valetism* can be obnoxious'. Donne was also present on the first night on 27 October, following which he was able to reassure Lord Sydney that the performance contained nothing which might 'reflect on present times or on illustrious personages', though he recognised, too, that 'the plot is an awkward one and some ten or fifteen years ago it would have been desirable to exclude the Drama from the stage'.[47]

II

In the assiduous concern of the Lord Chamberlain's Office to exclude from the stage all material injurious to the dignity of established institutions or of anything which might be said to encourage disaffection with or disturbance of the existing political and social structure, the latter years of George Colman's career — the decade of Reform agitation — were dangerous times. But positively to exclude all references to Reform, machine-breaking, incendiarism, riotous assemblies, and other equally sensitive issues was a virtually impossible task, especially as the minor theatres (outside the Lord Chamberlain's control unless he also happened to be the licenser of the theatre), whose audiences in the main comprised the more volatile lower classes, exercised more or less unchecked a degree of political freedom that would certainly have horrified Colman if he ever took the trouble to attend the performances. It is at such minor theatres as the Coburg, Surrey, and other transpontine sources of theatrical entertainment that any serious claim that the Victorian theatre possessed a distinct political dimension must be finally tested. One of the most outspoken dramas of the period was John Walker's *The Factory Lad* (Surrey, October 1832), which deals in remarkably uninhibited language with the problems of machines supplanting traditional human labour, incendiarism, the rough justice meted out to the poor, and the glaring inadequacies of parish relief. We may be quite certain that Colman would never have given official approval to such arousing sentiments as expressed by the villain Squire Westwood, the erring employer, who dismisses his loyal workforce in favour of steam-driven machines: 'What have I to fear or dread? Is England's proud aristocracy to tremble when brawling fools mouth and question? No; the hangman shall be their answer.' Nor, indeed, on the other side of the political fence, to the rabble-rouser's declaration that 'the slave abroad, the poor black whom they affect to pity, is not so trampled, hunted, or ill-used as the peasant or hard-working fellows like yourselves, if once you have no home nor bread to give your children'.[48]

As in the later part of the century, the bolder forms of political allusion and satire often found freest expression in the popular pantomime, both in the dialogue (which was frequently added to after licensing) and in the stage business. The majority of pantomimes were performed at the minor theatres but, interestingly enough, one of the most audacious examples, John Baldwin Buckstone's *Grimalkin the Great* (Adelphi, 1830), was licensed by the Lord Chamberlain. It may be doubted, however, that full official sanction was given at the time of licensing to the events of the opening scene, which has been described as 'the most politically allusive of Reform Bill pantomimes' dramatising 'the confrontation of a sovereign, a manufacturer, and workers who, like the Luddites, destroy the manufacturer's machinery and products'.[49] Much later in the century J. R. Planché went far in realising his ambition 'to lay the foundations for an Aristophanic drama'; and in his extravaganza *The Seven Champions of Christendom* (1849) indulged unchecked in unmistakable allusions to the Italian Revolution, bloodshed in Paris, the German insurrection, the Rebecca riots in Wales, and the potato blight in Ireland.[50]

In those cases of the minor theatres outside the Lord Chamberlain's immediate control, the range of political reference was sometimes tempered by an indignant press, which in severe instances prompted visits to offending theatres by the licensing magistrates. This is certainly what happened at the Coburg Theatre in 1832 when, in its advertisement of Henry Fielding's classic burlesque *Tom Thumb the Great*, the management, emphasising that any similarities between the characters of the play and the current domestic situation of the King, his consort, and the Duke of Wellington were 'merely casual', succeeded in their obvious intention of promoting the parallels even further. As reported in the prejudiced columns of the *Age* (3 June 1832), the playbill announced that 'the character of the good-natured, hen-pecked, *King Arthur* may appear like that of a certain distinguished Personage', 'the termagent breeches-wearing Queen Dollalolla' like that of the same distinguished person's wife, and Lord Grizzle like 'a well-known notorious Duke', who was opposed to all talk of Reform. The same newspaper commented, in its usual vociferous manner, that the advertisement was an 'unprecedented compilation of indecency, common outrage, and downright rebellion', full of 'the grossest allusions ... made in the most unblushing manner'. Immediate action was demanded in the shape of a visit by the licensers, the Surrey magistrates, 'to strip the Coburg Theatre TO-MORROW OF ITS LICENSE'.[51] Such matters were out of Colman's hands but his own actions were frequently designed to prevent such journalistic outbursts. Only the year previously he had ordered a change in title of a comedy from *Nettle Whigs All; or, the Majority of Ten to One* to the much less provocative *Nettlewig Hall; or, Ten to One.* Afterwards the *Courier* commented approvingly (2 April 1831) that the play's 'palpably sinister name was most judiciously reformed . . . by the able hands of the Deputy-Licenser', who had also cut out all the pro-Tory allusions.

Colman's judiciousness and powers of discrimination seemed to have temporarily deserted him, however, in the licensing (with only very minor cuts) of Douglas Jerrold's 'domestic drama' *The Factory Girl* (Drury Lane, October 1832). The *Times* reviewer (8 October) was moved to comment sourly that 'a more ticklish subject (colonial slavery alone excepted) could not have been selected for scenic representation'. Scarcely concealing his satisfaction, the reviewer went on to note that the audience had shared his misgivings about the play so that by the time the curtain fell it had become patently annoyed at the absurdity of the plot and the exaggerated picture given of factories and their owners. 'Some gentlemen in the dress circle', he observed, 'were remarkably violent in their disapprobation, and at one time there was every appearance of an approaching battle royal.' A few days later the play was discussed in the columns of the *Age* (14 October), and the management of Drury Lane was severely reprimanded for ever having allowed such a play to disgrace its boards and thereby turn the theatre 'into *a scenic Rotunda* for the promulgation of republican principles'. (The word 'Rotunda' had especially emotive connotations for the contemporary Tory press since it was at the Rotunda in Blackfriars Road that such notorious radicals as John Hunt met with others of like mind to discuss subversive topics and plot the overthrow of established government.) As might be expected, George Colman received his fair share of the blame and the newspaper made the most of its opportunity. 'What', it enquired, 'are we to say of that model of morality, the devout Deputy Licenser, who expunges the word "angel" as if it were an abomination, and blots out harmless and unmeaning ejaculations . . . whilst he sanctions . . . the most indecent attacks upon the Clergy of the Established Church, and the Aristocracy of the land?' It was a question to which many critics (Whig and Tory) and dramatists would have been delighted to have received an answer.

The 1830s and 40s were violent times. Reform agitation, Chartism, and such manifestations of civil unrest as the Rebecca riots continued to make the licensing authorities nervous of any dramas founded on plots, conspiracies, and social upheaval. It was for this reason that John Mitchell Kemble refused to licence Edward Stirling's adaptation of Ainsworth's novel *Guy Fawkes* under the title *Guido Fawkes; or, the Prophetess of Ordsall Cave* (1840) until extensive revisions had been effected. There are two MSS. of the play in the Lord Chamberlain's collection, the refused version and the revised text licensed some ten days after the date of the original submission.[52] Apart from some relatively minor textual differences between the two versions, the principal alteration concerns the opening scene, in which citizens discuss the significance of current events, particularly the recent burnings at the stake for profession of the Roman religion. Some speeches calling the citizens to arms are considerably modified in the revised text. A writer in the *Literary Gazette* (20 August 1840) described *Guido Fawkes* (no doubt somewhat exaggeratedly) as 'having given the Young Licenser of dramas such a twist as will make him remember (the fifth of November and) the office he holds to the last day of his life'. Rumours had gone abroad that the text had suffered severe pruning at the hands of the licenser; but, the reviewer continued, the production of the play at the English Opera House had been attended 'without any ill effects whatever. This extraordinary fact must have either proceeded from the people in authority having discovered and countermined the author's plot; or from the author's never entertaining any dangerous plot at all; which we cannot tell.' The Lord Chamberlain's Office had perhaps overreacted to Stirling's play; yet John Frost's Chartist uprising at Newport in November of the previous year must have been still fresh in people's memories. Fawkes's conspiracy itself and the whole atmosphere of martyrdom and discontent that pervaded the play must have been reckoned as rather too emotive for contemporary theatre audiences. After all, Fawkes's offence was against the whole principle of parliamentary government.

The vexed question of Irish politics, an area which provided the licensers with a number of awkward problems in the first half of the nineteenth century, has an obvious relationship with the authorities' proscription on the more general topic of revolution. As far back as 1826, George Colman prohibited a drama called *The Guerilla* 'on account of the numerous situations which agreed with present affairs in Ireland'.[53] Later, in 1840, John Kemble was obliged to reject a play entitled *Lord Edward*, based (it must be assumed since no MS. survives) on the career of the colourful Irish patriot Lord Edward Fitzgerald.[54] His agitation for Irish insurrection eventually triggered his arrest in

1798, shortly after which he died a martyr's death from a gunshot wound sustained at the time of his capture. Political activities of that kind were judged as best forgotten when, forty years after the Act of Union, the problem of Ireland seemed as far off as ever from solution. Similarly, George Dibdin Pitt's 'Hibernian domestic drama' *Terry Tyrone (the Irish Tam O'Shanter); or, the Red Beggar of Ballingford*, submitted by the Britannia Theatre in 1847, was also interdicted for taking as its hero another Irish patriot, the rebel and political intriguer Robert Emmet, who had taken a leading part in the 1798 rebellion.[55] (Indeed, the prohibition on Emmet lasted at least until 1881–2, when Frank Marshall completed his long-awaited play on the Irish hero — Henry Irving had already agreed to take the title-role — only to discover that the Lord Chamberlain of the day, the Irish Catholic peer Lord Kenmare, refused to entertain the idea of licensing a drama which, in the words of Bram Stoker, 'might have a dangerous effect on a people seething in revolt'.[56] Such blatantly objectionable cases apart, Ireland was not, of course, a totally prohibited topic. All hinged on the subject-matter and the treatment, so that a dramatist like Dion Boucicault in such popular plays as *The Colleen Bawn* (1860) and *Arrah-na-Pogue* (1864) was permitted to use specifically Irish settings without any interference from the Lord Chamberlain.[57]

To the early Victorians the spectre of bloody revolution (not only in Ireland but at home) was real enough. During 1848, the year which marks the climax of the revolutionary spirit, the government, anxiously watching events on the European continent, took alarm at isolated but nonetheless disturbing manifestations of political disturbance in England. For a time political censorship became more stringent than at any period since George Colman's. J. Stirling Coyne's *Lola Montes* (Haymarket, 26 April 1848) was an early victim. The official explanation for its being stopped within two nights of the first performance was the discovery that it contained material likely to embarrass a foreign government. But its temporary interdiction may well have had more to do with the fact that Coyne's heroine, by means of her insidious political and sexual influence, was seen to be directly responsible for the citizens' insurrection which led to the enforced abdication of Louis I of Bavaria. (And it could hardly have helped Coyne's case that his adventuress claimed Irish birth.) On those terms, the play was clearly an uncomfortable reminder of the instability of monarchical government in the turbulent times of 1848. However, after various modifications (including the removal of all allusions to the King) *Lola Montes* was safely defused and allowed to continue its run under the new title *Pas de Fascination; or, the Prince of Horses*.[58]

A similarly watchful eye was kept over the production of Alexandre Dumas' *Monte-Cristo* at Drury Lane, where Alfred Bunn had engaged a French company for the occasion. The text was subjected to special scrutiny and a number of cuts were made (the whole of IV, viii, for instance) before the Lord Chamberlain – still with some misgivings – agreed to licence it. A member of the St James's Palace staff was directed to attend the first performance to report whether any objectionable material had been inserted in defiance of the Lord Chamberlain. As it turned out, his task was impossible for the theatre was full of 'protectionists', who made apparent their violent antipathy to the engagement of foreign actors. Their howls of derision and the resulting general commotion in the house were reportedly as bad as anything since the notorious 'Old Price' riots at the same theatre forty years before. After the enforced transfer of the play to the St James's – the traditional home of French-language drama – the performance proceeded 'without the slightest interruption, and the actors on their appearance were treated with marked respect'. Again the Lord Chamberlain's representative was present, carefully following the authorised text, aided by a separate list of excisions provided by Kemble. His task, as he afterwards noted, was two-fold: 'I was ... ordered privately not only to check the words, but to remark the nature of the scenery & drapes, also the *Music*, & to report if any of the revolutionary airs as the Girondin, & the Marseillaise etc. should be given – in fact if any political tendency should be evinced.'[59] Clearly, the fear was that *Monte-Cristo* might provide a convenient opportunity for some display in favour of French republicanism; and, indeed, there seems to have been some political motive behind the production on the part of the actors. The play was given in two parts, each on separate nights, and the official report shows that certain passages struck out from the licensed text were spoken on the stage – 'three sentences' on the first night but 'many more' on the second. No further action was taken, however, as the play was not to be repeated and the French company was returning home. But the authorities' reaction is a further reminder of their extreme sensitivity to anything which might inflame political passions in the critical period of 'the Year of Revolutions'. The drama was constantly encouraged to play in a minor key.

In times of political tension, the censors were especially mistrustful of patriotic plays. The patriot, characterised by Samuel Johnson as 'a factious disturber of the government',[60] was a man with a clearly defined but suspect idealism. By its very title, George Dibdin Pitt's play *The Revolution of Paris; or, the Patriot Deputy* must have immediately aroused suspicion when it was submitted for examination in March

1848. The drama was loosely based on the events of the Paris uprising of 1659; but unfortunately for Pitt (who was unlucky more than once with his choice of subject-matter), it also happened to be a mirror of contemporary events in that city. In an effort to convince the licensers that his play was inoffensive, the author (or perhaps the theatre manager) prefaced the text with a short note stressing that the piece was free from 'political allusions to Monarchy. No *names*, or persons introduced of the Present time; the danger of placing too much power in the hands of the Indiscreet and the Character of a *Red* Patriot Exemplified unbiased by Party feelings.'[61] The subtitle is heavily scored out from the title page and on the verso is another note again emphasising the play's irrelevance to the current situation in Paris:

Notice / This piece does not in any way touch on the Present Crisis — except the Appointment of a *Provisional* Government. It is originally an Italian story — and the title given to it the most apposite to the leading Topic of the day; the *Monarch's name* is never mentioned, no notice of *ministers* ... The title has be [en] suggested, *since* the piece has been wrote [sic] but as it will be seen — tis a *stage Revolution* not that of *Paris 1848* — and with the addition of some lines in the part of the Deputy — the Italian revolution of 1659 in Milan.[62]

Pitt could hardly have provided a better set of reasons for the suppression of his play. On advice from the Examiner, the Britannia Theatre was induced to withdraw the play from examination. In return its manager Samuel Lane received an appreciative note of thanks from the Comptroller of the Lord Chamberlain's Office: 'such conduct', he assured him, 'on the part of those holding Licenses from His Lordship, affords The Lord Chamberlain an additional Reason for contriving to encourage the Drama, with a due regard to the Interests of the Managers who uphold the respectability of their Establishments by good discretion and rightmindedness'.[63]

Pitt's play, far from encouraging thoughts of revolution, explicitly advocates non-violent change. As the hero declares in Act I: 'I would open the eyes of the King as well as those of the people for he is no true Patriarch that would deluge his natural land in Blood or seek to destroy its commerce & content by Anarchy & War.' The Lord Chamberlain could hardly have objected to such sentiments; but the speaker, Victor Roland, is arrested at the end of the act and his betrayer thereupon incites the mob to insurrection with the cry 'The hour is at hand — tear up the Pavement. Attack the Palace, Down with the Prison, up with the Tricolour. A bas le Bourbon.'[64] Recent events in Paris — the overthrow of Guizot's conservative regime following the popular uprising of 22 February (only a week or so previous to the arrival of the play for official examination) and the enforced abdication of Louis Philippe — were uncomfortably close parallels with the events of Pitt's drama, which was itself the terrifying image of what might take place in Britain. The authorities' objection to the play lay not in the treatment of the subject but in the subject itself.

At home the advocates of change were becoming more and more articulate and in April 1848 the monster Chartist petition, allegedly containing the signatures of millions of people (including the unlikely name of Queen Victoria) was presented to parliament, only to be summarily rejected. Such an emotive and potentially inflammatory subject could never have been accepted as fit for stage representation in 1848; and the manager who submitted the anonymous two-act drama *The Chartist; or, a Dream of Every-day Life* was either very bold or else naive to have supposed otherwise. Again, as with Pitt's play, the text was accompanied with a note remarking upon the non-political nature of the work:

Notice. The Drama of the Chartist is in no degree political but is merely intended to illustrate the evil consequences that young misguided men may bring upon themselves by associating with the idle and the depraved — and how be [ing] led away by bad example the unthinking may involve themselves in inextricable ruin . . . [how they] woo their own destruction by the vain attempt to seek into matters and raise questions they neither comprehend nor can answer.[65]

In its sympathetic account of the ruin of the Victorian ideal of the honest craftsman by the evil of commitment to radical politics, *The Chartist* does set out to be an anti-political play. George Maxwell ('a working Jeweller') is persuaded by Robert Rockley ('a member of a Political Club, Profligate and Gambler') to attend a Chartist meeting, where, Rockley tells him, 'You'll hear speeches about social order and the constitution untill [sic] you'll feel yourself a patriot from the crown of your Hat to the heel of your boots . . . I shall never be satisfied untill I've enrolled you a member of "The Friends of Liberty"' (fol. 575). Under Rockley's dubious influence, Maxwell becomes a Chartist, robs his former employer (who had earlier dismissed him for his political affiliations), deserts his wife, takes to drink, and is falsely arrested for murder. In its limited way, *The Chartist* is about the nearest that the early-Victorian drama comes to the probing inquisition of the social-problem novel of the 1840s. The play was never performed because Lord Breadalbane refused to licence it. Indeed, he must have had little choice, since the text is full of potentially damaging references to the weakness of authority and of appeals for Chartist objectives: 'You'll join the friends of liberty wont you?' says Rockley, 'You'll be a patriot and knock down the Police and everything else. We'll have plenty of money and nobody shant do nothing but help himself to what he pleases and no paying' (fol. 581). With such sentiments the Lord Chamberlain's Office could have had precious little sympathy. Dr Johnson's aversion to 'patriotism' was something that the licensing authorities wholeheartedly shared.[66]

4

THE OPPOSITION TO NEWGATE DRAMA

The image of Newgate gaol figures prominently in many of the most popular dramas and novels of the 1830s and 40s as a reflection of society's continuing obsession — inherited from the previous century — with the activities of the criminal. The eighteenth-century taste for public executions, shared by every strata of society including the intellectual circles of Johnson and Boswell, survived well into the nineteenth century. So long as public execution remained it was inevitable that the gallows (particularly at Newgate, to which site hangings had been transferred from Tyburn in 1783) should be surrounded by legend, superstition, and even a degree of romantic glory.[1] The atmosphere and ritual of Newgate inspired a wealth of literature devoted to the criminal way of life, which, with its usual reward on the scaffold, appealed directly to the current taste for sensationalism.

One of the most fruitful sources of material on burglary, highway robbery, murder, and swindling for the hack writers of the nineteenth-century stage was the Newgate novel, a sensational form of the historical romance in which writers like Bulwer Lytton and Harrison Ainsworth — to name only the most prominent — brought vividly to life many of the more interesting characters whom they found in the various editions of the *Newgate Calendar*.[2] Bulwer Lytton in *Paul Clifford* (1830), *Eugene Aram* (1832), and Ainsworth in *Rookwood* (1834), and, more particularly, in *Jack Sheppard* (1839), exploited fully the sensational elements in the careers of notorious criminals of the past. Their romanticised treatment of such well-known figures as Dick Turpin (in *Rookwood*) and Jack Sheppard served to confirm their mythological and legendary aspects and convert them into folk-heroes. It was specifically this tendency to elevate and romanticise the criminal which involved the Newgate drama in heated controversy during the second quarter of the nineteenth century.

The drama of crime, like the Newgate novel (itself the offshoot of the picaresque novels of Defoe and Smollett), has its roots in the eighteenth century. Jack Sheppard was already portrayed on the stage within a year of his execution at Tyburn in 1724;[3] but the two most important examples of the dramatic use of the criminal theme in the century are Lillo's *The History of George Barnwell; or, the London Merchant* (1731) and John Gay's *The Beggar's Opera* (1728). The former provided such a salutary moral lesson about a young apprentice led into the paths of crime by his infatuation with 'a lady of pleasure', that from mid century until 1819 the play was performed every Christmas and Easter holiday for the edification of generations of London apprentices.[4] But it was *The Beggar's Opera* which exercised the more lasting influence on the novel and drama; it has been described as 'the first [play] to make the English drama of rascality really popular'.[5] Popular it certainly was, but Gay's roisterous heroes also aroused much suspicion on account of their allegedly subversive moral influence. Dr Johnson, though approving the play in general terms, conceded that 'at the same time I do not deny that it may have some influence, by making the character of a rogue familiar, and in some degree pleasing'.[6] Johnson's reservations were duplicated in the nineteenth century in the storms of protest which greeted the descendants of the heroes of *The Beggar's Opera* in the strangely humourless Newgate novels and plays of the 1830s and 40s.

George Colman readily agreed in 1832 that it was his duty as Examiner of Plays to recommend refusal of licences 'to such things as tend to justify or encourage crime'.[7] But the only play which suffered that fate during his term of office was *Forgery; or, Mary and Henry Le Roy* (1824), based on the events leading to the arrest of the celebrated master-forger Henry Fauntleroy, a banker of Berners Street in London.[8] Much as he would have wished to, Colman had no power to interfere in the case of the manager of the Surrey Theatre who announced that in *The Gamblers; or, the Hertfordshire Tragedy* (January 1824) he would be using certain props (including a horse and chaise) actually employed by the murderer John Thurtell in his brutal killing of his gambling companion William Weare. But according to Edward Fitzball, the play was quickly suppressed – probably by the licensing magistrates – 'to the great satisfaction of the respectable members of that and every other parish in London'.[9]

The real onslaught of Newgate drama came in 1839, shortly after the publication of Harrison Ainsworth's *Jack Sheppard*, which led to an excessive number of stage adaptations of the life of one of the most daring of eighteenth-century criminals. The real Jack Sheppard, born in London in 1702, was first apprenticed to a carpenter but he quickly fell into bad company and, with the encouragement of dubious friends like

Blueskin and two women of the town, Edgeworth Bess and Poll Maggot, was easily persuaded into a life of crime. Before long he was engaged in a host of activities ranging from simple pocket-picking to house-breaking and highway robbery. Never one to be deterred by iron bars, Sheppard made daring escapes from Newgate gaol on three separate occasions until he was finally arrested and executed on Tyburn Tree in 1724 at the tender age of twenty-two. At Newgate he was sketched by Thornhill and his hanging was attended by thousands of spectators, who much pitied his end.

Ainsworth's version of Sheppard's career is unashamedly sensational. It has everything: a fast-moving plot, a liberal sprinkling of horrors, a dramatic rescue from the Thames during a thunderstorm, and a touching scene of death-bed reconciliation between Jack and his mother, who has been shut up in a madhouse from worry over her son. Above all, at the centre is the daring picaresque-like hero who skilfully outwits his captors on every possible occasion except the final, heartrending drama on the scaffold at Tyburn. In these respects the novel was admirably suited to the needs of the stage adapters, who stressed even more the horrors and violence of the original. Before the end of 1839, no fewer than eight adaptations (and this must be a conservative estimate) were running at various London theatres.[10]

Of the two London versions licensed by the Lord Chamberlain – the rest were performed at minor theatres outside his jurisdiction – the most important was undoubtedly John Baldwin Buckstone's for the Adelphi (28 October 1839). The press reaction was favourable enough. *The Times* (29 October) agreed that Buckstone had made the best of a rather indifferent novel in constructing a play which 'met with the almost unequivocal approbation of an overflowing audience'. Singled out for special commendation was the horrific 'well-hole scene', where Sir Rowland Trenchard is savagely murdered by Jonathan Wild and the Jew Abram Mendez. Together with the final scene when Wild's house is set on fire by the angry mob attending Sheppard's execution, these were considered to be the most effective and spectacular episodes in the play. But John Forster, seizing on the implications of popularising Newgate novels in the theatre, commented in the *Examiner* (3 November) that the stage versions had served up 'the worst passages of the book' and made them attractive to young people. Thackeray, also concerned about current trends, described the popular reaction to *Jack Sheppard* in the form of a Sheppard craze at the theatres:

I have not read this … romance but one or two extracts are good: it is acted at *four* theatres, and they say that at the Cobourg [sic] people are waiting about the lobbies, selling *Shepherd-bags* — a bag containing a few pick-locks that is,

Plate 5   Mary Anne Keeley as 'Jack Sheppard' at the Adelphi Theatre, 1839

a screw driver, and iron lever, one or two young gentlemen have already confessed how much they were indebted to Jack Sheppard who gave them ideas of pocket-picking and thieving wh. they never would have had but for the play.[11]

What was even more disturbing to many contemporaries — though it was hardly surprising — was that the craze was taken up by the low saloons and penny gaffs, so that *Jack Sheppard* quickly became the focus for the attack on the Newgate drama.

Given the unexpected public reaction to *Jack Sheppard*, the Lord Chamberlain's Office was probably never long in doubt that some kind of control over crime drama was necessary. But in mid 1840 further and startling evidence came to light concerning the influence of plays like *Jack Sheppard* on the impressionable young, as a result of the bizarre murder trial at the Old Bailey of a Swiss valet named François Benjamin Courvoisier, who was accused of stabbing his employer, Lord William Russell, with a carving knife. At the end of the three-day trial Courvoisier was found guilty and sentenced to be hanged.[12] However, while awaiting his fate in the condemned cell at Newgate, Courvoisier (according to a report in *The Times*, 25 June 1840) made the extraordinary admission that the idea for the crime had come to him after reading Ainsworth's *Jack Sheppard* and seeing a performance of J. T. Haines's adaptation at the Surrey Theatre. As a direct result of this new evidence, it seems that the licensing authorities decided to prohibit the licensing of any further adaptations of the novel and to discourage performance even of those stage versions which had already received the Lord Chamberlain's sanction. William Donne pointed out to the 1866 Committee that during the 1840s the Lord Chamberlain 'had a great many letters from parents and masters requesting that such pieces should not be exhibited because they had such an ill effect on their sons and apprentices'.[13]

The theatrical fortunes of Jack Sheppard are paralleled by those of stage adaptations of *Oliver Twist*. The latter, frequently (and unjustly) linked in criticism with Ainsworth's romance, had appeared on the London stage by 1840 in at least five versions. None was by Dickens himself; he had shelved the idea late in 1838 on being advised by Macready — for what reasons it is not clear — 'of the utter impracticability of *Oliver Twist* for any dramatic purpose'.[14] The Lord Chamberlain licensed two versions, one by Gilbert A'Beckett and the other by Edward Stirling.[15] As Kathleen Tillotson points out, the *Literary Gazette* 'commented with some truth that [Beckett's version] was "unfit for any stage except that of a Penny Theatre" and it appears to have been given only one or two performances'.[16] Dickens's novels almost always appeared on the stage in debased form as crudely sketched melodramas. And, as Philip Collins observes, in degenerate theatrical versions '*Oliver Twist* probably seemed much more like *Jack Sheppard* and *Paul Clifford* than it really was'.[17] Thackeray, in 'Another Last Chapter' to his novel *Catherine* (itself intended as a burlesque of the Newgate novel and serialised in *Fraser's Magazine*, 1839–40), insisted on linking *Oliver Twist* and *Jack Sheppard* in his condemnation of the whole Newgate school, 'which gives birth to something a great deal worse than bad taste, and familiarises the public with notions of crime'. With Fielding and Gay, he continued, the moral direction of their works is not in doubt

[b]ut in the sorrows of Nancy and the exploits of Jack Sheppard, there is no such lurking moral, as far as we have been able to discover; we are asked for downright sympathy in the one case, and are called on in the second to admire the gallantry of a thief ... [I]n the name of common sense, let us not expend our sympathies on cutthroats, and other such prodigies of evil![18]

Many contemporaries echoed his sentiments, some to the extent of refusing to allow the existence of a 'lurking moral' even in Gay's *Beggar's Opera*. Dickens himself was convinced that no one would take warning from the example of Macheath 'or will see anything in the play but a very flowery and pleasant road, conducting an honourable ambition in the course of time, to Tyburn Tree'.[19]

Jack Sheppard did not disappear entirely from the London stage in the 1840s, though the authorities lost no opportunity to discourage its appearance. By accident, following a series of police visits (instigated by the Lord Chamberlain) to several of the humbler minor theatres in the summer of 1845, it was discovered that the play was being performed at the City of London Theatre, where the manager, Frederick Fox Cooper, was exciting the patronage of the poorest classes of society by admitting two people for the price of one. This objectionable practice was stopped at once on orders from the Lord Chamberlain's Office and, according to Cooper, he was obliged to give up his theatre since he could not make it pay at standard prices.[20] The first record of any formal prohibition on *Jack Sheppard* and *Oliver Twist* dates from 1848, when the managers of the Surrey and Haymarket Theatres were apprised of the Lord Chamberlain's refusal to sanction any further versions of the plays in question.[21] *Jack Sheppard* did not return to the West End until 1852; and then it was permitted only in the classic Buckstone adaptation, which, as the playbill reminded spectators, had never been formally interdicted:

This statement is rendered necessary by the numerous unlicensed imitations that have been acted under the same title, and in which scenes and situations have been presented to the Audience that, however harmless when followed by the context in reading the novel, were deemed unfit for delineation on the stage. In the present adaptation all objectionable passages are carefully expunged, and whilst every care is taken to illustrate the striking incidents of the Drama, the most scrupulous may rest assured that in 'adorning the tale' the great end of Dramatic Representation — 'to point a moral' — has not been forgotten.[22]

The announcement of the Haymarket production (with Mrs Keeley, the original Jack Sheppard of the Adelphi performance, again in the title role) encouraged plans from other theatres to stage versions of the same play. But the Lord Chamberlain's Office was not prepared to open the way for a new 'Sheppard craze' and the applications from the managers of the Pavilion Theatre and the Bower Saloon were both summarily refused. In a letter to the former it was pointed out that 'the Drama of Jack Sheppard having been licensed some years back for the Adelphi Theatre, his Lordship [Lord Exeter] does not think it right to revoke a Licence granted by one of his Predecessors, but it is not his intention to grant any further licence for its performance'.[23] The strength of Buckstone's play lay in the licence granted in 1839; and it was this reason alone — not that his adaptation was any less 'dangerous' than the others, or even artistically more successful — which guaranteed its immunity from an official veto. The Adelphi *Jack Sheppard* in fact continued its charmed life for another six years, with a revival at Sadler's Wells in 1855 and at the Surrey Theatre in 1858 (to which the Adelphi company had moved temporarily during the rebuilding of their theatre). This production has been noted as 'the last representation in London' of Buckstone's play in anything like its original form.[24]

Official intransigence over *Jack Sheppard* and *Oliver Twist* in the period after 1840 extended, though less absolutely, to a great many dramas involving highwaymen, thieves, burglars, and murderers, most of them using the *Newgate Calendar* as source. In 1844, the year after the Theatre Regulation Act of 1843 extended the Lord Chamberlain's control as licenser of plays to the ubiquitous minor theatres, John Kemble referred as many as four plays from the category defined (in 1866) as 'the swell mob and burglary school'. They included W. L. Rede's *The Old House of West Street; or, London in the Olden Time* (which is recorded as 'withdrawn' in Kemble's fee book), T. P. Taylor's *George Barrington; or, the Life of a Pickpocket*, George Dibdin Pitt's *The Murder*

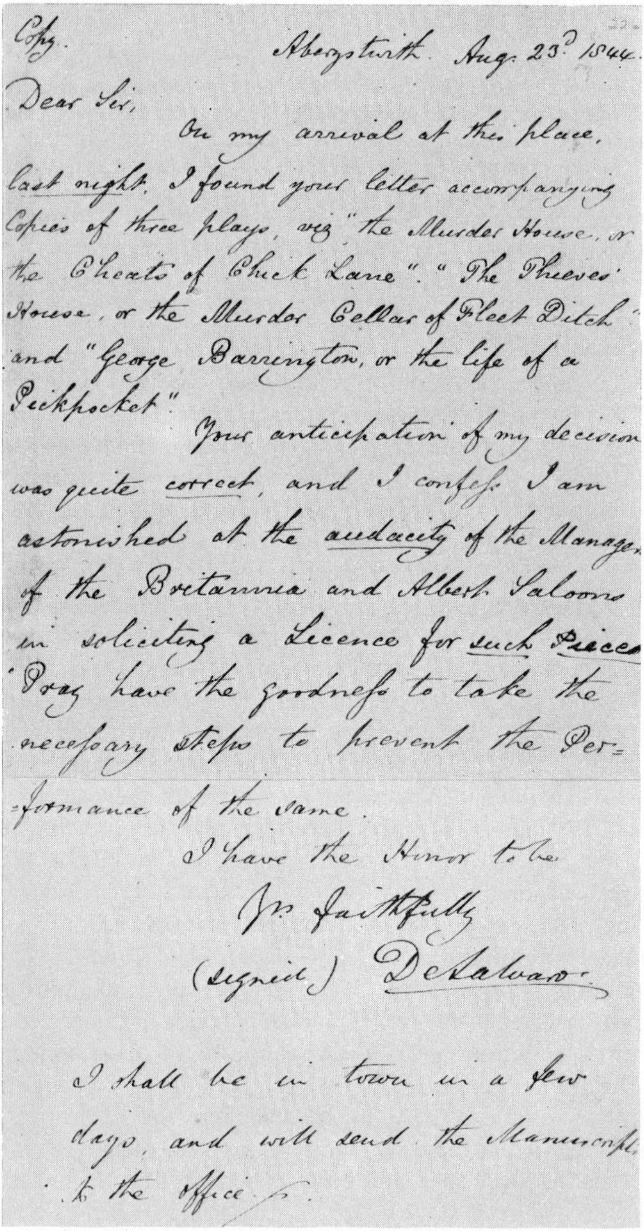

Copy.

Aberystwith. Aug. 23rd 1844.

Dear Sir,

On my arrival at this place, last night, I found your letter accompanying Copies of three plays, viz: "the Murder House, or the Cheats of Chick Lane". "The Thieves' House, or the Murder Cellar of Fleet Ditch" and "George Barrington, or the life of a Pickpocket".

Your anticipation of my decision was quite _correct_, and I confess I am astonished at the _audacity_ of the Manager of the Britannia and Albert Saloons in soliciting a Licence for _such Pieces_. Pray have the goodness to take the necessary steps to prevent the Performance of the same.

I have the Honor to be

Yrs faithfully

(signed) De Alwar

I shall be in town in a few days, and will send the Manuscripts to the office.

Plate 6   Letter from Lord De La Warr to John Mitchell Kemble confirming the ban on three Newgate plays, 23 August 1844

House; or, the Cheats of Chick Lane, and Samuel Atkyns's *The Thieves' House; or, the Murder Cellar of the Fleet Ditch*,[25] all of them striking examples of the Newgate school, crowded with sensational incident, violent crime, and brutal murders. All were interdicted on instructions from Lord De La Warr, who was outraged at the grossness of the plays. As he told Kemble: 'Your anticipation of my decision is quite *correct*, and I confess I am astonished at the *audacity* of the Managers of the Britannia and Albert Saloons [who had submitted the last two plays] in soliciting a Licence for *such Pieces*. Pray have the goodness to take the necessary steps to prevent the performance of the same.'[26]

The Lord Chamberlain's Office believed that it had a special responsibility to provide its protection for the frequenters of the lower class of theatre in London; and there is evidence to support the contention that in doubtful cases the class of theatre for which a play was intended could be the decisive factor. The theatres of London's East End were accordingly subjected to more rigorous censorship in this regard than were the theatres of the more sophisticated West End. In 1852 a play for the Pavilion Theatre (in the Mile End Road) called *The Swell Mobsman* was prohibited. No MS. survives but the title is sufficient indication of its content.[27] In the following year *Wrath's Whirlwind; or, the Neglected Child, the Vicious Youth and the Degraded Man* was refused licence for the Britannia Theatre and, in a letter to William Donne, a member of the Lord Chamberlain's staff wrote to express the Lord Chamberlain's full concurrence in the Examiner's recommendation to interdict the play, which, like others of its type, tended to degrade dramatic art. 'It is highly desirable', he continued, 'to elevate the tone of the drama and it is specially necessary in the case of the saloons, who have a tendency to lower the morals and excite the passions of the classes who frequent these places of resort.'[28] Again, in the summer of 1854 the Pavilion Theatre encountered further trouble with James Elphinstone's *Rotherhithe in the Olden Time; or, the Female Housebreaker*. In its original form (which was refused a licence) *Rotherhithe* is a sensation drama, full of rather gruesome murders, though relieved by some slight comic effects.[29] The MS. in the Lord Chamberlain's collection shows that a large proportion of it was considered highly unsuitable for public representation, especially at a theatre which attracted the lower classes. 'Damme' and 'damnation' are excised throughout, together with all references to house-breaking and robbery from the person. One scene in particular caught the Examiner's eye in Act II, where two thieves lie in wait in a churchyard while an old dame and her coachman cross through the tombstones:

Cockey:　――What say you, Dickey Duff? shall I knife the pair of 'em, or bind
'em together with a rope and throw 'em into the adjoining ditch?
Dickey:　Tut! Isn't the water covered with ice strong enough to bear an elephant ... Do as I said before — Nobble them — give each a top on the
nut with the cudgel.

They then confront the dame and her coachman with the words (underlined in red ink in the original for the Lord Chamberlain's benefit, and
here italicised):

Cockey:　Give us all the money you've got about you and *we'll let you off with
nothing more than the lop of a few brains or a broken rib or two.*
Dickey:　*Your money or your life.*

As neither victim has any money the thieves strip the coachman of his
breeches and the old woman of her dress. The stage direction (also
underscored in red ink by the Examiner) reads: 'Pulls off her gown and
discovers her in a short petticoat.' Donne's comment on the scene in the
margin of the MS. was, 'All this is in a churchyard.' When the play was
returned from Lord Breadalbane, Donne was informed by the Lord
Chamberlain's Comptroller that his Lordship:

quite concurs in your view of the gross nature of the incidents, & general
impropriety and mischievous tendency of the whole piece. The Lord Chamberlain is of the opinion that a mere representation of a gross and extravagant
crime should as far as his authority is concerned be always excluded from the
Stage. The difference between the fair dramatic use of a criminal incident
& a mere exhibition of vulgar crimes is too obvious to necessitate any pre-
scribed rule or instructions.[30]

Yet, despite his evident distaste for the play, Breadalbane was indulgent
enough to consider a much-revised version and this second text was
duly licensed for performance. It omits the subtitle (which was probably regarded as too offensive) and the whole play has a very much
more sober, less violent, tone. All the cuts marked by the Examiner in
the original were retained.[31] Presumably, Lord Breadalbane considered
that the revised text now made 'fair dramatic use of a criminal incident'.

William Donne was sufficiently convinced of the evil effects of such
plays that in the following year he suggested that the Lord Chamberlain
give thought to banning from the stage all dramas 'turning on the subject of Burglary, Highway robbery, stealing from the person etc.'. Unwilling as Lord Breadalbane was to give his 'positive mandate' for bidd-
ing such topics, he did propose that his Examiner confer with the managers of the principal London theatres (and write to the rest) in order to
urge upon them a proper understanding of the impropriety of sen-

sationalised forms of crime drama in the hope that they 'spontaneously withdraw from performance licensed plays of that character, and refuse to accept for their Houses, in future, MSS. of a similar kind'.[32] Although the ban was as yet unofficial, the way was opened for Donne to pursue a much more rigorous policy in the general area of Newgate plays with the eventual aim of achieving a full-scale official interdiction.

When William Donne became official Examiner of Plays on the death of John Mitchell Kemble, he embarked on a campaign to remove Newgate drama from the theatrical scene. His first opportunity of putting his views to the new Lord Chamberlain, Earl De La Warr, came in 1858 with the submission of a play entitled *The Blood Spot; or, the Maiden, the Mirror, and the Murderer*, which, as he pointed out to his superior, 'belongs to a class of Dramas now nearly extinct on the stage, and never introduced as novelties – to the class in which highway-robbery, burglary, and larceny form the staple of the interest and action'. These kinds of play, he maintained, were 'extremely prejudicial to the younger portions of the Pit & Gallery audiences at the Minor Theatres'. At the same time Donne tried to enlist the support of the Comptroller, Spencer Ponsonby, in suppressing the play. 'I have nearly "scotched this snake"', Donne declared, 'and should be sorry were it to revive in the form of the adventures of Jerry Abershaw' (a criminal from the *Newgate Calendar* on whose career *The Blood Spot* was founded). Lord De La Warr was very sympathetic to Donne's appeal and wrote of his objection to '"the Old Bailey Character" running so strongly through the whole structure of the drama'.[33] The same play was submitted a second time in April of the following year with the horrors of the second act (one of the principal sources of complaint) much tempered; but it was again turned down, this time even without reference to the Lord Chamberlain, whom Donne 'declined to trouble . . . with a Manuscript which he has already condemned'.[34] The Examiner's uncharacteristically harsh (and illegal) action over the play suggests the force of his dislike of Newgate drama and his determination that it should all be banned from the stage.

Naturally, the cornerstone of any such policy must have been the suppression of *Jack Sheppard*. Accordingly, during the spring of 1859, after 'a partial revival of *Jack Sheppard, Oliver Twist, & Turpin's Ride-to-York*' at the Grecian, Marylebone, and Astley's Theatres, Donne again put the suggestion of a blanket prohibition to Lord De La Warr. (He no doubt recalled that De La Warr had been Lord Chamberlain during the first controversy over *Jack Sheppard* and had possibly been responsible for the original ban). His reply was terse and explicit: 'It may be doubtful how far it wd. be expedient to revive the Ban agst. all the "Highway Pieces", but I have no doubt that *Jack Sheppard* might be interdicted.'[35] Elated at his success, Donne managed to extend the Lord Chamberlain's directive to include all versions of *Oliver Twist*, which by virtue of its instructional examples of thieving, pocket-picking, and house-breaking he considered quite as dangerous as *Jack Sheppard*: 'it is highly objectionable in its moral, more especially as it is performed at Theatres where the Gallery is the main resort, and the greater portion of its frequenters consists of apprentices and young persons of either sex'.[36] In consequence, after 1859, both *Jack Sheppard* and *Oliver Twist* virtually disappear from the London stage, at least under their original titles.[37] However, the licensing authorities did allow some indulgence to such plays as *The Idle Apprentice* and *The Young Apprentice* (both none-too-well disguised variations on the Sheppard theme performed during the early 1860s), acceptable so long as the names of Jack Sheppard and his associates were not mentioned.

During the 1860s, with the suppression of familiar, well-loved heroes like Sheppard and the exhaustion of suitable new material in the *Newgate Calendar* (the last nineteenth-century edition of which was published in 1845), dramatists began to look for other sources to satisfy the continuing demand for sensational crime drama. Playwrights turned instead to the exploitation of the contemporary fascination with real-life murder, accounts of which were readily available and reported in gruesome detail in the newspapers. For its part, the Lord Chamberlain's Office, alarmed at this unexpected extension of an already objectionable school of drama, took steps to discourage such notions by refusing to licence a two-act drama called *The Money Lender* (Standard Theatre, 1861) and severely pruning *The Usurer; or, a Struggle for Life* (City of London Theatre, 1862). Both plays were founded on the same grim murder that took place in July 1861 when Roberts and Murray, a money-lender and a solicitor, fought to the death in law chambers off the Strand. It was a particularly savage encounter, which shocked the whole of London.[38] In the case of the former play, the Lord Chamberlain had no doubt of its unfitness for the stage; but Donne, aware that an interdiction on the latter would mean certain financial ruin for the City of London company, did his best to expurgate the details relating to the actual crime. He reported to the Lord Chamberlain that:

one scene is cancelled, another changed from the struggle in a room to a quarrel and a duel in a Gaming House, in fact the scene from a long ago licensed play of *Thirty Years of a Gambler's Life* [1827]. These are the only two scenes in which the *soupçon* of the recent case occurs: all the rest are common melodramatic business acted and licensed over and over again . . . [but] I shall go to the first representation to see that my instructions are carried out.[39]

A year later, the Marylebone Theatre's *The Gipsy of Edgware; or, the Crime in Gill Hill's Lane* was found to be open to much the same objection because it revived memories of the notorious murderer Thurtell, executed in 1824. Donne wrote to the Lord Chamberlain saying 'the case is so flagrant that unless desired I will not trouble your Lordship to read [it]' and seeking Lord Sydney's permission to administer 'a severe rebuke to Mr Cave for accepting such a Manuscript'. In reply, the Lord Chamberlain agreed that all stage representation of recent real-life murders was 'very undesirable' since 'it . . . gives the public a morbid feeling & encourages mischievous ideas in their minds'.[40]

A sudden revival of interest in *Oliver Twist* in 1868 occasioned some temporary embarrassment for the licensing authorities when W. H. Liston of the Queen's Theatre, having received notice of their reluctance to licence any version of it, demanded official evidence of its supposed earlier proscription. As he pointed out to William Donne, he was 'not aware that either the press or the public have ever complained of Mr Dickens' novel being an immoral work'. Donne hurriedly scoured the records but was forced to admit to Spencer Ponsonby that he could find no trace of the original ban: 'I am afraid there is little chance as JMK [John Kemble] kept no memorandum.' However, it was Donne's memory that was at fault for, as he soon afterwards discovered, its interdiction dated from a suggestion he had made himself in a letter to Lord Breadalbane in 1855, later converted into a formal ban by Lord De La Warr in 1859. The Examiner's argument for the continued suppression of *Oliver Twist* failed to convince Lord Bradford, who, no doubt reflecting on the current state of Dickens's reputation and the fact that the MS. submitted by Liston was an entirely new version, directed that the play 'should be licensed for any one who submits [it], subject to excisions'.[41] The performance of *Oliver Twist* in John Oxenford's adaptation at the Queen's Theatre (11 April 1868) has thus the distinction of being the first licensed production for nearly ten years.[42] It marks the first substantial break in the licensers' prohibition on Newgate plays.

But the interdiction on *Jack Sheppard*, by any standard the principal villain of the genre, proved much less easy to remove, even in expurgated and moralised versions like *Jack Sheppard; or, Vice and the Punishment and Virtue and the Reward* (1868) which, to all appearances, had the qualities of a moral *exemplum*. The preface to the MS. declares:

This version of the work is exempt from all obnoxious scenes, characters and brutal murders: the part of Jack Sheppard stripped of the honours and heroics by which he has been surrounded by the novelist and stands forth in his true light – in boyhood envious vicious and treacherous; in manhood vain and desperate, sinning but suffering both mentally and physically – and the last closing scenes of his life a fearful lesson and warning to youth never to be tempted to the first false step – that step which can never be retracted. Thames Darrell [Sheppard's virtuous contemporary] by avoiding the tempter triumphs – proving that Vice and Virtue meet their just reward.[43]

The Examiner was not persuaded. He produced for the Lord Chamberlain's benefit a list of reasons why the play should continue to be suppressed. Recent experience over *Oliver Twist*, he argued, had shown how curious the public were to see 'restricted pieces', and other theatre managers, in trying to satisfy public demand, would be induced to submit new versions of *Jack Sheppard*, all of which it would be impossible to refuse licences once the precedent had been set. Even with large-scale expurgation, Donne maintained, the main point of the play – that Jack shows that crime does pay as long as you don't get caught – still remained:

He is the hero of the highway: the object of admiration to the young and adventurous, the dashing brilliant cutter of purses, and where it cannot be helped, throats also. I fear his penitence and sufferings 'moral and physical' will not outweigh his other attractions. He is surrounded by his old associates Blueskin, Jonathan Wild and Co. though Bess Edgworth is left out.

It was an impressive argument and a deeply felt one on Donne's part; and much to his delight Lord Bradford supported him and refused the play a licence.[44] The reappearance of 'Jack Sheppard' on the London stage was staved off for another five years.

The reiterated ban on *Jack Sheppard* did not prevent some theatres trying their luck with disguised versions of the original play. Sometimes they were successful, as in 1870 when *The Grand Hurly-Burly-esque, The Idle 'Prentice, A Tyburnian Idyll of High-Low Jack and his Little Game* was officially approved after all reference to Sheppard's name had been carefully excised,[45] though in the following year another burlesque *Jack the Joiner; or, The Appropriating Apprentice*, 'being "Jack Sheppard"', was summarily suppressed.[46] But the climax of the licensers' preoccupation with Jack Sheppard came in 1873, when Sheppard-fever reached disturbing, if short-lived, proportions. In February of that year at least four different versions were submitted for examination; all received the most careful scrutiny and were heavily cut for performance. In the Victoria Theatre's *The King of the Mint* Donne even insisted on a signed statement from the manager guaranteeing scrupulous adherence to the cuts imposed. Among the Examiner's required deletions was the passage: 'We will make him the most expert pick-pocket in London, and we will guarantee no one shall catch him where after his labours he should wish to deposit the fruits of his industry here in the Mint.' Donne further warned that there 'must be no allusion to pocket-picking in word or act'.[47] Similarly, in another version called *Lantern Lights* (for the Elephant and Castle), the excisions noted in the Day Book occupy a whole page. Again references to pocket-picking were deleted as were all references which tended to romanticise the criminal way of life — such comments as 'My father [is] a Tyburn hero.' Donne commented severely: 'Keep all such kind of heroism out of the representation of the piece.' And he further directed that the name of Jack o'London (for Jack Sheppard) should be 'struck out wherever it occurs in the Drama'.

Perhaps stimulated by the sudden rash of *Sheppard*-like plays, Benjamin Webster of the Adelphi Theatre made an application to stage the old (and now for many years banned) version of *Jack Sheppard* by John Buckstone — the Adelphi original, in fact, of 1839. The first response of the Lord Chamberlain's Office was decidedly negative. Webster was simply informed that Lord Sydney 'does not consider himself justified in reviving the permission to play a piece which has been found to be an incentive to crime on former occasions'.[48] But not to be outdone, Webster persisted and eventually sent in a modified text under the title *The Stone Jug*, the old slang term for Newgate gaol. In reply, the Examiner, having recognised it for what it was (merely the old Adelphi version with a new title and new names for the characters), explained that he was disappointed with *The Stone Jug* since he had expected an entirely new adaptation. If Webster wanted a licence for his play, he went on, certain conditions would have to be observed:

You will see by the notice herewith sent that I do not object to the burning of Sampson Savage's [i.e. Jonathan Wild's] house as a finale but a march to Tyburn cannot be passed: that is a glorification of the highway . . . [T]he burglary and highway element must be excluded.

In my opinion, you have weakened your drama by omitting the original first act. In that lies the pith of the story, and in it, there is nothing, except perhaps a word or so, objectionable. Restore that act, 'banish Peto, banish Pistol, banish Poins', and more especially Chance's [i.e. Sheppard's] 'two wives' and then there will be no impediment towards recommending *The Stone Jug*.[49]

Although Donne's conditions of licence, in effect, required the radical remodelling of the drama, Webster complied with them readily enough and in March 1873 *The Stone Jug* was approved by Lord Sydney.

Donne's considerable efforts in suggesting the necessary expurgations for the play are a reflection of the often good-natured relations which existed between the Lord Chamberlain's Office and those theatre managers who showed a willingness to maintain a standard of decorum on the stage. A somewhat sour note was, however, soon injected into the proceedings when, despite all Donne's attempts to suppress the link between *The Stone Jug* and *Jack Sheppard*, Webster advertised the new play as founded on the Adelphi original. The Examiner lost no time in making his feelings plain: 'It may be a clever stroke of business', he wrote, 'but it is a bad reward for the pains that have been taken, before licensing *The Stone Jug*. I must leave the matter to your conscience — but I do so in the hope that you will see the impropriety in departing from the conditions which I fully explained to you, made by me, and fully accepted by yourself.'[50] But even without the assistance of Webster's advertisement it seems unlikely that the model for *The Stone Jug* would have escaped detection by the reviewers. The majority reaction was hostile. The *Illustrated London News* (29 March 1873) remarked on the curiously anomalous policy of the licensers in now releasing *Jack Sheppard* under a new title after the original had been so roundly abused. 'Will not', it asked, 'the example of Bob Chance be as bad as that of Jack Sheppard?' Although prepared to give full credit for the competence of the production, the same reviewer dismissed *The Stone Jug* as a 'morally objectionable' play, 'the acting of which is now regarded by the judicious as a social offence'. When Benjamin Webster came to publish the text of the play later in the year, the Lord Chamberlain's Office insisted on a prefatory note indicating that 'this is the only form in which the escapades of the popular hero of Ainsworth's Romance are allowed to be enacted on the Stage; but under the present title, and with the present characters, its representation has been specially sanctioned by the Lord Chamberlain'.[51] Jack Sheppard was clearly still an awkward subject; but at least by 1873 the licensing authorities were making some attempt to discriminate between good (that is, moralised) and bad (socially undesirable) versions of the story.

In one way Webster's staging of *Jack Sheppard* in only a thin disguise was a victory; yet the public's reactions to the play seemed fully to endorse the authorities' long battle to keep it off the stage. Although there were signs in early 1873 of a massive revival of interest in 'the hero of the highway', particularly at those theatres catering for the lower classes in London, the year marks in fact the virtual extinction of popular interest in Jack Sheppard. Even Webster's *Stone Jug* lasted only for thirteen performances. The reasons for the decline are not altogether clear; but it may be suspected that audiences were becoming more sophisticated in their demands and that the abolition of public hanging in 1868 had robbed the gallows of its strange mystique. What is apparent, however, is that neither *Jack Sheppard* nor any other Newgate play ever regained its former ascendancy after 1873. There were, it is true, occasional revivals of *Jack Sheppard* in various forms during the 1880s and 90s, but most were comparative failures.[52] Newgate plays as a whole seemed to lose their focus with the disappearance of their colourful hero; and the licensers, relieved at the improvement in public taste, relaxed their restrictions on the Sheppard theme. After 1873 the Lord Chamberlain's Office ceased to be interested and the few revivals licensed under Donne's successor Edward Pigott were approved as a matter of course.

The swaggering heroes of Newgate plays attacked the very fabric of society. They had small regard for individuals or for property; few were daunted by the shadow of the gallows. *Jack Sheppard*, the eponymous hero of which was the worst offender, was attacked more fiercely by the censors and by responsible authority than perhaps any other drama of the mid-Victorian period. Its very popularity with juvenile audiences (who might be so easily swayed by its specious morality) was seen as an index of the danger to society in general and to the moral health of the theatre in particular. Consistently, it was the policy of the Lord Chamberlain's Office to channel the mis-directed hero-worship lavished on Jack Sheppard and his associates to objects more worthy of respect and imitation.

5

EARLY CHALLENGES TO
VICTORIAN MORALITY

It is a common assertion amongst writers on the early nineteenth-century drama that, if it was nothing else, it was moral.[1] The majority of theatre-goers might well have agreed with Miss Prism's observation on her own creative effort in *The Importance of Being Earnest* (1895) that the meaning of art was that 'the good ended happily, and the bad un-happily'. Certainly, a great deal of the drama of the period satisfied that simple criterion. But the theatre was, of course, moral in the sense that it was expected to adhere to the standards of behaviour and conduct which had become identified with social respectability. And given such a preoccupation with morality (or decorousness, or propriety – the words were more or less interchangeable) it might be supposed that moral censorship would have accounted for much of the burden of work for the censor during the first half of the century. Yet, until as late as the mid 1860s this is just not so. When questioned at the 1832 Committee, the dramatist W. T. Moncrieff contended that the Examiner of Plays was 'much more severe on any political allusions' than on morality, since theatre audiences themselves could be safely relied upon to show their displeasure at anything which they felt exceeded the bounds of decorum.[2] The drama has always had a special responsibility to its audience because its success depends entirely upon its reception in the theatre. For that reason it is closer to what is commonly called 'popular taste' than perhaps any other art form. Until recent times, the drama has been necessarily inhibited in its description of personal and sexual relationships (the area in which the restrictions are most obvious) in consequence of the belief that what is seen and heard on a public stage before a mixed audience must remain less explicit than what is read individually and in private.

The Victorian theatre lay under special restrictions in a climate in which even the novel – normally 'much less sensitive to the censorship of public attitudes than the stage'[3] – operated under strict taboos. There was a well-defined threshold over which a novelist ventured at his peril; but few of the novelists, still less the dramatists, found the existence of such a barrier in any way restricting.[4] This is an indication of the extent to which they all wrote from a common moral standpoint, although, admittedly, there were some novelists who were accused of sailing rather too close to the wind for comfort. As one contemporary critic observed of Thackeray, for example: 'he never violates a single conventional rule; but at the same time the shadow of the immorality that is not seen is scarcely ever wanting to the delineation of the society that is seen'.[5] Yet no dramatist would have dared attempt the portrayal of a character modelled on 'Tom Jones' such as Thackeray painted in *Pendennis* (1850), pale though it was in comparison with Fielding's original. If the censor had not made that certain, then the public would have done so. Indeed, the reason for the paucity of moral censorship in the drama until the 1860s seems to lie in the fact that few playwrights in England had the inclination or the temerity to offer their audiences morally exceptionable plays.

Of course, it is a commonplace amongst literary historians that the strict moral code of the Victorian period proper has its origins long before Victoria's accession to the throne in 1837. To look no further back than the opening years of the century, there is ample evidence of increasingly puritanical attitudes to morality. Many of Thomas Bowdler's 'improvements' to Shakespeare's text in his 'family edition' of 1808 were effected in the cause of moral propriety; and when Mrs Inchbald published her series of notable British plays in the same year, her introductory remarks to the much-modified texts of Restoration and early eighteenth-century plays show that their moral tone was no longer acceptable. Of Farquhar's *The Beaux Stratagem* (1707), she comments that it is 'an honour to the morality of the present age, that this most entertaining comedy is but seldom performed'.[6] Plays like *The Provok'd Husband, The Relapse*, and *The Recruiting Officer* fell much out of favour as the century advanced. On the rare occasions when they were performed, the texts were subjected to stringent managerial censorship. Sometimes even that was insufficient. Francis Place, in evidence to the 1832 Committee, recalled recent performances of *The Recruiting Officer* and *The Beaux Stratagem* in which 'Mr Kemble and Mr Keeley used words which were much softened from the original yet they caused a sensation in the house which prevented their using them any more.' Place commented: 'I thought the rebukes they received wholesome and sufficient.'[7] And when Rowe's *The Fair Penitent* (1703) was staged in 1831, a reviewer expressed his 'indignation at the revolting indecency of the text, and the bad taste of the manager'.[8]

But the early nineteenth-century censors could be reasonably confident that modern dramatists would never be guilty of such offences against taste, and that the majority of MSS. submitted for licensing would have already undergone such moral censorship that might be required. What official censorship there was was generally minor in degree and small in quantity. George Colman admitted in 1832 that it was part of his function to guard against 'downright grossness and indecency',[9] which is presumably why he insisted, much to the author's surprise, that the word 'thighs' should be omitted from Moncrieff's play *The Bashful Man* (1824).[10] For similar reasons of propriety Colman required (among other small excisions, notably a reference to members of the royal family as 'all stout Gentlemen') the removal of the following song from a 'dramatic sketch' entitled *The Stout Gentleman* (Theatre Royal, Bath, 1824):

> I've heard of good times, but they've long been over,
> When Adam & Eve were living in clover.
> When she was a Belle & he was a Beau,
> In a neat first floor in Paradise Row.
> She was an applewoman, fat & fair, & sizeable,
> Never wore a petticoat unless 'twas an invisible.
> He never feared Dun, Creditor, nor Jailer,
> For he never bought his small clothes of any London tailor.[11]

Such suggestiveness Colman was sure would not be tolerated on the stage, but his moral sensibilities seemed rather more robust than those of the theatre manager who submitted the MS. of Michael Lacy's *The Two Friends* (an adaptation of Scribe's *Rodolphe; ou, frère et sœur*) in 1828 and disclosed his unease lest the phrase 'ship's bottom' should be found indelicate. He was anxious, too, about the propriety of 'little affair' in the sentence 'Now, the little affair that I wish to speak to you about is this' — for which he suggested 'something' as a safer and more decorous alternative. Surprisingly, Colman ignored all the manager's queries and, with the usual deletion of a few oaths, licensed the play as adapted by Lacy. In performance, however, the slightly equivocal subject-matter gave grave offence to the critic of the *Dramatic Magazine*, who, alluding to the relationship between the brother and sister (later shown to be perfectly innocent), described the piece as 'one of the most immoral and dangerous dramas' ever produced.[12]

Despite such growing prudery — in this case more that of the public at large than the Examiner's — and despite Colman's reputation for moral bigotry, the evidence suggests that the licensing authorities were more tolerant in this respect than some of their later-Victorian counterparts. So far as can be ascertained from the official records, not a single play was banned in Colman's time as censor on exclusively moral grounds.[13] John Howard Payne's historical drama *Richelieu* (submitted by Charles Kemble for performance at Covent Garden in 1825) came closest to that fate; but, even then, there were other objections involved. The first version was actually prohibited at the behest of the Lord Chamberlain himself, who was affronted at its apparent libel on the aristocracy and by the treatment of the sexual misconduct of the principal character, the Duc de Richelieu, seducer of a merchant's innocent wife. Kemble made concession after concession in attempts to satisfy officialdom, including three changes of title, the substitution of the name 'Duke of Rougemont' for Richelieu, and some tempering of Payne's rather heartless depiction of the sexual relationship.[14] Eventually, all objections were overcome and Colman was permitted to licence the play under the title *The French Libertine*. But the press were unanimous in their condemnation. *The Times* (13 February 1826) shuddered to think what the original text must have been like when first submitted to the Examiner. After a lengthy *résumé* of the 'extremely tiresome, vulgar, stupid, [and] commonplace' plot, the reviewer concluded that the theme of libertinism was 'carried forward with a perfect disregard of all the limits which decent taste and respectable feeling have been used to set to such discussions'. Such gross miscalculation of public feeling was rare at this period and, burdened by the severe moral disapprobation of its critics, Payne's play lapsed into swift oblivion.

II

It was a matter of general agreement among witnesses at the 1832 Committee that moral censorship was the least of the worries of the licensing authorities, since the taste of the times was for plays which respected contemporary notions of decorum and respectability. So matters continued for a time after Colman's death. Except for the suppression of two foreign-language dramas – Scribe's *La Famille Riqueborg; ou, le mariage mal assorti* (in 1845) and Vittorio Alfieri's late-eighteenth-century tragedy *Mirra* (in 1856)[15] – moral censorship under Charles and John Kemble seems to have been virtually dormant. But from the early 1850s onwards, with the importation of increasingly large numbers of plays from France, the morality of the stage began to assume a new importance for the Lord Chamberlain's Office. French drama had long been suspect in England for its adventurous approach to personal relations. As far back as 1834 Robert Southey was complaining of its iniquities as boldly exemplified in the plays of the elder

Dumas and Victor Hugo, which were characterised by a preponderance of adulteresses, prostitutes, seducers, bastards, and foundlings. Such 'accumulations of horrors', Southey observed, were fortunately unknown in England, where, despite the occasional coarse expression or gross scene in our earlier drama, 'the taste of modern audiences has long since prohibited the exhibition of any such indelicacy'.[16]

The notoriety of the younger Dumas' *La Dame aux Camélias* (published as a novel in 1848, then as a play in 1852) spread to England well in advance of the first application for a licence to perform it. Accompanied by his courtesan heroine Marguerite Gautier, Alexandre Dumas had made forcible entry into one of the proscribed regions of Victorian morality. This, coupled with the fact that the theme of 'the fallen woman' was coloured by an explicitness which had startled even sophisticated French audiences, made the play completely unacceptable in the English theatre. George Henry Lewes, a usually liberal critic if ever there was one, found the piece so intolerable as to describe it as nothing less than an 'idealisation of corruption' and a 'hideous parody of passion'. He fully supported the Lord Chamberlain's suppression of the drama, submitted in English translation under the title *Camille* for performance at Drury Lane Theatre in March 1853. Lewes commented:

Paris may delight in such pictures, but London, thank God! has still enough instinctive repulsion against pruriency not to tolerate them. I declare I know of few things in the way of fiction more utterly wrong, unwholesome, and immoral, than this *Dame aux Camélias* ... I am not prudish, nor easily alarmed by what are called 'dangerous' subjects, but *this subject* I protest against with all my might; — a subject not only unfit to be brought before our sisters and our wives, but unfit to be brought before ourselves. The very skill with which young Dumas has treated it, makes his crime all the greater, because it tends to confuse the moral sense, by exciting the sympathy of an audience.

There was no fear, Lewes concluded, of any Lord Chamberlain being 'supine enough to licence it'.[17] He was more right than he knew. Dumas' play, the archetype of courtesan drama, remained under official interdiction for over twenty years.

Yet Dumas' *La Dame aux Camélias* did achieve early success in Giuseppe Verdi's operatic version, *La Traviata*, which had its first performance in England at Her Majesty's Theatre in May 1856. William Donne, who had recommended the refusal of *Camille*, had been temporarily displaced as Examiner following John Kemble's return from Germany and it was on the latter's advice that the opera was licensed. Commenting on Kemble's decision, Donne wrote to Fanny Kemble: 'My old enemy La Dame aux Camélias has at last escaped from her four years' bondage, and is now performing at the opera *La Traviata,* in the full bloom of her original horrors!'[18] Contrary to many expectations, however, it did not create a scandal. Indeed, the *Illustrated London News* (31 May 1856) concluded that, as far as the morality of operas in general was concerned, *Traviata* was hardly more improper than many others that were previously licensed and regularly performed. It commented approvingly that the details of Dumas' play were 'softened down' and that the opera as a whole was 'irresistibly pathetic', for 'he must be a stern moralist indeed who can witness unmoved the sorrows of the erring but most interesting heroine'. And in the *Times* review (24 May 1856) the morality of the piece passed entirely without remark. Opinions on the opera were generally so favourable that within the month the Lord Chamberlain felt justified in allowing an English translation under the title *La Traviata; or, the Blighted One* to be performed at the Surrey Theatre. Evidently, the addition of music to a morally questionable plot was sufficient to turn the balance in its favour; the licensing of *Traviata* in both Italian and English versions illustrates the much greater degree of tolerance which the Lord Chamberlain's Office permitted to nineteenth-century opera in comparison with the straight drama. As Donne pointed out in 1866, when questioned on the anomalies such a policy encouraged: 'it makes a difference, for the words are then subsidiary to the music'.[19]

Various attempts were made in mid century to persuade the authorities to licence Dumas' original for the English stage. But on each occasion they refused to countenance a play which, in the words of the Lord Chamberlain himself — he had seen the play in Paris — 'in all its undisguised licentiousness' was so obviously unfit for presentation. In his report on the MS. of the play submitted by the St James's Theatre in 1859, Donne described it as 'a glorification of harlotry [which] in the last act ... profanes the sanctity of death';[20] and, though he was aware that the licensers might be accused of inconsistency in having already allowed *La Traviata,* the Examiner had no difficulty in winning Lord De La Warr's permission to refuse the application. Pleased by his success in preserving the ban on the French prose version of *La Dame aux Camélias,* Donne proved equally anxious to extend the prohibition to English versions as well. He was amply supported in his view both by Lord De La Warr and his successor, Viscount Sydney, and by the Comptroller of the Lord Chamberlain's Office, Spencer Ponsonby, who declared in unequivocal terms at the 1866 Committee that Dumas' play, as a general matter of policy, should never have been licensed in any shape or form (including operatic versions) for any theatre in England.[21]

Nevertheless, the licensers could claim no absolute ban on the play, since (like its ubiquitous parallel in crime drama, *Jack Sheppard*) performances did take place occasionally in the provinces, where the Lord Chamberlain's authority proved sometimes difficult to exercise.[22] At least one performance of *La Dame aux Camélias* (unlicensed) even took place in London, at Sadler's Wells in 1860; but Donne, after hasty consultation with his superiors, wisely decided not to interfere as the theatre was closing within a few days and he wished to avoid a confrontation in the press. 'I don't care for the Examiner', he wrote, 'but I don't like the Lord Chamberlain's running on a rock at the close of a season . . . Policy not mercy, inclines me to think that just now, *no notice* might be best. But I am quite ready to push the bolt, should you think otherwise.'[23] Spencer Ponsonby sensibly agreed, but Donne warned the theatre management that 'the *Dame* must never show her face after this present week'. Indeed, at this juncture, Dumas' play—together with his hardly less-notorious *Le Demi-Monde*, interdicted in the same year[24]—seems to have acted as a touchstone for the licensers' judgment of the permitted boundaries between morality and immorality. In May 1860 Donne prohibited a number of French plays announced for inclusion in M. Félix's season of French drama at the St James's Theatre and came close to banning one further play (entitled *Redemption*) which appeared on superficial examination to be of similar import to *La Dame aux Camélias*. But, as Donne reported to the Lord Chamberlain, the position of the heroine was 'not brought prominently forward' like that of Marguerite Gautier and she did not actually belong to 'the demi-monde'. The supper scene in the fourth act, he maintained, was 'not more, perhaps less objectionable than a similar scene in [Dion Boucicault's] *The Corsican Brothers*'.[25]

Alexandre Dumas' plays apart, the general tone of the drama in the early 1860s was remarkably 'moral'. The licensing authorities interfered only occasionally and then in no very serious way. It was with some considerable measure of satisfaction that William Donne was able to report to the 1866 Committee that 'all the excisions which I made in 1865 would not occupy more than [a] sheet of paper; not because I overlooked what was wrong in them, but because they did not require it'.[26]

III

From about 1866 onwards, the seemingly endless importation of morally questionable French literature gave rise to increasing pessimism over the drama and, in consequence, over the fate of English society. Spencer Ponsonby in his evidence to the 1866 Committee observed plaintively that 'the modern French drama is almost entirely immoral'.[27] And just two years later, W. R. Greg pointed out that 'French fiction, always more or less diseased and indecorous, has in recent years passed through several distinct phases of disease, and may now almost be said to have left simple indecorum far behind.'[28] The sexual irregularity of the French novel — and thus of the drama, since the two forms developed very nearly simultaneously — seemed already to have gnawed away at those values which the Victorians held to be the very basis of their society; the majority of articulate opinion was convinced that the moral debates at the core of so much contemporary French literature were damaging to the whole fabric of society. Indeed, the treatment of seduction and adultery in the *demi-monde* of Alexandre Dumas and his imitators was not interpreted as a warning about the nature of modern society but blamed as an active agent for its imminent moral dissolution.

During the late 1860s and early 70s there was a concerted campaign on the part of the licensing authorities to ensure that as little as possible of the insidious corruption of French drama reached the London stage. In swift succession no fewer than four French plays were refused licences in 1867 and all without reference to the Lord Chamberlain, since they were pieces which, in the Examiner's opinion, would 'shock (I think) *justly* an English audience'.[29] But Donne, always insisting that it was his 'desire to accord all possible liberty to the stage consistent with public morals or even prejudices', was prepared to argue the case for those plays which seemed to offer pointers in the right moral direction. In his advocacy of a new Parisian seduction drama *Le Supplice d'une Femme* (scheduled for the St James's season of 1867), he stressed that the piece contained 'much that was good in principle'. The wife did pay for her indiscretions with 'a heavy expiation' and her lover was 'not a worthless character'. Even more importantly, there was 'no attempt to gloss over vice, or to make wrong appear right'. Unluckily for Donne, however, the new Lord Chamberlain did not share his Examiner's favourable opinion and the play was declined a licence.[30] Lord Bradford's moral conservatism sealed a similar fate for Augier's *Paul Forestier* in the following year, even though Donne had been again at pains to point out that the moral resolution of the play was quite without objection.[31]

Behind William Donne's official *persona* as censor of the drama, one senses a conflict between his personal opinions and his clearly marked public duty. Private opinions were strictly of no account in his work as Examiner, whose duty it was to interpret public opinion and thus to operate within the limits of what he thought the public would tolerate. In terms of public notions of propriety and good taste much of the French drama which came under his notice was necessarily condemned; but, as Donne found out, it was becoming more and more difficult to discriminate between the merely indelicate and the actually immoral. This is the explanation of the long, often involved plot summaries that Donne began sending to the Lord Chamberlain from the late 1860s. A second opinion was always desirable even if, on occasion, that opinion proved something of a surprise. But, in any case, Donne's policies as moral censor increasingly struck a more personal note, since attitudes were changing rapidly. Indeed, there was no longer a commonly accepted standard to which the Examiner could safely refer.

Offences against the Victorian moral code were rare in the case of native English dramatists. But the tone of the authorities' attitude to French drama (still the most common source of trouble in the 1870s) was set by Donne's experience of the heated controversy which greeted the performance of Dion Boucicault's *Formosa; or, the Railroad to Ruin* (1869), the first excursion by a native author into the realm of the courtesan play. The first night reviews were generally very favourable. Boucicault was an established playwright and *The Times* (7 August 1869) considered the piece superior to most of his earlier efforts, almost matching in quality *The Colleen Bawn* and *Arrah-na-Pogue*. There was general agreement that the difficult central character of a reclaimed prostitute had been 'most inoffensively treated'. A long run was predicted.

The first hint of trouble came on 25 August, when John Heraud of the *Illustrated London News* — which periodical had in an earlier review (14 August) praised the play for its clever adjustment of an 'equivocal subject' to the taste of a modern audience — surprised all concerned by calling for the Lord Chamberlain 'to protect the public even against itself, and prevent the prevalence of bad taste, which now threatens the whole of society with demoralisation'. Boucicault's claim that his play was founded on the life of the notorious 'Anonyma', the courtesan of Rotten Row, made *Formosa* even more objectionable; and Heraud demanded immediate action to remove it from the stage. Alarmed at the reviewer's importunity, the Lord Chamberlain (who, of course, had never seen the MS. of the play) insisted on his Examiner's providing an explanation for having licensed on his own responsibility something which was apparently so indecent. Donne's considered and persuasive reply offered a full justification for his action on the grounds that, while the play was 'vulgar, foolish, and improbable', it did not actually offend moral propriety. The heroine, he claimed, underwent appropriately severe mortification for her sins, showed genuine remorse, and, unlike *La Dame aux Camélias*, Boucicault had made no attempt to hold up his sinful characters as worthy of imitation or respect. On the contrary, 'vice was throughout represented under a repulsive aspect', and the play gave a very sound illustration of the maxim that 'to have been weak and guilty was to be miserable also'. For these reasons, Donne concluded, 'it appeared to me that . . . there was a fair, although a painful, dramatic element: and none of the immoral casuistry that disfigures so many French comedies. Again in *Formosa* there is no intrigue that affects family-life, makes the husband profligate and ridiculous, and the wife nearly worthless or quite foolish.' With such a confident set of reasons Donne was able to acquit himself from the controversy with some degree of dignity. But worried voices were still being raised in the press and even in parliament; and as a consequence Donne was directed to attend a performance of *Formosa*, after which he reported to the Lord Chamberlain that he had been struck merely by its 'improbability and absurdity'. And in an attempt to assuage Lord Sydney's continued anxiety, Donne gave the further assurance that he would lose no opportunity of making it known that, had the Lord Chamberlain been aware of the contents of the play, he would never have sanctioned it. The Examiner's error of judgment seems to have strained for a time the normally cordial relations between Donne and Lord Sydney; but it was a mistake that the former attributed to 'a miscalculation of public feeling, though with the honest intention of doing even-handed justice to both the public and the stage'.[32]

Not unexpectedly, the immediate result of the *Formosa* affair was that Donne became much more cautious in his assessment of the latest novelties from across the English Channel. For his own protection he tried to involve the Lord Chamberlain more directly in the decisions made. In 1871, for example, he asked for his superior's advice on six French plays, not because any of them was 'positively indecent, coarse, or *au fond* immoral', but because they raised certain moral questions which Donne feared an English audience might not fully appreciate or understand. As Donne put it, 'every one of [these] comedies now on trial turns or treads upon some domestic or social theme, and the English moiety of spectators are either scandalised or bewildered by this class of entertainment — more frequently indeed "bewildered", since they often stop at the postulate and do not take into account the Q.E.D.'[33] Possibly the Examiner's estimate of the intellectual capacity of English audiences was a little pessimistic, but certainly there was a growing body of opinion ready to protest strongly at any introduction into the drama of what Donne might have called 'painful problems' of sexual and domestic relations. The Examiner envisaged himself – appropriately enough for the classical scholar he was – in the invidious position of 'steering between the Scylla of those who demand a decorous drama and Charybdis of those who require the contrary'.[34]

The last three years William Donne spent at the Lord Chamberlain's Office were without doubt the most fraught of all his experience as Examiner of Plays. The principal source of trouble was the season of French plays regularly performed from 1871 onwards by M. Félix, whose choice of pieces almost invariably conflicted with official notions of propriety. Of Jacques Offenbach's *La Vie Parisienne* (proposed for 1871), Donne commented with some feeling that 'the less that is said and shown of its *vie* the better'. Moreover, there were distinct fears that whatever cuts were made in the plays submitted would be ignored by the French manager. Accordingly, the endorsement to the operatic spectacle *Fleur du Thé* (1871) carried the following warning:

The objections to this Opera in the 3rd Act having been removed by Songs substituted for the original ones, and by excision of several passages in the dialogue, a License is granted for its performance. But the Manager is desired to take notice that this License applies to the Opera as amended and altered: and that any return to the former *songs or dialogue* will render the permission – void.

Even so, reports from the theatre indicated that certain indecencies had crept back into the dialogue and Donne prophesied that 'unless some decided action be taken with the Director of the Lyceum Plays, it will be quite impossible to maintain the Lord Chamberlain's authority as Licenser'.[35] The time had clearly come for some show of strength and during the rest of 1871 and on into 1872 the Examiner was given permission to pursue an even more stringent policy with regard to the French drama. Bristling with his new authority, Donne reported in July 1871 that he had 'scored [Offenbach's] *La Belle Hélène* for the Gaiety Theatre even more than I did for the St James's three years ago'.[36] Several French plays were refused licence during 1872, including *Le Timbrale* and a comic treatment of the amorous adventures of Byron under the title *Une Fantasie; ou, les amours de Lord Byron*, about which Donne remarked that it was 'extremely profane & profligate and cannot under any pretext be authorised for the English stage'.[37]

From 1873 M. Félix's season of French plays was inherited by Messrs Valnay and Pitron, who took leases on a succession of London theatres

Plate 7 *AUT CAESAR AUT NULLUS*. Caricatures of Spencer Ponsonby
and William Bodham Donne

and who seemed intent on challenging the licensing authorities by their
choice of programme. Before long Donne was confiding to the Lord
Chamberlain that the pair were 'most slippery to deal with', especially
since their arrival at the Princess in May 1873, where, having 'made
loud protestations of a desire to raise, by their choice of pieces, the
moral character of the Anglo-French theatre . . . they seem to me to do
all in their power to keep it at a low standard'.[38] In fact, very few of
Valnay and Pitron's plays were actually refused licences, but a great

many underwent correction at the hands of the Examiner; and it was this petty interference, as they themselves saw it, which proved the source of much frustration and acrimony. In most cases, Donne was cautious enough to supply outlines of the plays to the Lord Chamberlain before recommending them for licence. It was not until the 1874 season that the smouldering frustrations finally erupted and, in apparent desperation, Valnay and Pitron made the whole matter public. Early in that year, Donne recommended the suppression of one of the newest Parisian pieces *Le Chef de Pevision* and the two Frenchmen promptly retaliated by advertising their substitute play as forced upon them by the action of the Lord Chamberlain.[39] At the end of their lease of the Holborn Theatre in early April 1874, Valnay and Pitron secured advertising space in *The Times* (2 April) to assure the public that they had done all in their power to provide the best possible entertainment over the past few months but that their efforts had been continually upset by '"les riguers inexplicables et inexpliquées" of the "censure"', without which they 'would have been enabled to give still better satisfaction to the public'.

But this gibe proved only a mild prelude to the much more vigorous (perhaps even vicious) campaign that they launched against the Lord Chamberlain's Office as a result of their experiences during the immediately succeeding season at the Princess Theatre. Just as it was about to open, Donne prohibited on his own authority Lecocq's *opéra bouffe Giroflé Girofla* (Brussels, 1854), which, as he afterwards informed his superior, he had found 'so thoroughly indecent & unfit' that 'on this occasion I think it unnecessary to trouble you by wasting your time in reading it'.[40] And a few days later, Donne caused further dismay at the Princess by advising the managers to withdraw *La Jolie Parfumeuse* from their projected repertoire as he was certain that no licence would be forthcoming, having heard from various quarters of 'its gross indelicacy & unfitness'. As the Examiner later remarked to Spencer Ponsonby, Valnay and Pitron had been given fair warning 'that expurgation would not suffice; nothing short of destruction would'.[41] Given the climate of opinion at St James's Palace, the two managers must have known they were tempting fate by advertising Alexandre Dumas' notorious *Le Demi-Monde* for inclusion in their summer programme. The play had already been banned in 1860 and, although Donne was personally prepared to compromise by suggesting various excisions and agreeing to a new title, the Lord Chamberlain was in no mood to reverse a decision of fourteen years' standing. The news that the play would not be licensed roused Valnay and Pitron to new fury and they used their summer advertisements at the Princess Theatre as the medium for a bitter attack on the Lord Chamberlain:

Notice. Madama PASCA. Until now, Messrs VALNAY and PITRON had the hope of presenting this artiste to the British Public in her great part of La Baronne d'Ange, in the celebrated play, 'Le DEMI-MONDE' by Alexandre Dumas, fils. Unfortunately, the Licensing Authorities have not condescended, *because this piece had been prohibited by one of their predecessors*, to withdraw the veto put on its representation fifteen years ago, — notwithstanding that it had, by their own admission, NEVER BEEN READ; — notwithstanding that it has been represented with great success in most of the civilized capitals of Europe, and in the presence of THE MOST EMINENT PERSONAGES; — notwithstanding that an alteration of Title and innumerable excisions were proposed by Messrs Valnay & Pitron solely to remove the apparent susceptibilities of the Licensing Authorities.[42]

While not totally unfounded, Valnay and Pitron's accusations were certainly neither disinterested nor even quite accurate. But wisely the authorities did not take the proffered bait and chose to remain silent on the whole business. At the same time, Donne observed privately that 'it is next to impossible now to find a French Play which is not of questionable morality, and perhaps as impossible to *veto* all that are sent for examination — such wholesale prohibition being equivalent to closing the French Theatre in London'.[43] Admittedly, this is the remark of a tired man, who had completed a quarter of a century as Examiner, but one cannot fail to sense the note of near defeat. Donne's successors could have no illusions about the magnitude of the task ahead in salving the morality of the English stage.

6

RELIGION AND THE STAGE

Nineteenth-century objections to the stage representation of religious and scriptural themes were deeply rooted in the theatrical and religious climate of the age. Since at least the middle of the seventeenth century a strong body of opinion had been resolutely opposed, not only to the principle of religious drama, but to the theatre itself. Polemics such as Prynne's *Historio-mastix* (1633), Collier's *Short View of the Immorality, and Profaneness of the English Stage* (1698), and William Law's *Absolute Unlawfulness of the Stage Fully Demonstrated* (1726), together with countless lesser but nonetheless provocative and often influential works, had respectable counterparts in the nineteenth century.[1] The growth of nonconformity in the previous century was one of the main reasons why the enemies of the theatre gained so much support, especially among the middle classes, in the early years of the nine-teenth. The strength of the Puritan element in Victorian society was something that the theatre could not afford to ignore. As has been pointed out by one social historian, 'the English did not cease to be Puritans when they stopped believing in Puritanism'; and Matthew Arnold could still write truthfully in the 1870s of 'the prison house of Puritanism' in which the English consciousness had been shackled for the past two hundred years.[2]

Prejudice against the theatre expressed itself in varying forms. Despite the efforts of David Garrick and others in the eighteenth century, the acting profession still retained its age-old stigma as the resort of vagabonds and debauchees. The whole morality of the stage and its drama was called seriously in question when prostitution was known to be tolerated, if not openly encouraged, at almost every play-house in London. A contributor to the *Edinburgh Review* in 1833 re-marked sadly on 'the glaring indecencies of our playhouse lobbies and saloons ... [which] have made the theatre of moral England a byword of Continental wonder and reproach'. Ironic comparison was drawn between the fastidiousness of a censorship (under George Colman) which prohibited 'damn it' and 'my angel' and the officially licensed theatres of London 'where open profligacy revels with a freedom scarcely known in other civilized lands, and which the wives and daughters of our citizens can scarcely enter without a blush'.[3] (The analogy with Law's description of the theatre as 'the *Sink of Corruption and Debauchery*' needs no elaboration.) The supposed low character of the actors, the encouragement of prostitution, and the triviality of the entertainment provided were put forward as compelling reasons for large sections of the community to turn away in righteous indignation from an institution which by its whole nature seemed inconsistent with the profession of the Christian faith.

The course of religious censorship from 1824 to 1901 was determined, like other attitudes adopted by the Lord Chamberlain's Office, by reference to public opinion (which generally meant no more than the views expressed by the press). The major difference, however, between religious and other forms of censorship was that the former became more and more inflexible as the century progressed. Naturally, there were occasions when the rules were temporarily modified (or even in very rare instances relaxed) but the mere whisper of public criticism produced a speedy reversion to the enforcement of the authorities' former policy even when, at the turn of the century, it was becoming clear that public opinion was reordering its attitudes towards a cautious acceptance of some forms of religious drama. When in 1832 George Colman stated his belief that 'all Scripture is much too sacred for the stage, except in very solemn scenes indeed', there was at least the possibility (admittedly more illusory than real) of the legitimate use of religious allusion. By 1866 William Donne, having experienced the strength of public opinion on the issue, was forced into a more rigid statement of the Lord Chamberlain's position, observing that 'both as a matter of morality, and as a matter of taste, I never allow any associations with scripture or theology to be introduced into a play'. But it was left to George Redford, in evidence before the 1909 Committee, to articulate what had by then become a rule with quasi-legal status, namely, that he had 'no power as Examiner of Plays to make any exception to the rule that scriptural plays or plays founded on, or adapted from, the Scriptures are ineligible for license in Great Britain'.[4]

George Colman's notoriety for a rooted objection to all references to heaven, God, Lord, and even angels (on the grounds that they are mentioned in the Bible)[5] was no figment of the imaginations of the Examiner's enemies. In a letter to the playwright Thomas Morton respecting his play *A School for Grown Children* (1827), he advised cutting

Please to omit the following underlined words, in the representation of the Tragedy called

"Caswallon, or the Briton Chief."

Act 1.

Scene 2. —— . "Now sustain me, Heaven!

Do. "Aye, — I think Heaven — 'tis living, blooming — Eve," &c

Do. —— "by you Conscious Heaven I swear it"

Do. "Will then ask? — awful Heaven! — he turns away."

Act 2.

Scene 1. —— — "by all my hopes Here, and hereafter!"

Do. —— "Mysterious Heaven!"

Scene 2. —— . "lifts the adoring heart in grateful wonder To Him who thus hath ordered it."

Do. "Heaven in its mercy! is thy heart of stone?"

Do. "Almighty Power! I've warned them," &c

Do. "Stay yet, thou heavenly maid!"

Do. —— "who in her confident oisfears, to Heaven,"

Act 3.

Scene 1. — "Oh Heaven! it is himself"

Do. —— —— "Oh Heaven! my wretched Country!" (turn over)

Plate 8   George Colman's list of cuts required in *Caswallon, the Briton Chief* (1829)

Scene 3.

D? "By Heaven while ~ "Damned thought!"

"By Heaven while left, I will not see thee left."

D?
                — "Tis Heav'n
Inspires the thought, & Heav'n will prosper it."

              Act 4

Scene 1.   — "Now God ha' mercy! kneel —"

D?   "Heav'n! & must we know it now!"

D?   — ..."in Heaven's name,
What is't your purpose?"

D? — "Damned wretch!"

D?   — "I thank Heaven,
At Chester."

D? "By the deep horrors of that Hell thou caus'st."

              Act 5

Scene 1.. "I come to tell thee, — but, by Heav'n, thy youth" &c

D?   — ...."Oh Heaven!
Suffering one," &c

D?   "Heaven in its mercy,
Preserve, or quickly end me!"

Scene 2.. "All Angels, starting from their light abodes,"
         Behold & guard her!

D? Thank Heaven! thank Heaven! I have not sped in vain!"

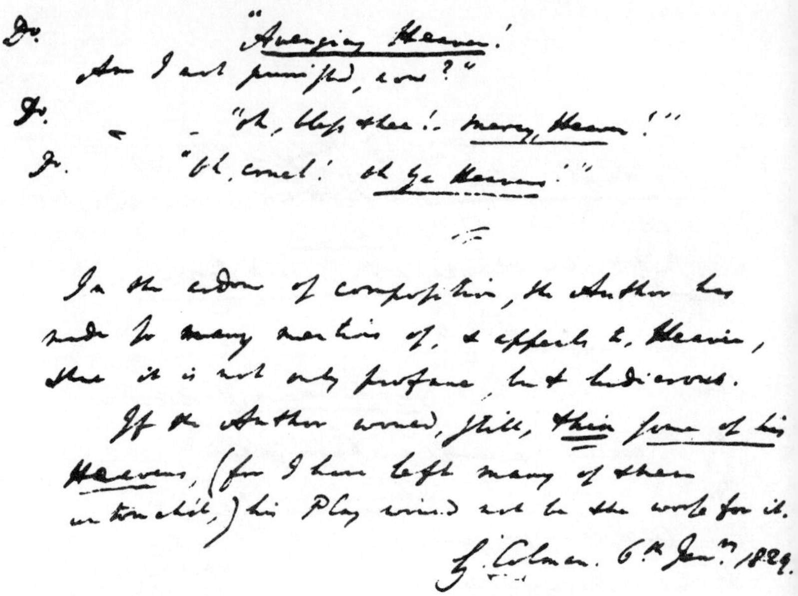
Do. "Avenging Heaven!'
Am I not punish'd, now?"
Do. – – "Oh, bless thee! – mercy Heaven!"
Do. "Oh, cruel! oh ye Heavens!"

In the ardour of composition, the Author has made so many mentions of, & appeals to, Heaven, that it is not only profane, but ludicrous.
If the Author would, still, thin some of his Heavens, (for I have left many of them untouch'd,) his Play would not be the worse for it.
G. Colman. 6th Jany 1829.

Plate 8 George Colman's list of cuts required in *Caswallon, the Briton Chief* (1829)

out three uses of 'Heaven forbid' and one 'By Heaven', expressions which he agreed were 'in daily colloquial use'; but, he went on, 'surely, if they mean anything, they are sacred Invocations, and improper for the Drama at least upon *light* and *ludicrous* occasions'.[6] As might be expected, a large number of the MSS. licensed by Colman, if they show no other mark of censorship, invariably have any stray 'sacred Invocation' boldly excised in red ink. But perhaps an exceptional case is that of C. E. Walker's tragedy *Caswallon, the Briton Chief* (1829), in which the unfortunate author suffered no fewer than twenty-three excisions of references to 'Heaven', the phrase 'Almighty Powers', two uses of 'damned', and the lines 'All Angels stooping from their bright abodes, / Behold & guard her!' And, if that were not enough, Colman also appended this advice: 'In the ardour of composition, the Author has made many mentions of, & appeals to Heaven, that it is not only profane, but ludicrous. If the Author would, still, thin *some of his Heavens,* (for I have left many of them untouch'd,) his Play would not be the worse for it.'[7]

The Examiner's missionary zeal was by no means confined to such minor oaths and references to angels but to any phrase which might remotely recall the language of the Bible. He was evidently anxious that audiences' sensibilities should be protected from such shockingly irreverent phrases as 'reduced to the misery of Lazarus', 'the father of Abraham's promise', 'the blessing of Jacob be on thee', and even 'May the protecting hand of Heaven be stretch'd to preserve him.' Excisions of that kind — they are all from M. R. Lacy's *The Knights Templar; or, the Maid of Judah* (1829) — begin to show the comprehensiveness of Colman's religious censorship.[8]

There were inevitably times when the mark of Colman's fanaticism went too far even for contemporary taste. The only recourse for a disaffected dramatist was to make an appeal over Colman's head to the Lord Chamberlain. Few playwrights ever made use of such an opportunity, since it was only when a reasonable and sympathetic Lord Chamberlain was in office that there was any hope of a reversal of the Examiner's decision. The Duke of Devonshire, a man of rare distinction, was such a person. When the author of *Ben Nazir the Saracen* (1829) applied to the Lord Chamberlain for his veto on the cuts imposed on his play, the Duke immediately ordered the restoration of all the passages excised. One of Colman's objections concerned the speech by Emerance, daughter of the Duke of Aquitaine, who has married the Saracen hero of the play:

> Have I done wrong? Oh all-creating Power!
> Why hast thou given each individual mind
> Thoughts, faculties, and feelings of its own?
> Why not for all alike traced one wide way,
> If one alone is virtue? I've wed a Moor:
> Am I less a Christian? Heaven thou know'st
> How firm my faith is. Oh! Could the sacrifice
> Of this most lowly form lead his soul
> To thy true worship . . .[9]

Colman's blanket prohibition on religious allusion meant that he was unable to discriminate between the legitimate and illegitimate use of such references in drama. It is, of course, an argument which would exclude *Othello* from the stage. The Duke of Devonshire's intervention on behalf of the author confirms his recognition of the parallel.

Given George Colman's generally cavalier attitude to his work, it is less than surprising that an occasional major inconsistency disturbs the otherwise clear pattern of rigorous religious censorship. As might be expected, the suppression of a play with the title *The Prodigal Son*

(1828) was virtually guaranteed, even though the New Testament parable was a relatively popular subject at many of the minor theatres outside the Lord Chamberlain's control.[10] But Colman's licensing (with excisions) of Thomas Wade's *The Jew of Arragon; or, the Hebrew Queen* (1829) is a good illustration of just how capricious the censor could sometimes be. Although the plot of Wade's play was derived from the biblical story of Esther, the author had cunningly transported the action into thirteenth-century Spain during the reign of Alfonso XIII and thereby sufficiently disguised its origins for Colman to feel justified in granting it a licence. Yet the cuts that Colman required were so extensive and, to the author's mind, so ludicrous and absurd that when the play came to be performed at Covent Garden in October 1830 (some twelve months after licensing) Wade attributed at least part of its failure – it ran for just one night and was booed off the stage for its supposedly pro-Jewish bias – to Colman's censorship. In self-vindication Wade then published the full text with all the Examiner's cuts printed in italics.[11] The press were totally mystified at Colman's censorship since it appeared to adhere neither to rules nor to any discoverable principles. According to the *Literary Gazette* (6 November 1830), lines such as 'Before the Red-sea miracle' had been struck out yet 'They shall not, by the Cross' was allowed; Colman prohibited 'Heaven keep your grace' while he retained 'By Judah's God! my liege, it makes me mad' – anomalies (amongst many others) which led the reviewer to suspect, not unreasonably, that the Examiner had read only alternate pages of the MS. Certainly, Colman's hasty excisions did nothing to improve what was already a rather indifferent work; *The Times* (1 November 1830) declared imperiously that *The Jew of Arragon* at its first and only performance was 'most unequivocally and justly condemned, because it was a bad play'.

As one recent critic has pointed out, 'the significance of Colman's judgments is that it only exaggerated – it did not run counter to – the prevailing opinions of the time'. By the time of the Examiner's death the rules by which he had governed the stage had taken on almost legislative force and under the relaxed regime of his immediate successor public opinion and the Press ... now lacking a Colman ... had to impose their own check upon dramatists by public clamor'.[12] Bulwer Lytton was one of the first victims of the new sense of public responsibility. His first play, *The Duchess de la Vallière* (1837), was denied a fair hearing by the reviewers because of the prominent religious element, which provoked impassioned outbursts of religious indignation. Charles Kemble had evidently considered that the final scene (V, vi), where the heroine takes the veil within the chapel of a Carmelite convent, was perfectly admissible. (The stage directions require that 'the altar . . . is partially seen through the surrounding throng', 'officials pass to and fro, swinging censers', and the scene opens to the accompaniment of solemn music and a hymn.) But it was the whole texture of the play which gave offence. A critic in the *Monthly Review* remarked that the recurrence of invocations to heaven throughout the play were 'shockingly irreverent' and to be condemned along with the rest of the religious vocabulary:

There occur such words as these, 'O Father, bless her', which we are happy to learn were received by the audience . . . with the most unqualified testimonies of disapprobation. Really novel and play-writers should remember, that if they spend their days in catering for public amusement, the least thing that can be demanded of them is that their words be harmless — that they offer no glaring indignity to the most solemn and precious feeling which religion has fostered.[13]

But it was left to Alfred Bunn to comment in his autobiography (what was apparent to all) that *La Vallière* would never have had the sanction of 'the ever regarded and ever regretted' George Colman as the play contained such allegedly outrageous passages as 'And seek some sleek Iscariot of the Church. / To *sell* SALVATION *for the thirty pieces*!' and 'My heart's wild sea is hush'd, and o'er the waves / *The* SAVIOUR *walks*!'[14] Admittedly, Bunn was no friend of Bulwer Lytton and his objections may not have been wholly sincere; but his point was nevertheless sound enough, since the play is full of speeches that would have horrified Colman:

Lanzan	Damn you!
Montespan	Damn *me*! What! damn a Marquis! Heaven would think
	Twice of it, Sir, before it damn'd a man
	Of *my* rank! Damn a Marquis! there's religion! (V, ii)

Outraged public opinion soon forced Bulwer Lytton into making some concessions. About a week after the first performance at Covent Garden he wrote to Macready suggesting that in Act II 'Merciful Heavens' be substituted for 'Lord of Hosts'. Other more substantial changes followed: 'Heaven is less merciful' became 'Fate is less merciful' and, in later editions of the play, 'all stage-directions referring to crucifixes and other holy objects, and a number of lines suggestive of Divinity [were] altered or suppressed'.[15] In Bulwer Lytton's case, the activities of the censor pale into insignificance when measured against the pressure of public opinion in establishing its own criteria of religious decorum. He might well have pondered on the truth of his own prologue to *The Duchess de la Vallière* that (echoing Dr Johnson) 'the mightiest critic is the PUBLIC VOICE'.

II

With the exception of Charles Kemble's short career, those of Colman's successors follow a pattern of religious censorship substantially similar to Colman's own. It extended to the deletion of all passages and phrases quoted directly from the Scriptures or even implying any such association. Religious censorship embraced the whole of the spectrum from the comic or irreverent biblical tag to the most serious and devout references. That included semi-religious jokes like 'Collect my Labourers from the Vineyard — I mean the cowshed', lines such as 'He would tell a lie to the Bishop of London' (which also offended against the rule on personal allusion), as well as the serious use of biblical style as in the line 'And from the innocent blood that shall be shed I here do wash my hands before all men & him.'[16] In the Strand Theatre's version of Dickens's *Bleak House* (1854), Jo the crossing-sweeper was prevented from being taught the words of 'The Lord's Prayer' on his death-bed. At this point, too, the Bible could not be used as stage property, or even mentioned on stage; and as late as 1870 a crucifix was forbidden in the theatre, though an unadorned cross was usually permitted.[17] That the censors were not being over-particular is attested by Dion Boucicault, who recalled at the 1866 Committee an incident at a performance of his comedy *Old Heads and Young Hearts* (1844) when the audience hissed the line 'I came to scoff, but I remained to pray' (from Goldsmith's *The Deserted Village*) because they thought it came out of the Bible.[18] And Boucicault himself, like countless other Victorian dramatists, suffered minor censorship for religious exclamations, as in *The Colleen Bawn* (1860), the Day Book entry for which bears the instruction 'for the word "God" substitute "Heaven"'.

The uncompromising nature of the rule against religious drama was dramatically illustrated during the Examinership of John Mitchell Kemble, with the suppression in 1847 of works by the two pillars of French classical drama, Racine and Corneille. In March that year *Athalie* (1691) was prohibited and in April Corneille's *Polyeucte* (1641–3) suffered the same fate.[19] The refusal of the former is easily accounted for since it violates the rule banning subjects taken directly from the Scriptures — it is based on the narrative of Athaliah and

Joash (2 Kings 11 and 2 Chronicles 22—24) — but the rejection of *Polyeucte* could not have been defended on like grounds. Corneille's source-material — a medieval text relating the conversion of the hero to Christianity and his subsequent martyrdom in Armenia during the reign of Decius about 250 A.D. — was not specifically scriptural and so he could hardly have been accused of profaning Holy Writ. Ironically, however, neither drama need ever have been submitted to the Lord Chamberlain, since they both pre-date the 1737 Licensing Act; and in any case *Athalie* had already received a licence (albeit unnecessarily) from George Colman in 1827.[20]

The injustice perpetrated against Corneille's play was redressed three years later when William Donne, having recently taken over as acting Examiner from John Kemble and lacking the official record books, granted it a licence. Donne stoutly defended his action before the 1866 Committee (to whose members the reversal of the ban seemed to savour of caprice) on the perfectly legitimate ground that *Polyeucte* had no specific connexion with any scriptural text.[21] Racine's *Athalie*, however, remained under official interdiction.

William Bodham Donne attempted to inaugurate a somewhat less inflexible policy on religious drama even though at times this proved a hazardous enterprise, since he could be sure of no support from the dignitaries of the Church — the Bishop of London was resolutely opposed to any form of religion on the stage — and little enough from the press. Yet he was prepared to explore, where possible, ways of compromise. In the case of *The Hebrew Sacrifice* (1852) the objections were confined solely to the third act, which embodied the story of Jephthah's daughter (Judges 11 :29—40); but after revisions the rest of the play was licensed and performed under the title *The Hebrew*.[22] In other instances no amount of remodelling would suffice, as the Olympic Theatre found to its cost in March 1852 when a licence was refused for *The Hebrew Son; or, the Child of Babylon*. The Day Book records that the piece was nothing more than 'a dramatic version of the Scriptural account of Joseph and his Bretheren'. A second version (with the highly improbable title *Robert; or, the Fiend of the Volcano*) proved equally unsuitable.

What the period of Donne's Examinership does prove is that, for a time at least, it was possible for religious plays to be granted the Lord Chamberlain's licence as long as the directness of the scriptural parallels was obscured sufficiently to satisfy the letter rather than the spirit of the prohibition on scriptural drama. Much also rested on the degree to which the biblical source-material was regarded as divinely inspired. In other words there were parts of the Bible (the Apocrypha, for example) which, being less highly esteemed, were occasionally permitted as subject-matter. On the face of it, the problem with *The King of Persia; or, the Triumph of the Jewish Queen* (1855) was a simple one. The play, based on the biblical story of Esther, offended the well-defined ruling on the use of biblical material and Donne wrote to the Lord Chamberlain advising its suppression on the grounds that it might afford, if licensed, 'a dangerous precedent'. As he explained, 'several even of the names in the Bible are retained viz. Haman, Mordecai, Vashti, Esther etc. With the treatment of the subject I have no fault to find; my objection lies against the employing a portion of the Bible which moreover is occasionally read in the Church-Service, as a dramatic theme.'[23] Donne's firm attitude towards the play's unsuitability for the stage is, however, a little surprising. The book of Esther (part of the Apocrypha) had been long regarded as of possibly dubious canonical worth and there was a degree of uncertainty as to its historical truth. Furthermore, Esther was a fairly popular subject with earlier dramatists, among them Racine, and, nearer Donne's own time, Thomas Wade, who had used it (in a disguised version) for a play already discussed in 1830. Also, Elizabeth Polack's *Esther, the Royal Jewess; or, the Death of Haman* had been performed — unlicensed since it was a minor theatre — at the Pavilion in 1835. (Miss Polack's play has been described in error by the most recent writer on religious drama in England as 'the sole recorded exception to the ban on biblical drama during a period of some three centuries'.[24] Such persuasive precedents seem to have been ignored both by the Examiner and the Lord Chamberlain, for on 31 August 1855 *The King of Persia* was formally refused a licence.

But within two weeks the Lord Chamberlain's Office had second thoughts about the play. A revised version was submitted to the Examiner by the City of London Theatre and a licence granted. The amended text — there is only one MS. in the Lord Chamberlain's collection — reveals that the revisions amounted to very little more than the substitution of less-emotive names for the scriptural characters: for example, 'Vashti' loses her biblical identity completely and becomes merely 'the Queen', while 'Haman' is altered to 'Orodes', and 'Esther' is transformed into 'Marianne'.[25] This curious juggling with the *dramatis personae*, though not a particularly common practice, had evidently been sufficient to satisfy the scruples of the licensing authorities on previous occasions. All operas based on biblical themes suffered in this way. Rossini's *Mosè in Egitto* (1818) became *Pietro L'Ere-*

mita for its premiere in England in 1822, while Verdi's *Nabucco* (1842) was permitted only under the title *Nino* for its first production at Her Majesty's Theatre in 1846 and as *Anato* for its subsequent performance at Covent Garden in 1850.[26] William Donne clearly found the practice somewhat ridiculous, but he was obliged to comply. As he wryly observed to Fanny Kemble when the famous Mme Ristori was to play the heroine in Paolo Giacometti's tragedy *Giuditta* in the summer of 1858:

[T]o please the thick-skulled superstitious British public I have been obliged to find her a new name for the Tragedy, and new titles for the characters, and all because the book of Judith happens to be bound up with the Bible, being all the while as much inspired as 'Tom Jones'. When shall we be a wiser people?[27]

Giacometti's play was founded on the Apocryphal story of Judith and Holofernes; but, as Donne pointed out to the Lord Chamberlain when he argued his case for licensing the tragedy, the book of Judith 'has never been reckoned among the Canonical Scriptures, and is simply an historical record or legend (without any pretensions to divine inspiration or ecclesiastical authority) of a Jewish heroine'. The main objections to the play, Donne observed, would come from the Established Church, but he stressed that *Giuditta* should not be excluded from the stage merely by the application of '*a priori* grounds'.[28]

Lord Breadalbane was as anxious as his Examiner to accord all reasonable liberty to the stage and he himself suggested a solution whereby the play might be granted a licence while yet silencing all religious objection. The Comptroller of the Lord Chamberlain's Office outlined Breadalbane's scheme to Donne:

He would not of course wish this to be publicly announced, but he desires me to request you to convey unofficially to the Author of *Judith* or to whomsoever has applied to you on the subject that while [the Lord Chamberlain] must decline to licence a Play founded on the Biblical story of Judith and Holofernes he would not be unwilling to take into consideration a Play the plot of which might closely resemble that story.[29]

It was extremely unusual for a Lord Chamberlain to offer a solution in such terms, or, indeed, to offer any solution at all. The impression forms of a liberal Examiner of Plays and a liberal Lord Chamberlain whose joint responsibility to public opinion — Donne's 'thick-skulled superstitious British public' — gave little opportunity or encouragement for such tolerant attitudes. The authorities were reduced to sleight-of-hand methods in an attempt to disguise the dramatisation of a scriptural story. But there could have been few who were deceived and it provides an insight into the Victorian ethos that such superficial camouflage should remedy all religious objections.

III

Under the powers granted to the Lord Chamberlain by the 1737 and 1843 Acts on theatrical licensing the libretti of operas were also subject to his jurisdiction; but, as in other areas of censorship, the standards applied were in general rather less rigorous than in the case of non-musical forms of drama. Certainly, opera was not immune from censorship but the authorities allowed considerable latitude in the use of religious backgrounds and settings. Throughout the MS. of Edward Fitzball's *The Favourite* (a translation of Donizetti's *La Favorite*) licensed in October 1843, John Kemble deleted a variety of Roman Catholic allusions — to the Pope, priesthood, confession, even to cloister, while one seemingly harmless enquiry 'To join the mass goest not thou my son?' was reformed by the substitution of 'bretheren' for 'mass'.[30] But the opera did retain its religious atmosphere and it became a popular piece with the public. Fitzball later commented in his autobiography on the fickleness of English audiences, who had been greatly affronted at the use of a crucifix in Bulwer Lytton's *The Duchess de la Vallière* (1837), yet, in the scene in *The Favourite* 'where Miss Rosmer . . . personated the heroine at the foot of the cross, the utmost approval prevailed'. However, his assumption that 'the prejudice respecting the appearance of a cross on stage is judiciously exploded' was premature, as there remained in the minds of both the public and the licensers a crucial difference between what was appropriate to musical and non-musical drama.[31]

One of William Donne's first problems after taking over as acting Examiner in 1849 was the English libretto of Meyerbeer's *Les Huguenots* (Paris, 1836), which was everywhere acclaimed as the composer's greatest work. The substance of the opera concerned the St Bartholomew Day massacre of the Huguenots in Paris in 1572. It was a sensitive historical subject and its apparently anti-Catholic prejudice had already necessitated changes in plot and title for performance in Catholic countries abroad.[32] The opera had enjoyed three previous runs in England (all of them at Covent Garden and all in foreign languages) in 1842, 1845, and 1848, though only the 1845 version had been considered doubtful enough to be referred to the Lord Chamberlain.[33] The MS. licensed by Donne in 1849 excludes a number of anti-Catholic allusions, like the description of the soldier Marcel as 'inspired with religion, a deep hatred of the Pope and the fair sex' and a song directed 'against the Papal power, bigot Monks / and Women'.[34] Encouraged no doubt by the success of the Royal Italian Opera's production at Covent Garden, the English version was staged a number of times during 1849 and generated no religious ill-will. The licensing of *The Huguenots* illuminates the proposition that, while a religious subject of this nature would have no chance of official sanction as a straight drama, the very same subject could silence all objection in musical disguise.

Such curiously naive rationalisation explains the apparent discrepancy between the licensing of Edward Fitzball's *Azael the Prodigal* (a translation of Auber's opera *L'Enfant Prodigue*) for Drury Lane in February 1851 and the proscription in the same month on the drama *The Prodigal*, which was, on official advice to Samuel Lane of the Britannia Theatre, 'withdrawn' from official examination as unacceptable.[35] The plot of the opera retails the story of Reuben's son Azael, who abandons his father and his betrothed for the superior attractions of the city of Memphis and the traveller Nepte, until prevailed on to return by the 'Spirit of the Desert'. While the *Illustrated London News* (22 February 1851), which described the piece as 'one of the most gorgeous spectacles ever witnessed on the London stage', made no mention of the religious interest of the opera, its biblical atmosphere really is unmistakable. There are obvious echoes of the parable of the Prodigal Son (Luke 15) and Reuben (as chief of an Israelite tribe) is mentioned in the Bible on a number of occasions. The Church, much less convinced than the press of the propriety of the opera, marshalled its forces into action and some days later one of its self-appointed watch-dogs, the Bishop of London, protested to the Lord Chamberlain that *Azael* was quite improper for the stage. As a precaution against enquiries into the Bishop's allegation, the Lord Chamberlain immediately requested suspension of the licence, a directive that James Anderson of Drury Lane rather surprisingly ignored.[36] In the event the opera was judged to be harmless enough and its run proceeded without further interruption. Fitzball later remarked:

Eventually, *religious* people of almost all denominations came to witness this spectacle, and I am quite sure, from the general burst of tears, into which I have seen, over and over again, the house dissolve at its conclusion, that if religious pieces were allowed to be produced *by proper people, at proper* seasons, in this country, it would do more to soften humanity, than all the lectures that the finest orator ever yet poured forth from the rostrum.[37]

The encouraging public reaction to *Azael the Prodigal* might have prompted a more reasonable attitude to religious drama in general, but in fact quite the opposite occurred after the appearance at the Olympic Theatre in October 1851 of George Rodwell's burlesque *Azael; or, the Prodigal in London*. Perhaps unwisely, in retrospect, Donne licensed the piece without reservation, only to find that he had inadvertently provided the Bishop with fresh ammunition for his attack on religious drama, and that he himself was under fire from his superiors for having 'sanctioned a Performance described as so objectionable'. More serious than that, however, was that the Lord Chamberlain's Office, in seeking to appease the Bishop, accepted that 'to connect the vulgarity & ribaldry of a Burlesque was in every way offensive to good taste', and was forced into stating in the most uncompromising terms that for the future 'no sanction should be given to any Drama or Burlesque founded on Scriptural Incident'.[38]

IV

The fact that from a purely *quantitative* view religious censorship continued to dominate the whole of the Victorian period is an important index of public attitudes. Not surprisingly, it was the Church which took the lead in moulding public opinion. As late as 1878 its attitude, not only to religious drama but to the theatre itself, was, to say the least, equivocal. Admittedly, the Anglican Church had never condemned the theatre outright (in contrast to certain nonconformist sects) but even at this juncture it contained within its ranks a number of stalwart and influential clergy who were opposed to the theatre, whose burden of association with levity and immorality proved stubbornly difficult to shed. Yet there were, too, some more hopeful signs. One contributor to *The Theatre* noted enthusiastically that the Church Congress of 1878 had actually discussed the Church's responsibility to the drama.[39] The tentative but increasingly sympathetic attitude of the Church to the theatre in the 1880s and 90s was a formal recognition of the transformation which the theatre had undergone in its search for respectability. But the Church did little or nothing to promote the advent of religious drama.

Edward Pigott and George Redford continued more or less unmodified the policies of their predecessors in the Examinership. Indeed, the comment of the former on the frequency of the exclamation 'My God' in the play *Zana* (1883) might have come directly from the Colman era half a century before:

This bold translation of a French idiom has an entirely different signification in English, and addressed to an English audience. The frequent repetition of the name of the Deity on the most trivial occasion is irreverent and offensive. There are of course occasions when even upon the stage, it is the right word to use. But these are rare, and only where the prevailing strain of thought is high and solemn.

Pigott's incidental 'even upon the stage' serves as a revealing illustration of just how far apart, in the Examiner's view, religion and the theatre really were. Certain theatre managers, too, were no less assiduous in their concern to remove all religious oaths and other religious allusions from their plays even before submission to the Examiner. In 1879 Wilson Barrett of the Grand Theatre, Leeds, advised the young Henry Arthur Jones to delete, among other things, all oaths (religious or otherwise) from the text of his comic drama *Harmony Restored*: 'All oaths should be expunged; "this is your darnation old mother again" would probably provoke and certainly deserve a hiss, all the expletives do not strengthen but disfigure a charming piece. I do not think Barry's conversion and singing the Moody and Sankey hymns advisable — I abhor cant as much as any man living.' And later, writing of Jones's *A Clerical Error* (1879), Barrett suggested the excision of many allegedly offensive expressions, such as 'Neither in earth nor in heaven nor in hell.'[40] The ban on associating religion and drama extended even to the advertising of plays. When the manager of the Olympic Theatre was rash enough to publicise his production of Wilkie Collins's *The New Magdalen* (1873) accompanied by an appropriate scriptural text (Luke 15:7) on repentance, the Examiner requested the immediate removal 'of this unprecedented and unnecessary allusion to a verse of scripture'.[41] And the announcement of Robert Buchanan's dramatisation of his own novel *God and the Man* by the Adelphi Theatre in 1883 stirred Edward Pigott to write to the theatre indicating in no uncertain terms that a play with such a title 'would be a most unjustifiable offence to the religious feelings of the country and nothing less than a scandal ... [and] an outrageous piece of profanity'.[42] The ferocity of the Examiner's reaction was apparently enough to deter any thought of performing the play, even with a different title, and under the heavy burden of official disapproval the whole project lapsed.

The hostile reaction of the licensing authorities in the 1880s and 90s to any suggestion of religious drama has, in retrospect, little enough to recommend it; but what does redound to their credit is that it was not only the Christian faith and the Established Church that came under their protection. In the winter of 1890 rumours that Henry

Irving was about to perform the title role in a play called *Mahomet* provoked the Lord Chamberlain's Office into issuing a denial that they would ever contemplate licensing a work which might give so much offence to the Muslim community in Britain.[43] Jewish sensibilities were also protected in 1901 when it was discovered that the Hebrew operetta *Isaac; or, the Angel's Message* contained 'a highly realistic representation of the Sacrifice of Isaac calculated to offend many strict Jews, and possibly produce a disturbance in the theatre'. The licence was withdrawn and the Lord Chamberlain, in order to avoid future mistakes of this kind, directed that all Yiddish plays submitted for licensing were to be accompanied by a certificate confirming that its English transcript was a literal translation.[44]

English minority interests were similarly afforded the benefit of the Lord Chamberlain's concern. The Salvation Army, for instance, which had commenced operations in 1878, though it undoubtedly suffered as the butt of jokes in Christmas pantomimes and the like, was sheltered from unwelcome allusions in the serious drama. In the endorsement to the licence for *Baffled*, a play for the Variety Theatre in 1884, Pigott commented:

Omit in representation all allusions to the Salvation Army. It is not permissible to insult & vilify a considerable number of people who are perfectly well-meaning and worthy of respect (however eccentric in some of their manifestations) by identifying them with a felon and a heartless hypocrite, as in this piece. Nor is it desirable, in the interests of the Stage that the religious feelings of any portion of the public should be offended. Although the Blue Ribbon Army may be considered hostile to the trade of a publican, it is not desirable that a Licensed Theatre should be used as a platform for advocating intoxication and sneering at temperance.

'This pandering to vicious tastes and habits', Pigott roundly concluded, 'is a degradation of the stage.' The patronising comments aside, there is evidence for the assertion that Edward Pigott was genuinely convinced that he was instrumental in improving the moral and religious tone of the drama.

Ridicule of any form of religious faith was serious enough but when ministers of the Christian religion were brought into venal contempt on the stage, the breach of decorum aroused cries of disgust and outrage from the leaders of the Anglican Church. The crusade against presentation of clerics in unbecoming situations was headed by the new Bishop of London in July 1882, following the portrayal of priests in Sydney Grundy's comic opera *The Vicar of Bray*. As spokesman for the many people who had written to him in complaint, the Bishop

protested at clergymen 'singing comic songs & the like' on the grounds
that 'such an exhibition is not only objectionable in point of good taste,
but not without danger in its bearing on reverence for sacred things,
& thus indirectly on even religion itself'. In France, he claimed, it was
unlawful even under the Republic to represent ministers of religion on
the stage; and he expressed the hope that the Lord Chamberlain would
bring the whole matter before the Examiner of Plays 'with a view of
preventing the recurrence of performances which shock, if not a larger,
yet a better class of persons than of whom they amuse'.[45] But Grundy's
opera was not the first occasion when clergymen were represented on
the stage, though in all probability this was the first time they were
shown in the guise of music-hall comedians. Nevertheless, it is true
that Church of England ministers were only rarely portrayed in the
early- and mid-Victorian theatre. In 1831 Douglas Jerrold was shocked
to learn that his play *The Bride of Ludgate* was to be refused a licence
at Drury Lane because the plot required the character of Charles II
'to wear the disguise of a clergyman'; and it was only after lengthy
remonstration with the Examiner, who settled for the lame substitute
of a lawyer's outfit, that it received official approval.[46] Not until as late
as 1873 (in Wilkie Collins's *The New Magdalen*) was a clergyman introduced into a play in anything other than a peripheral role. Few nineteenth-century dramatists (or novelists, for that matter) were much
inclined to probe to any depth the religious convictions of the characters they created. Anglican ministers, as the embodiment of all
Christian ideals, were shrouded in an aura of sanctity which the
creative writer disturbed at his peril. Such reticence was deliberately
fostered by the licensing authorities, who successfully prevented the
depiction of the Anglican clergy on the stage until late in the century.
Even after the early 1880s both Pigott and Redford were careful to
preserve the dignity of the Church by prohibiting unseemly characteri-
sations. As the former remarked in his endorsement to the licence for
George Comer's *Till Death Do Us Part* (1885) 'to represent the character
of a drunken vagabond as that of a clergyman, is a gross and unwar-
rantable libel on the English Church, and calculated to give offence
to a considerable portion of a respectable mixed audience'. Arthur
Pinero encountered similar resistance when in his farce *Dandy Dick*
(1887) he attempted to show a dean, the Very Reverend Augustin
Jedd, D. D., 'yielding under the stress of a pecuniary embarrassment,
to temptations of a sporting kind'. Although, as Pinero later recalled,
he was not refused a licence for the piece, Pigott 'deplored in strong
terms my want of taste in holding a dignitary of the Church up to

ridicule'.[47] Oscar Wilde's amusing caricature of a country rector in the person of Canon Dr Chasuble (in *The Importance of Being Earnest*, 1895) was about as far as most playwrights were prepared (or allowed) to go in the portrayal of the Anglican clergy.

A remarkable exception to the censors' general policy in matters of religion was Henry Arthur Jones's *Saints and Sinners* (1884), which emerged unscathed from Pigott's hands yet 'in its crude sentimental way ... reintroduced the possibility of religion as a serious consideration in the English drama'.[48] But its reception in the theatre lends weight to William Archer's argument that religious topics would always be vetoed by public opinion. Jones's portrayal of the pettiness and hypocrisy underlying the ultra-religious façades of provincial middle-class dissenting life was something of a new departure for the drama. His attack was not on nonconformist religion as such —Jones was himself a Methodist — but on the narrow, unimaginative way of life it could demand of its adherents. The delineation of the two chapel deacons Hoggard and Prabble, whose religion counts for nothing more than the material and financial advantages they derive from it, was for some a little too near the truth and on the first night the play was given a very mixed reception: '[S]ome of the pit and other parts of the house objected to the scriptural quotations used by the characters, and the audience hissed and booed loudly. The notices were favourable on the whole, the papers agreeing that the work was sincere, but nearly all the reviews commented unfavourably on the use of quotations from the Bible.'[49] In fact *Saints and Sinners* has the distinction of shattering the hitherto inviolable rule of the licensing authorities that the Bible should not be quoted on the stage. In the play Hoggard and Prabble habitually quote from it in order to support their materialist philosophy Hoggard remarks: 'We must be sharp in business nowadays. Business is business. What does the Bible say? "Seest thou a man diligent in his business? He shall stand before kings!"' Later, in the preface to the published text, Jones commented: 'Half the audience thought I was canting, and the other half thought I was blaspheming.' Even so, the play, having attained a certain notoriety, ran for nearly two hundred nights at the Vaudeville Theatre, 'some of its success', Jones observed, 'being doubtless due to the discussion it raised as to the playwright's right to portray contemporary religious life'.[50] As a result of his experience with *Saints and Sinners* Jones continued to press for more tolerance from the public — it was this, not the official censorship, which seemed to him to be the real restricting influence on the development of English drama — and to argue for the intrinsic right of the drama to 'possess itself of the whole of human life' and not to feed 'decrepit prejudices'.[51] Jones undoubtedly scored a minor triumph over public opinion with *Saints and Sinners*; he had shown that, given courage, 'decrepit prejudices' could be overcome.

Henry Arthur Jones made further excursions into the realm of religion in *Michael and his Lost Angel* (1896), which occasioned George Redford some heart-searching before he recommended the play for the Lord Chamberlain's licence. The Examiner confided his difficulties to Spencer Ponsonby:

It is very strong, well written, but pitched in a very low key and has preaching. It turns on a clergyman, after having compelled a young girl of his flock to make 'open confession' of a lapse of virtue, falling into an exactly similar fault, and himself having to openly proclaim it to his congregation assembled. The idea seems sometimes familiar to me in a novel, I think, but it is certainly very originally treated and without any of the coarseness so prominent in 'Triumph of the Philistines'. I should have no hesitation in licensing it, but I wish they would not write plays on such extraordinary subjects, and I fancy this will be the feeling with nine out of ten who see it. Surely the idea of open confession is extremely rare in the English Protestant Church even in the highest circles! The part has evidently been written for Mrs Pat Campbell, but there have been ructions at rehearsal and Miss Marion Terry will play it — a great loss to the piece I should be afraid.[52]

Jones's play was of a sufficiently controversial turn for Redford to be present at the first performance and afterwards he reported to Spencer Ponsonby that he was now convinced that the subject was one 'which, personally, I think quite unsuitable for the Stage, but given the subject, the dramatist has treated it with the greatest delicacy and refinement'. Redford went on to observe: 'I take it that as "Examiner of Plays", I am not concerned with questions of taste, and as for the central situation in the play there are numerous precedents both on the stage, and unfortunately in real life.'[53] But even though the Lord Chamberlain's Office appeared to be satisfied that *Michael and his Lost Angel* fell within the bounds of religious decorum (somewhat redefined, it might be noticed, since the 1880s, for the Examiner was no longer concerned with matters of taste) a minor storm blew up over the alleged impropriety of the procession in the church scene at the end of Act IV. Bernard Shaw, in defending Jones's point of view, concluded that what the public (or a certain section of it) was really objecting to was 'Michael's treatment of religion as co-extensive with life: that is, as genuinely catholic'; and he prophesied that English drama would steadily annex all the territory on which the religious bigot now felt so uncomfortable.[54] Right at the end of the century the Lord Chamberlain, Lord Clarendon, went so far as to suggest to the Bishop of London (who had complained about the use of the marriage service in *The Price of Peace*, 1900) that the 'demand of the age is for realism ... [but] I will however give directions to guard against realism of this description from going too far'.[55] The authorities' retreat from legislating on matters of religious taste was almost complete.

V

No parallel concessions were made on the topic of scriptural drama. Until the end of the century there was no question of licences being granted for any play manifestly based on any part of the Bible. Few dramatists had the temerity to contemplate writing such plays; but the one important exception of the early 1890s was Oscar Wilde. Wilde's *Salomé* (1892), written originally in French, was possibly never intended for the stage, but Sarah Bernhardt read it, was immediately attracted to the part of the heroine, and she herself encouraged the idea of its production in England. Rehearsals were in somewhat premature progress when the MS. was submitted to Edward Pigott for licensing. The Examiner read it with growing incredulity and felt compelled to treat it as nothing more than a joke. He wrote confidentially to Spencer Ponsonby:

I must send you, for your *private* edification & amusement, this MS. of a 1 act piece ... written by Oscar Wilde! It is a miracle of impudence; and I am bound to say that when Mr Abbey, his Acting Manager, called on me, in answer to my summons, he lifted up his eyes with a holy shudder of surprise, when I described the piece to him, & recommended him (as Uncle Toby advised the father of the juvenile Poet) to 'wipe it up & say no more about it'.

Pigott then went on to outline the basic details of the plot, stressing the 'incestuous passion of Herod for his step-daughter' and that of Herodias for John the Baptist; but the latter's

love turns to fury because John will not let her kiss him *in the mouth* – and in the last scene, where she brings in his head – if you please – on a 'charger' – she *does* kiss his mouth, in a paroxysm of sexual despair.
The piece is written in French – half Biblical, half pornographic – by Oscar Wilde himself.
Imagine the average British public's reception of it.[56]

But Pigott did regard the play seriously enough to refuse it a licence. *Salomé* stood condemned both on the grounds of immorality (the incest theme) and on its biblical foundation. Naturally enough, Wilde was incensed at the prohibition of his play by what he described as 'a common-place official – in the present case a Mr Pigott, who panders to the vulgarity and hypocrisy of the English people, by licensing every low farce and vulgar melodrama'. Shortly afterwards Wilde wrote to a friend expressing his hurt 'not merely at the action of the Licenser of Plays, but at the pleasure expressed by the entire Press of England at the suppression of my work'.[57] The sole exception was William Archer, whose letter condemning the ban appeared in the *Pall Mall Gazette*.[58]

Once more the press had vindicated the action of the censors, who were again confirmed in the belief that public opinion was staunchly opposed to the representation of the scriptures in performance. But as Henry Arthur Jones put it in his article of 1893 advocating the dramatisation of scriptural themes, the objections to such things were as unreasonable and as illogical as objections to religious pictures, sculpture, or architecture. 'It is not a matter of judgment or reason', he wrote, 'it is only a matter of prejudice.'[59] Jones's point of view found little favour elsewhere in the periodical press and a contributor to the *Spectator* (4 February 1893) reiterated the view that biblical subjects were totally unsuitable material for the stage because the only effect could be to degrade religion by 'blending the solemn histories of the Bible with the poor melodramatic tricks of the histrionic art'.

Nonetheless, public attitudes were undergoing slow reorientation. Wilson Barrett in *The Sign of the Cross* (1896), without using any specific scriptural episode and without ever quoting directly from the Bible – these were, of course, the reasons why Redford was able to licence the play – 'managed to capture enough of the Doré Bible, the popular chromo-lithograph, and the *Sunday at Home* to wrap an atmosphere of profound religiosity around a splendid and sensational melodrama'.[60] The popular success of *The Sign of the Cross* (which turns on the conflict between Roman paganism and early Christianity) persuaded even some of the clergy to extol its praises from Metropolitan and provincial pulpits. So encouraged, Barrett tried a further experiment in quasi-religious drama with *The Daughters of Babylon* at the Lyric Theatre in 1897; but this production, as Shaw put it, suffered 'a good deal from our religious prudery'.[61] Barrett's plays, however, did nothing to move the licensing authorities from their own extreme religious prudery. In the same year George Redford refused licences to *The Conversion of England* (described by the Examiner as 'a series of tableaux with dialogue of a very religious tendency unsuitable for representation in a licensed Theatre') and a four-act drama *Barabbas* ('a Scriptural Play involving the trial and crucifixion of Christ').[62] Redford even felt obliged to seek his superior's opinion on the propriety of the titles *A Crown of Thorns* and *No Cross, No Crown*, even though the dramas in question had no religious or scriptural foundations.[63]

The boldest expression of the increasing public interest in religious drama was the production in July 1901 of the medieval morality play *Everyman* — its first performance for about four hundred years — by the Elizabethan Stage Society, under the direction of William Poel. The play did not require the sanction of the Lord Chamberlain — it would certainly have been refused licence if it had — and after its initial trial at Charterhouse was transferred to the Imperial Theatre, where it ran for a whole month before being taken on tour around the main provincial centres to be 'received with the same hushed enthusiasm'.[64] Under his powers granted by the 1843 Act, the Lord Chamberlain could have interfered and stopped the performance. That he chose not to do so made nonsense of the official policy on religious drama. There is no doubt that for much of the nineteenth century the stringent rules applied were a true reflection of majority opinion. But the gradual changes in attitude to the theatre and (quite as important) changes in attitudes towards religion and the Bible stimulated no corresponding alterations of policy. By the late 1890s the censors had fallen well behind public opinion in stubbornly clinging to the belief that scriptural drama was inappropriate and unwanted in the theatre. Those objections still being raised to religious drama were being voiced by a part of the community no longer broadly representative of the whole; and it is to the discredit of the Lord Chamberlain's Office — and still further evidence of its inherent conservatism — that it chose to listen to minority opposition rather than to be persuaded by the growing tolerance of the majority.[65]

7

POLITICAL AND PERSONAL
SATIRE

Much of the political nature of later Victorian drama expresses itself through the medium of satire, which could be both personal and more generally political in application. To the licensing authorities political satire was potentially quite as damaging to the fabric and dignity of government and its institutions as was the superficially more serious form of criticism implicit in earlier prohibited plays, like Martin Shee's *Alasco* (1824) or George Pitt's *The Revolution of Paris* (1848), which seemed to attack the notion of state authority. As James Sutherland has remarked of satire in general, 'it has always been unwelcome to people in authority' for it can be 'destructive, either of the individual, or of the party, or of the ideas and traditions on which established institutions are based'. But satire in personalised form 'is perhaps most immediately dangerous in the theatre, for there its explosive qualities are greatly increased by the presence of an audience in whom excitement is easily generated . . . and as the feelings of each individual are communicated to his neighbour the mass emotion may rapidly become overwhelming'.[1] Such is the rationale behind the political censorship of the drama. In the nineteenth century there was ample evidence to suggest the volatility of theatre audiences[2] and this was an important factor in the calculations of the licensers. The preservation of decorum in the later Victorian theatre was seen to rest in large measure on the exclusion of personalised political allusion.

Most of the witnesses at the 1866 Committee who were not opposed to the whole principle of stage censorship repeated the opinions of their counterparts in 1832 and confirmed their dislike of any form of politics in the theatre. The tradition of personal allusion had long been lost to the serious drama and, as William Donne observed in 1856 (the year before he became official Examiner of Plays), 'an Athenian playwright would have revelled in impersonations of Chatham's gout and flannels; of Pitt's crane's-neck; of Sheridan's ruby nose, and Fox's shrill tones and bushy eyebrows. [But] the modern dramatist who should reproduce them, would not cause even the injudicious to laugh, and would be rewarded for his attempts by a general sibilation.'³ Political censorship had all but effectively achieved the removal of public personalities from the stage in the early Victorian period. Donne's argument rested on propriety rather than politics, but it is nonetheless true that personal allusion was frequently linked with political allusion, so that in forbidding the one, the other more important objective was gained as well. The strict rules outlawing the portrayal of notable personalities on the late Victorian stage, as conceived by Donne and his successors, were primarily motivated by political concerns.

The list of personalities whose names were proscribed on the stage is extensive. It ranges down from the Queen and the royal family to members of the government, foreign sovereigns and dignitaries, contemporary theatrical personalities, indeed, to anyone whose name was a topic of public interest. All references to Queen Victoria were ruthlessly excised even if they were complimentary. So, too, with members of the Cabinet. In the Adelphi pantomime *The Loves of Cupid and Psyche* (1857) the endorsement bears the instruction: 'Omit the Trick in which the Cabinet pudding turns into Lord Palmerston'; while in *Prince Pygmy* (1860) for the Grecian Theatre, the manager was directed to omit the business in the last scene, which involved an auction prefaced by the line 'Now here is Napoleon to be had cheap, he has sold a good many in his time.' Other, less illustrious, personalities were protected by applying the same rules. For *Harlequin and Little One Eye* (1854) the Day Book lists the following cut in the comic business:

A man enters with a large Bird Cage labelled 'A Present to Britannia'. Clown and Pantaloon come forward to receive it. They peep inside. Clown says '*Oh it's a Bird*' . . . the cage door opens — a young lady rushes out — the cloth over the cage is removed and the words 'A true British Nightingale' appear. A man enters with a Placard 'Wanted Nurses for the East' [and] he is followed by six old women hobbling with sticks, the first of whom bears a flag inscribed 'British Granny-dears'. Clown introduces them to Miss Nightingale.

Impersonation was regarded as particularly distasteful, especially when it involved the royal family, as in the Effingham Saloon's pantomime *Tit, Tat, Toe, the Three Butcher Boys all of a Row* (1858), where, in a nursery scene, 'Flower pots are brought down and the Two Royal Children appear, one dressed as a sailor, the other as a Soldier.' William Donne pointed out that 'the Rule is *that a Pictorial Representation* is permitted: but Members of the Royal Family must not be represented on the Stage by Male or Female performers'.

Charles Kean in 1848 achieved a notable success in preventing the Strand Theatre from performing Alexandre Dumas' *Edmund Kean* by making a direct appeal to the Lord Chamberlain, stressing that the play 'places my father in a most false and degrading position'.[4] And much later in the century, Henry Irving heard that he was being ridiculed on the stage of the Gaiety Theatre in 1889, whereupon he informed the Lord Chamberlain's Office, who intervened at once and threatened not to renew the theatre's licence if the offensive make-up continued.[5] Oscar Wilde was, of course, an obvious target for caricature; but presumably because he did not complain when he was parodied in W. S. Gilbert's comic opera *Patience* (1881) — he seems to have been rather more flattered and amused than offended — the authorities chose not to interfere in 1892 when, as Wilde described it to a friend, in a burlesque of *Lady Windermere's Fan* 'an actor dressed up like me and imitated my voice and manner!!!'[6] In contrast to William Donne, Edward Pigott believed that many prominent individuals actually revelled in the thought of stage caricature and, if there were no direct political intent, the Examiner was usually prepared to let the matter pass without notice. Following a report that Lord Randolph Churchill was being impersonated at the Gaiety in 1891, Pigott commented to his superior that 'many public men like to be pilloried in this way, for the sake of the advertisement'.[7] If that was so, then the Lord Chamberlain's Office was apparently content to sanction the publicity.

As a number of the examples of personal satire have so far indicated, it was the pantomime, together with the re-emergent burlesque— extravaganza, which provided most of the opportunities for political reference in the later Victorian theatre. Both forms proved very difficult to control by means of pre-production censorship, since both relied on being up-to-date and generally allusive to the times. In 1872 James Planché (one of the foremost exponents of the burlesque genre before Gilbert) observed somewhat gleefully that the censor was at a severe disadvantage in trying to exercise his authority over such essentially ephemeral pieces: 'Any profane expression or indecent situation, any coarse allusion or personal insult to those in authority over us, may be, and *has been*, foisted into a burlesque or pantomime after its performance has been sanctioned by the licenser.' In the recent 'Christmas harlequinades', he continued, the Examiner's instruction 'to omit the common-place jokes upon certain members of the Cabinet ... were never paid the slightest attention to, but continued to excite the roars and plaudits of the galleries to the last night of re-presentation'.[8] Thus what may sometimes appear to be extreme indulgence on the part of the licensers in the matter of political al-lusion was often the result of management (or actors') interference with the text after official examination had taken place.

The 1871–2 pantomime season to which Planché referred was an especially sensitive one for the Examiner of Plays. Robert Lowe, the Chancellor of the Exchequer, had recently imposed a tax on matches, in the face of much bitter opposition, in order to raise money for arms in the event of the spread of the Franco-Prussian war,[9] and the pan-tomimes were full of none-too-complimentary references to the tax and its author. Following the publication in the *Era* of a letter to a theatre manager disclosing that the Examiner had 'struck out Lowe's name and the matches' from all pantomime scripts submitted during the season, the press took up the case and howled its derision at the authori-ties' interference in such 'innocent pastimes'. Donne, much against his better judgment and on the instructions of his superiors,[10] publicly defended his action. In a letter to the *Era* (14 January 1872), the Examiner pointed out that the deletion of allusions to the match tax was not the result of any special instructions from the Lord Chamber-lain or any member of the government (both of whom had been sug-gested as originators of the ban) but that he was merely carrying on with an established practice:

I have acted with regard to the excisions, which are comparatively few in 1871, exactly as I have done during the last fourteen years, therein following the example of my immediate predecessor Mr Kemble. He, as well as myself, uniformly cut out from manuscripts sent for examination 'personal or per-sonally political questions', as well as passages or words, names and phrases, in such manuscripts as were likely to give offence on religious or moral grounds.[11]

However, far from disarming public criticism, Donne's letter served only to lay the Lord Chamberlain's Office open to further ridicule and recrimination when, published in the same issue of the *Era*, was a letter from no less a light than W.S. Gilbert, who claimed that on three separate occasions after the Examiner had interfered in his plays he, Gilbert, had 'systematically declined to take the slightest notice of his instructions'. It was an embarrassing admission for the Lord Chamberlain's Office to hear; but nevertheless it was an accurate statement of the practice of some authors and numerous theatre managers who found it profitable either to add topical matter to plays already licensed or to ignore, like Gilbert, the directions of the licensing authorities altogether.[12]

After the uncomfortable publicity of the 1871–2 season Donne was anxious to avoid 'such an absurd storm' in the following year and he wrote directly to the Lord Chamberlain for instructions on the policy that he should follow:

The Press in 1871–72 fell foul on me for *rigour*: had it laid its *venue* for *laxity*— that is to say, more tolerance or indulgence than my predecessors allowed themselves, they would have been nearer to the mark. In Dramas, Burlesques, & Pantomimes I have always lent more to the mercy than the justice-side, because I think that all reasonable liberty should be allowed to the stage. When however liberty has passed into licence, I have always tightened the curb. To strike out personal names, when they affect rank, office, or private character, I shall consider essential, unless otherwise instructed. When allusions to, or censure on public measures, of *recent* date are introduced I shall direct them to be 'omitted in representation'.

Donne forecast that the main sources of trouble, as far as pantomimes for the current season were concerned, would occur with references to the controversial Licensed Victuallers' Act and possibly Arbitration, 'lucifer matches being extinct'.[13]

Topical references abound in the burlesque—extravaganza, a form which attracted many of the most original talents of the Victorian period, not only J. R. Planché and Gilbert but others, less well known, like the Brough brothers, H. J. Byron, and Bronson Howard. In William Brough's *Field of the Cloth of Gold* (1868) there are allusions, among much else, to the recent extension of the franchise, arms policy in England and France, and nepotism within the Civil Service;[14] but it was not until the 1870s with the advent of Gilbert's *The Happy Land, The Realm of Joy*, and Robert Reece's *Richelieu Redressed* (all performed during 1873) that the burlesque took on a more openly political stance. Gilbert discovered that the peculiar strength of the form lay in the relative ease with which its politics could be sharpened by the subtle use of political caricature. During 1873 the licensing authorities were presented with a rigorous test of authority in political censorship, largely because, on Gilbert's part at least, his burlesques seemed to have been intended as a challenge to see just how far the censor could be pushed.

William Donne, little suspecting the political furore soon to be associated with the play, licensed W. S. Gilbert's and Gilbert A'Beckett's *The Happy Land: A Burlesque Version of 'The Wicked World'* in February 1873 without any hesitation, since, as he later claimed, the MS. contained only legitimate general satire. In performance at the Court Theatre under the able direction of Marie Litton, the political generalities of the text were translated into pointedly specific political gibes. So much so, indeed, that one historian has commented that 'not since

Plate 9   Scene from W. S. Gilbert's *The Happy Land* at the Court Theatre

Fielding's Pasquin had such a pungent satire been put upon the stage'.[15] Three members of the then current Gladstone administration (the Prime Minister, Lowe, Chancellor of the Exchequer, and Ayrton, Commissioner of Public Works) appeared in the burlesque labelled as Mr G, Mr L, and Mr A, a trio of mortals whose chronic mis-management of affairs on earth provokes similar chaos in fairyland (the 'Happy Land') when they try to show the inhabitants how a government should be set up. The trio arrive to the chorus 'We are three statesmen, old and tired'; they recommend that the new appointments for government office should be conducted on the model of earth, where they are made on the principle that those who are least qualified win the top jobs. As they observe to the preferred candidate for 'First Lord of the Admiralty': 'Nature has pointed you out as eminently qualified... *because* you don't know anything about ships. You take office – you learn about ships – and when you *know* all about ships, the Opposition comes in, out you go, and somebody else, who doesn't know anything about ships, comes in and takes your place. That's how we educate our ministers.[16] To make the burlesque even more audacious, the three main characters were made-up to look like their real-life counterparts.

As a recent critic has pointed out, 'where the authority of a government jealous of its dignity and tender about its shortcomings threatens, the political can be as *risqué* as the sexual',[17] and the spectacle of

120

Cabinet ministers and their policies being lampooned on the stage forced the Lord Chamberlain's Office into swift retaliation. Two days after the play opened Lord Sydney himself went to see the performance and on the following morning (6 March) Marie Litton received a brusque note informing her that the licence for *The Happy Land* was 'hereby cancelled in consequence of the manner in which it is placed upon the stage'.[18] Though Miss Litton, worried at the effect of the ban on her theatre, immediately made a substantial concession by agreeing to play the original text and remove the offensive make-up, the Lord Chamberlain decided that the matter needed much fuller investigation and ordered the prohibition to remain until further notice. The official directive was so slow in arriving at the Court Theatre that the doors were already open for the evening performance, which Miss Litton (in view of her concessions) had confidently expected would be permitted; and, in consequence, *The Happy Land* was performed that night in defiance of the Lord Chamberlain. A notice hastily printed during the day was circulated amongst the audience, begging 'to inform the public that the Lord Chamberlain has forbidden Messrs Fisher, Hill, and Righton to make up their faces in imitation of Messrs Gladstone, Lowe, and Ayrton' — a conveniently simple device for perpetuating the caricatures. In an address to the audience that same evening Righton insisted that the piece was nothing more than 'a good humoured skit' and that, while the actors had made 'certain unimportant alterations and additions' to the text during rehearsals, it had been thought unnecessary to trouble the licenser 'with an insignificant matter of detail' when his sanction had already been given to 'the general principle'.[19]

At an interview next day with Spencer Ponsonby at St James's Palace, Marie Litton made the startling admission (so the official memorandum records) that the whole episode had been 'a "try on" to which she had been urged by the Authors'. She was hardly in a position to deny that substantial alterations had been made to the licensed text and, on official request, supplied a copy of the play as performed for the Lord Chamberlain's inspection. A collation between the two texts disclosed that in the prompt copy there were no fewer than '18 quarto pages of additions, interpolations and deviations from the original'.[20] However, Miss Litton's acceptance of the authorities' interference was less absolute than the official records of the affair suggest. On 10 March 1873, by which time the burlesque was again on the stage (the Lord Chamberlain having satisfied himself as to Marie Litton's good behaviour for the future), *The Times* printed a statement from

Spencer Ponsonby outlining the official side of the argument; and on 11 March Miss Litton retorted with an announcement that she was preparing to publish the play with all of the Lord Chamberlain's excisions printed in capital letters. When the text did appear just a few days later it was prefaced by a hardly respectful note:

This book contains the EXACT TEXT of the piece as played on the occasion of the Lord Chamberlain's official visit to the Court Theatre, on 6th March, 1873. Those who will take the trouble to compare the original text with the expurgated version, as played nightly at the Court Theatre, will be in a position to appreciate the value of the Lord Chamberlain's alterations.

THE AUTHORS[21]

Copies of the play, on display at the box-office of the theatre, sold spectacularly well.

Although the kind of satire contained in *The Happy Land* appeared regularly in the columns of such periodicals as *Punch*, the play was a deliberate challenge to the widely held belief that the stage should remain, if not an instrument for established authority, at least silent on all controversial matters. But its success with the public – by October 1873 *The Happy Land* had run to over two hundred performances – encouraged further experiments in the same vein. Gilbert's second challenge to the authorities came in the shape of *The Realm of Joy*, submitted by the Royalty Theatre in October 1873. Donne decided that it was a matter for the Lord Chamberlain since 'it is written by the same Mr Tomline, who is the principal author of *The Happy Land* and who, I think your Lordship cannot fail to perceive, intends in this burlesque to single out the office of Lord Chamberlain for the special aim of his satire'.[22] Contrary to the Examiner's expectations, however, the Lord Chamberlain did not appreciate Donne's point and directed that 'the play sent to read may be acted. I return it by post: you can make the usual corrections.'[23] Donne received the news with dismay and wrote angrily to Spencer Ponsonby: 'What "the usual corrections" can be in a piece so utterly *incorrigible*, and so obviously meant to be an official, if not a personal insult, passes my understanding – perhaps the *Archbishop of Canterbury*, in the last page, may go overboard.' He reported that he would re-read the play when it was returned to him 'and if I *can* spike any word or phrase, I *will*; just to keep up the "right of way"'.[24] It was unlike Donne to be vindictive; but, understandably, he did feel incensed at a play which was set in the lobby of the Court Theatre, where another play to which the Lord Chamberlain had taken objection was being performed. The implied reference to *The Happy Land* — even to the parallel titles —could hardly have been missed; but Lord Sydney was perhaps wise in refusing to give *The Realm of Joy* a free advertisement by his interference.

Of rather more serious political importance was Robert Reece's burlesque *Richelieu Redressed,* which ran at the Olympic Theatre from the end of October 1873 concurrently with a revival of Bulwer Lytton's classic drama *Richelieu; or, the Conspiracy* (1839) at the Lyceum, with Henry Irving in the name part. The burlesque turned out to be yet another experiment in political caricature, a point seized upon by the *Daily News* (29 October 1873):

The appetite of theatrical audiences for political caricature has as yet only been whetted, and anything in the shape of a Premier making himself ridiculous, or a Cabinet Minister unfolding his schemes before the footlights, is always sure to find favour ... *Prime Minister Richelieu appears as an admirable imitation of Mr Gladstone attired in Court dress ... The Duke of Orleans — Richelieu's enemy — turns out to be none other than Mr Disraeli ...* The burlesque was received most enthusiastically, and it only requires an edict from the Lord Chamberlain to render it one of the successes of the season. [The passage in italic is underlined in black ink on the cutting preserved in the official records.]

Gladstone's popularity was at a very low ebb and the audiences at the Olympic especially enjoyed the 'Prime Minister's' reflections on the outcome of the impending elections:

> From the great limbo of past sessions rise
> The ghost of certain Legislative Acts
> To taunt me with my shifting policy;
> Amidst them, gaunt and frowning — Income tax
> Broods o'er my heart — I cannot take it off!
> While lesser demons, labelled — Sugar, Tea,
> Malt Hops, and kindred duties — hover round
> And gibber, 'Where's your popularity?'[25]

When Donne, who visited the theatre after the newspaper commentaries, made out his report for Lord Sydney, he indicated that there was 'little doubt that a good deal is *said* on the stage, and indeed *done* also' for which there was no authority in the licensed copy 'and, in short, the Olympic case is twin brother to the Court Theatre one'. There was, he reported, even one moment in the burlesque when the actor playing Richelieu (but made-up as Gladstone) came on stage to introduce himself, beginning 'as if it were a slip of the tongue — "I am Gla—" & then intimated by action that 'this won't do". I look upon this as a very significant instance of liberties taken with the authorized text.'[26]

But if Gilbert had intended *The Happy Land* as a challenge to the licensing authorities, Robert Reece, author of *Richelieu Redressed*, managed to persuade the Lord Chamberlain's Office that he had had no such purpose. On the contrary, his express wishes had been overruled by recalcitrant actors, notably Mr Righton (who, it should be noted, had played a chief role in *The Happy Land*). 'Every piece', the author explained, 'was scrupulously submitted to Mr Donne and I gave strict orders to the principal actors to avoid "make-up", as I wished the work to stand on its burlesque merits alone.' The author also claimed that there was no substance in the charge of political bias since 'the trifling allusions to the elections are perfectly harmless and the ultimate triumph of the existing powers clearly point that no political allegory is attempted'.[27] Reece's offer to make any alterations suggested by the censor and to remove all the offending make-up was gratefully and graciously accepted by the authorities, the Lord Chamberlain's Office having finally learnt the truth of the axiom about discretion being the better part of valour. Indeed, so diplomatically was the affair conducted that there was none of the usual furore in the newspapers and *Richelieu Redressed* continued on a much more conventional course. However, the experience with this play was a salutary one for the authorities, and William Donne kept a careful eye for any further attempts at hoodwinking the censor during the election period. His suspicions were momentarily aroused in February 1874 when the Court Theatre submitted Alfred Maltby's *Your Vote and Interest*, which at first sight seemed 'so like an electioneering squib', but was probably fairly harmless. Nevertheless, as he told Spencer Ponsonby, a visit to the theatre was indicated since 'it may be a plant as in the well-known case of *The Happy Land*'.[28]

II

Outside the predominantly comic forms of the burlesque — extravaganza and the pantomime, political comment in the later Victorian drama was comparatively rare and, where it existed, muted. But it is with playwrights like Tom Taylor and Charles Reade that some of the first tentative steps were taken into what might be called the realm of the socio-political drama. In the early 1860s both wrote plays which called attention to the highly serious problem of society's treatment of the reformed criminal, though, as Martin Meisel observes, 'the bluebook or critical portions are extraneous to the rest, whose dramatic values are altogether conventional'.[29] The Examiner of Plays was perfectly content with Reade's *It's Never Too Late To Mend* (1864), mainly because his social points were generally obscured in the dramatist's love of sensational effect. After a few performances, however, Reade was forced to modify the sordid details of the prison scene in Act II when he discovered that audience taste was insufficiently prepared for such realism.[30] In Taylor's case the Examiner was concerned with the title of *The Ticket-of-Leave Man* (1863), fearing that Lord Sydney 'might not fancy the present one'. But he had some minor reservations as well about the kind of play that Taylor had written and its probable unsuitability for the sophisticated middle-class audience of the Olympic. As he explained to Spencer Ponsonby, 'excepting the associations, The Ticket of Leave Man, barring a few follies in Act I, is a very estimable person, fallen into bad company. I think indeed Tom (& I shall tell him so on the very next opportunity) might as well keep from writing a kind of Victoria drama for the Olympic Theatre.'[31]

Reade made a further experiment with socio-political drama in the adaptation of his novel *Put Yourself in his Place* as *Free Labour* (1870), a study of the internal squabbles of modern trade unionism. While in the Examiner's view the play contained no objectionable political sentiments, he was anxious to avoid repeating his recent mistake of licensing a piece called *The Union Wheel*, which had been sharply criticised by the press — the *Standard*, for instance, had condemned it as an incitement to strikes and violence — and so requested the Lord Chamberlain's opinion on its suitability for licensing.[32] Like his Examiner, Lord Sydney fully approved the play but again the press reviews were very hostile. The *Athenaeum* (4 June 1870), one of the most critical, complained that the stage was in real danger of becoming a platform for political and social ideas, especially 'those disputes between labour and capital which form the most vexed question of the political hour'. Surprise was expressed that there had been no outburst of political feeling at the first performance and the reviewer concluded that the management must have exercised 'great care' in the admission of the audience. Yet, he continued, 'the play . . . seems like a grenade in the hands of one ignorant of its nature . . . the risk of an explosion and its probable consequences are unpleasant things for the by-stander to contemplate'. The storm of criticism prompted Donne's presence at the sixth performance of *Free Labour*, following which he reported back to Spencer Ponsonby that the recriminations in the newspapers were totally misguided:

Poor C. Reade had not enough at the Adelphi to excite any more riot than a single police-man might not have quelled. I . . . saw, what I never saw before — the Dress Circle quite empty — a sprinkling in the Stalls — ditto in the Upper Boxes — Gallery & Gallery slips pretty full — Pit not half full. There was no excitement at all. 'The Gods' were very discreet in their applause — clapping when Neville knocked on the head the Trade Unionists who had come to do *him* that favour but as far as regarded any interest in the 'political'! questions of Masters and Men the scene might have been laid in Timbuctoo — and with the claims of labour never heard. Charles Reade is very unpopular with a portion of the Press, and with much of the Theatrical World — *Hinc ille lacrymae* and in order to hit him, the writer [in the *Athenaeum*] opens with a solemn blaze of trumpets about the licensing power. *The Times* spoke quite fairly about the play.[33]

Both Taylor and Reade emerged virtually unscathed by censorship, but in those rare instances when a dramatist indulged in direct criticism of Victorian social institutions the censor was very ready to intervene. Some sections of Joseph Cave's *The Casual Ward* (1866), set within a workhouse, were heavily cut before the issue of a licence. Most of the deletions were designed to protect the workhouse authorities from Cave's attack, which includes the charge that they are morally unfit for their positions of trust:

Feeling and generous guardians that they are! What are the majority of them but men who have risen in trade by selling adulterated food at short weight, men who have cheated up to a minute or two of twelve on a *Saturday night* and then gone with long sanctified faces to Church on a *Sunday morning*.

At this point in the play the beadle (who has offered the speaker, a wayfarer named Philip Wilson, a morsel of bread and some gruel) interjects heatedly: 'Here's impudence! Here's owdaciousness!' Philip replies:

Truth you mean. I say fearlessly that three-fourths of those who call themselves *Guardians* of the poor are but their oppressors. Are these men, ignorant & overbearing, fit to measure out what *they* call justice to the unfortunate poor?[34]

The social point is made somewhat more courageously in this play than in either Taylor's or Reade's, though, as with its forebears, the critical matter is subsidiary to the main plot, which is a sentimental treatment of the events of one night spent by the hero in the 'casual ward' of a workhouse. Even so, the central social argument — 'let the administration of relief come from those who wish to see justice done to the unfortunate — educated in mind as much as in practice' — suffered under the censor's blue pencil, together with a further passage at the end of the play, which clinches the propagandist intent: 'The treatment that the deserving poor meets with at the hands of tyrannical and ignorant Guardians and officials.' The number and importance of the cuts was such that Donne was advised by Lord Sydney to visit the Marylebone Theatre during the performance; but so successful was the work of censorship that the Examiner was able to report to his superior that he had heard 'nothing that any guardian or relieving officer could justly object to'.[35]

Lord Sydney was nearly always prepared to attempt some kind of compromise with plays that offended against the establishment; but his successor, the Marquess of Hertford, was much more conservative and much less willing to engineer matters. When his Examiner submitted to him the MS. of a new play, *Lords and Labourers* by George Lander, in March 1874, the Lord Chamberlain confessed himself perplexed as to whether 'this trashy' play might not occasion more mischief by prohibiting it than by licensing it; but he concluded after careful consideration that the subject matter of relations between employers and employees was '*not* fit for representation on the Stage at any time, still less now when there has been considerable agitation on the subject among the inflammable part of the population'. He went on:

I quite agree with Mr Donne that even if there was no political objection, the burglary and throat cutting element are enough to condemn it — I might mention also that the clumsy attempt to disparage what the writer sneers at as 'the Virtuous Agricultural Reward Society' ought not to be countenanced by any one acting for Her Majesty who for the last 24 years has taken much personal trouble in a Society of that sort at Windsor & the neighbourhood — But you probably are not in the habit of giving reasons for refusing, & it is enough to say that this play is not a proper one for the stage and is not needed when the Government is doing its best by the appointment of a Royal Commission to meet some of the difficulties that have so long existed between the Employers and Employed.[36]

Lander's play was judged as untimely and unhelpful at a juncture when agricultural unrest was becoming a recurrent feature of the social scene;[37] and, what was perhaps more immediately important, when parliamentary elections were about to take place. The author, shocked by the suppression of his play, wrote directly to Lord Hertford complaining that it was 'very hard to have a play that has been carefully written, condemned without appeal, and consigned to the dark'. His offer to 'remodel the drama' in accordance with the wishes of the authorities was refused and the play was never performed. As Lander put it in his letter of complaint, he had thought the matter of *Lords and Labourers* 'a good one, inasmuch as it was a change from those subjects that so often form the backbone of dramas of which seducers and petty larceny characters are the heroes'. But what the author did not comprehend was that, particularly in the tense atmosphere of election-time, politics on the stage were considered far more dangerous than moral dubiety.

III

Any government-imposed censorship labours under the erroneous, but nonetheless embarrassing, implication that what it licences as suitable for the stage bears also the mark of official approval of the subject-matter. This was particularly uncomfortable for the Lord Chamberlain's Office when plays were discovered to make allusion to foreign affairs in times of war or in other delicate political situations. In the later Victorian period, as a necessary consequence of her growing imperialist interests, Britain's relations with various foreign powers began to assume a fresh importance. The licensing authorities were especially anxious that nothing licensed by the Lord Chamberlain should give offence to any friendly foreign government. For this reason a drama entitled *The Last Slave* was prohibited in 1865. Its background was the American Civil War and the assassination of Abraham Lincoln (though this was not shown on stage) and the play made use of other personalities involved in the struggle, authenticated by speeches quoted verbatim from actual accounts and reports. As William Donne observed to the Lord Chamberlain, 'this tragedy [is] so momentous in itself and its consequences actual and probable [that it] is not now and will not be for a long time, a proper subject for theatrical entertainment'.[38] But political circumstances often change more quickly than anticipated and within two years Donne recorded in the Day Book (18 June 1867) that the play had been granted a licence 'in consequence of change of American affairs'.

During the summer of 1870 the smouldering differences between France and Prussia broke into open conflict. Passions were running very high in Britain and the manager of the Surrey Theatre, E. T. Smith, decided to capitalise on popular feeling by submitting for licence a new play to hand, Henry Farnie's *A History of a Flag*, which dealt with the exploits of Napoleon. Donne conceived an immediate objection to it on the grounds that, while the drama had no direct reference to the Franco-Prussian war, it 'tends to represent war under a sort of heroical aspect, accompanied with glorification of conquerors'; and this was, the Examiner concluded, undesirable 'under the grave, mournful and terrible circumstances of the hour and the day'.[39] On appeal from the Surrey's manager, the Lord Chamberlain relented and granted the play a licence, only to discover a few days later that Smith had thought the better of his own position and had decided not to stage the play for the very reasons that the Lord Chamberlain had intimated in support of his prohibition.[40]

There the matter rested until January 1871 when Tom Robertson's drama *War*, licensed by Donne without prior reference to the Lord Chamberlain, was produced at the St James's Theatre. Many of the reviewers and first-night audience were persuaded of the play's application to the still current Franco-Prussian conflict. As the *Illustrated London News* (21 January 1871) commented, 'delicacy should have warned the author off that dangerous ground', and reported that the audience began, from the end of Act II (where there seemed an obvious allusion to the rout of Napoleon III's troops at Sedan) 'to express dissatisfaction, which grew and increased as the drama proceeded, and culminated in decided condemnation'. Likewise, *The Times* (18 January) remarked that at the end of the performance 'the curtain fell amid overwhelming sounds of disapprobation'. Incensed at the operation of an apparently double standard, Farnie reopened the question of the suppression of his *History of a Flag*, which had occurred less than five months previously. In a personal letter to the Lord Chamberlain, Farnie (with more than a hint of sarcasm) wrote that he was

grateful, now, that my drama was stopped; and I cannot but think that if the same restraint had been exercised in Mr Robertson's case, he too would have had reason for thankful acquiescence. In every respect his play, which I have witnessed, is as much a war drama as the MS. submitted to your Lordship by the Surrey Theatre in August last . . . I think that others should not be allowed to cross the boundary line clearly defined for me.[41]

Lord Sydney might well have argued that Robertson's play was unspecific in location and dealt with the theme of war in very general terms, yet there can be little doubt that, as with Farnie, the author expected to gain colour for his work from the inevitable recall of contemporary events. The licensing of Robertson's *War* strengthens the evidence for the authorities' discrimination between established dramatists — Robertson had been writing plays since 1845 — and those of more meagre, if prolific, talent. In such circumstances Farnie's protest was by no means unjustified.

The great patriotic fervour of the early 1870s returned to the English stage during the South African crisis of the 1890s; and in recognition of popular feeling topical allusions became more representative of imperialist concerns. At Daly's Theatre in 1896 the play *An Artist's Model* included some pertinent allusions to the Transvaal affair, the

Jameson raid, and to the German Kaiser, whose intervention in South Africa had occasioned much popular resentment in England. The theatre announced the inclusion of a jingoistic song 'Hands Off!' with the line 'Let Pinchbeck Caesar strut and crow'; but at the insistence of the Colonial Office the Lord Chamberlain intervened at the last moment, prohibited the song, and also demanded a number of further alterations and deletions. Nevertheless, the play managed to retain many of its references to the Transvaal crisis, which, according to *The Times* (13 January 1896) were the signal 'for loud outbursts of applause, the name of the German Emperor being loudly hissed and hooted, while cheer after cheer greeted the names of the Queen, Dr Jameson, the Chartered Company, and Mr Chamberlain. Several times cries of "Three cheers for Dr Jameson" and "Groans for the Kaiser" were raised in the gallery and responded to.'

At the end of the century Kaiser Wilhelm was frequently held up to ridicule in the music halls (where, of course, the Lord Chamberlain's control did not extend), but more rarely in the theatre. Those references which did occur were not licensed, but the Lord Chamberlain's Office was in no position to check on every reported infringement. However, in 1898 an official complaint via the Foreign Office spurred the licensing authorities into action. The objection was lodged against a new verse inserted into a song sung by Mrs Seymour Hicks during the production of *The Circus Girl* at the Gaiety Theatre, in which the Kaiser was represented as a doll worked by strings. Spencer Ponsonby gently pointed out to the manager, George Edwardes, that the song

was giving great offence to the Germans. Pray see if you can't drop it out quietly. Of course it is not licensed. Pray also let me know what you decide. I have not seen the song 'A little piece of string' but am told it is very offensive to the Emperor. Of course you will understand that it must be done very discreetly, as a fuss made about it would make it worse than the disease.[42]

Edwardes seems to have responded readily enough to this diplomatically phrased approach and no further action was taken.

The same kind of outside pressure dictated the Lord Chamberlain's course of action in the case of the play *Secrets of the Harem*, licensed first in 1896 and performed for four years without any official interference at a number of provincial theatres. The play did not appear in London until 1900, by which time, after many peregrinations round the provinces, it had accumulated a number of topical (and unlicensed) references in order to keep it up to date. The Turkish Embassy complained that the play involved a gross misrepresentation of Turkish affairs and of the country's involvement with the Armenian Massacres (which had long been an international scandal) and demanded immediate action from the Lord Chamberlain. At first the Lord Chamberlain confessed himself unwilling to interfere, arguing 'that more importance would be given to the subject if I were to pursue the very unusual course of withdrawing a Licence so long in existence'.[43] For a short time the Ambassador was mollified, but when reports indicated that the performance of the play at the Shakespeare Theatre in Clapham now contained, apart from 'many scandalous inventions, actual allusions to His Majesty the Sultan' more insistent representations ensued. The addition of offensive advertising material in the shape of placards, 'printed on so-called Khaki coloured paper bearing the . . . inscription in large letters "Sultan Abdul Hamid & his ladies"', determined the Lord Chamberlain on suspending the play's licence. The theatre protested so vigorously at this sudden withdrawal and the substantial financial loss it entailed that the controversy even spread to the House of Commons, where a sympathetic member tabled a question on the affair. The official response was that the piece had been considered 'offensive to the sovereign of a friendly state' but that Lord Hopetoun was quite willing to consider 'any revised version under a different title and with all the objectionable matter eliminated'.[44] Arbitrary and precipitate action on the part of the Lord Chamberlain could, it seems, no longer pass unchallenged; and in vindication of the rights of the theatre the play was relicensed under the title *Secrets*. Not unreasonably, the theatre management resolved to exploit as fully as possible the implications of the new title and advertised the piece as *Secrets* ----------, which, it has been claimed, was 'fifty times more suggestive and offensive than the original'.[45]

If later Victorian political censorship is less dramatic in tone and character than that of the earlier period, it does have the compensation of being rather more amusing. Except in the matter of personal allusion (and even that rule was less rigorously applied by the 1890s) there is no consistent pattern of political censorship after about 1850. In any case, not all political writers suffered equally from its effects. Notably W. S. Gilbert, apart from the celebrated case of *The Happy Land* (1873) and a few other minor frustrations, enjoyed what seems to have been an unparalleled freedom in gentle political satire,[46] while writers of pantomime often took (though were not necessarily granted) similar advantages. Political censorship is finally important because it helps to illustrate how close the Victorian theatre was to popular feeling on questions of immediate currency. The contrast between the nature of political censorship before and after 1850 is a pointer towards the slow but growing recognition of the social and political maturity of the stage.

MORAL DECORUM AND THE
ADVANCED DRAMA

At the end of his long career as Examiner of Plays in 1874, William Bodham Donne observed ruefully that the French drama was almost exclusively concerned with breaches of the seventh commandment. 'It seems to me', he wrote, 'that dramatic genius is very much on the decline in Paris. It has but one theme, and that adultery or *demi-monde-ism*.'[1] That was not to say that the French drama was not popular. On the contrary, the state and manners of Parisian society in the 1870s (perhaps characterised best in the music of Offenbach) held a strong fascination for English audiences. The drama fostered an image of Paris as an exciting city of aristocratic courtesans, secret assignations, seduction, and adultery. For many theatre-goers there was a sense of daring to be had from attending a 'fast' French play. Yet the question of how far the stage should be permitted to explore unconventional moral and sexual situations was one which increasingly absorbed the time and thought of the staff of the Lord Chamberlain's Office. Nor was French drama any longer the exclusive source of the trouble, for English playwrights began to treat of exactly similar kinds of problem; and it is from this point in the mid 1870s and onwards that moral censorship overtook in quantity and importance all other kinds of censorship. The difficulties to be faced were sensitive in the extreme and it was unfortunate that Edward F. S. Pigott, Donne's successor as Examiner, had little of his predecessor's tact, patience, or powers of real discrimination.

Pigott proved to be a perfect foil for the new Lord Chamberlain, the Marquess of Hertford, who was determined to curb what was currently being described as the growing license of the stage. Hertford intervened personally in the production of Offenbach's *Vert-Vert* at the St James's Theatre in 1874, where reports indicated that the skirts of the ballet girls who danced the audacious 'riperelle' were outrageously short, and he made an order that they were to be lengthened

PUNCH, OR THE LONDON CHARIVARI.—December 19, 1874.

SWEEPING THE STAGE. ("NEW BROOMS.")

Box Book-keeper. "STALLS, MADAM? WELL,—REALLY,—THE FACT IS, THE LORD CHAMBERLAIN,—THAT IS—AHEM!—WE'RE JUST NOW *CLEANING THE STAGE*, MADAM, AND HOPE TO HAVE THE THEATRE QUITE FIT FOR LADIES BY CHRISTMAS."

Plate 10   A satiric glance at Lord Hertford's attempt to improve the morality of the drama

to comply with accepted standards of decency.[2] It was the kind of crusade – the Lord Chamberlain's own description – which must have touched the sensibilities of many members of the public because for the next few months the Lord Chamberlain's Office received many further reports of indecencies in costume, all of which Pigott was required to investigate. At the Drury Lane Christmas pantomime of 1874 a number of complaints were lodged regarding the body-stocking worn by Harlequin, and Pigott was detailed to take the matter up with the theatre. As Hertford wrote privately to Spencer Ponsonby:

I hope Mr Pigott's remonstrance really has been attended to. I quite see our difficulty about entering on a crusade against individual dresses, but I am quite sure that if a disgusting dress of this sort is allowed just now after all that has been written and said we shall lose the prestige we have gained, so more must be risked now than usual.[3]

The Lord Chamberlain's stand on morality did not pass unnoticed by the Queen, who had apparently come to a similar conclusion that the contemporary stage was straining beyond the bounds of decency. Her private secretary wrote to Lord Hertford expressing Her Majesty's 'entire satisfaction at the steps you are taking to curb the License of the Stage, and [she] is glad to see that the response of the Managers generally shows that their opinions agree with yours. The Queen trusts that an improvement will be the result.'[4]

Encouraged no doubt by royal support, the Lord Chamberlain took a severely puritanical line with the newest (and most notorious) dance imported from France — the can-can. When it had first appeared in England about 1866, William Donne had written to the then Lord Chamberlain, Viscount Sydney: 'I am not very learned, as you know, in dancing or *ballets*, but I fancy *can can* dancing is rather *fast family* business even at Paris ... [and] it is occasionally alluded to in French novels as something rather lax.'[5] By the mid 1870s the popularity of the dance determined the authorities on preventing its appearance on the stage. The endorsement on the licence for Robert Reece's comic opera *Babiole* (1879), typical of scores of others of the period, contains the warning that 'nothing in the slightest degree resembling or characteristic of a Can Can is permitted in any piece licensed for representation by the Lord Chamberlain'.

Public taste in the late 1870s seemed to be much in favour of moral restraint, to the extent that the licensers made a substantial miscalculation of public feeling in permitting James Albery's comedy *The Pink Dominos* at the Criterion Theatre in April 1877. The play (adapted from *Les Dominos Roses* by Delacour and Hennequin) portrays a wife who suspecting infidelity on the part of her husband, puts him to the test by arranging a clandestine assignation, which she attends in a 'pink domino' disguise. Pigott licensed it without comment but the play caused an enormous outcry in the press reviews and in the correspondence columns of the newspapers. *The Daily Telegraph* fulminated that it is right to assert that conjugal infidelity has not yet become recognised as a trait in the national character, and that husband and wife are not, in this country at least, passing their existence in trying to deceive, dishonour, and detect each other. On the score of decorum it is, moreover, right to protest in the strongest manner against the transfer to the English stage of a piece in which the coarsest suggestions are made the provocative of merriment.[6]

The real trouble was not that *The Pink Dominos* was more morally unconventional than many of its contemporaries, but that it was much cleverer and made its point with added conviction. In a letter to the *Era* (15 April 1877) Charles Wyndham defended the play on the grounds that there were many other (better known) pieces, like Boucicault's *London Assurance* (1841) and Sheridan's *The School for Scandal* (1777), which were 'equally open to ungenerous misconstruction'. But another correspondent in the same issue of the newspaper argued that the censor, whose function it was to protect the morals of playgoers from corruption, had manifestly failed in his duty. He suggested that Pigott's office was merely 'a sham' and the fee charged for licensing 'a tax'. Although the authorities remained prudently silent throughout the whole affair, Albery must have sensed the Lord Chamberlain's unease and wrote to explain that the attacks on his play were the work of critics prejudiced against him. *The Pink Dominos,* he assured Lord Hertford, had been 'prepared with great care to avoid offence and there is no line or situation that should shock a pure minded spectator'.[7]

Yet the lessons learned from the spirited controversy over *The Pink Dominos* were ones which the Examiner could not afford to ignore and it is hard not to see some connexion with the suppression in the same year of no fewer than four adaptations from the French.[8] In 1878 and 1879 there were further prohibitions in the cause of morality, including *Niniche* ('an adaptation of a French piece notorious for its indecency ... which the English adaptation, while successful in removing all the wit of the original had vainly attempted to disguise'),[9] a comedy by Sydney Grundy and Joseph Mackay called *The Novel Reader,* and Arthur Matthison's *A False Step.* The proscription on the two former passed, for the moment, without further comment; but the enraged author of *A False Step* determined that the public should be allowed to judge for itself and published the play along with Pigott's letter explaining his reasons for refusing it a licence.[10] The piece was an adaptation of Emile Augier's *Les Lionnes Pauvres*, which attempts a study of the role of the courtesan, her power and wealth, and her inevitably demoralising influence on society. It was a serious play —

Augier had already gained some reputation as an exponent of 'la comédie serieuse' — and even Pigott acknowledged that it was 'profoundly moral in its ultimate purpose'. But he did have grave doubts about its reception in the theatre, fearing that 'the public and their critical guides would exclaim at the "situations" and say that the moral for the piece was only fit to be taught in the Divorce Court'. A reviewer for *The Theatre*, however, noted that most of the offensive material in the original had 'been judiciously eliminated or softened down by the translator' and that the regrettable suppression of the play was consistent with the authorities' policy of interdicting 'much finer plays' like *Le Supplice d'une Femme* and *Le Demi-Monde* which 'try to make us cry instead of laugh over marital infidelity, and . . . deal with adultery as though it were something more than a comic incident of daily life'.[11] The charge that the censor was much more tolerant of the comic treatment of seduction and adultery than its serious exploration is a recurrent one during the later nineteenth century — and for the most part it was entirely justified.

To the credit of the Lord Chamberlain's Office, however, it did have the courage to reverse a long-standing precedent by granting a licence for the performance of one of the most notable of contemporary French dramas even though it had been twice refused, in 1860 and 1874. The play was Alexandre Dumas' *Le Demi-Monde*, which the Comédie Française wanted to perform during their visit to London for a series of French plays in 1879. Pigott was favourably inclined towards it and endeavoured to persuade the new Lord Chamberlain to his point of view. He argued that precedent was not utterly inviolable and that there were occasions when it was right that it should be overturned:

Each case, as it arises, should be decided on its own merits, and subject to its own circumstances and conditions. It is one thing to avoid the appearance of capriciousness, and quite another thing to follow blindly some precedent which may be an unwise one; and not to have the courage to *create* a precedent under exceptional circumstances . . . I am convinced that the balance of *intelligent* opinion would be in favour of allowing such a play as *Le Demi-Monde*.[12]

Whatever Pigott's later reputation, it is clear that in his early career at least he was not wholly hostile towards controversial plays and that his mind was by no means closed to the demands of art. His argument on precedent was an important one, since it was the slavish authority of precedent which was at the root of the essential conservatism of nineteenth-century censorship. In this instance Pigott had his way and

Lord Mount Edgecumbe, in consenting to the licensing of Dumas' play, overthrew a prohibition which had lasted almost twenty years. When the news was conveyed to the director of the Comédie-Française, Spencer Ponsonby explained that the ban had been relaxed owing to the 'exceptional circumstances of the case & the fact that there appears to have been some misconception as to the character of the piece itself at the time when it was originally forbidden'.[13]

The resonances of the decision to permit *Le Demi-Monde* produced a much less inhibited policy towards French-language plays during the 1880s. Pigott maintained before the 1892 Committee that he was 'extremely indulgent' towards such plays, especially if performed by French companies. 'I made mistakes at first,' he concluded, 'but now if I accept a French play at all I never interfere with it.'[14] Even some English adaptations benefited from the loosening of the reins. In 1883 the Examiner recommended the licensing of *Niniche*, a play which at the time of its original prohibition five years previously he had branded as 'notorious for its indecency'. The veto on Sydney Grundy's *The Novel Reader* was also reconsidered, though not before the author had arranged a private performance, under the title *May and December*, at the Globe Theatre in 1882. The idea of a private performance (later to prove so useful to the Shelley Society and others) was a new one and the authorities were somewhat perplexed how best to deal with it. After consulting the Comptroller of the Lord Chamberlain's Office, Pigott decided to 'treat the matter with entire indifference';[15] but the publicity attaching to the production, and the large audiences which it attracted, made that rather difficult. None of the reviewers could find anything immoral in the play, including the critic of the *Morning Post* (29 September 1882), who commented that the ban on the original was hardly credible: 'it is difficult to discover why the gnats in "The Novel Reader" have been strained at' when it was considered 'how many imported French camels have been officially swallowed'. Not a little embarrassed by the affair, Pigott tried to rescue some dignity by the discovery, when Grundy resubmitted his play under its original title and with a few slight modifications of expression, that *The Novel Reader* was licensable after all, and after four years' prohibition it was released for public consumption.[16]

II

William Archer believed that the year 1885 or thereabouts marked a major turning-point in the history of English drama and, for contrary reasons, in the history of dramatic censorship. Up to that time, he argued, censorship had not produced 'any very depressing effect upon the English drama, because practically there was very little original English drama' but merely a succession of adaptations from the French. However, with the gradual emergence of a new and vigorous native drama, censorship 'has had a very distinctly and growingly depressing and repressing influence upon [its] development,' since 'it has prevented the development in the direction of the serious drama — the serious treatment of life'.[17] Archer's reference is to the beginning of the period which Henry Arthur Jones later called 'the Renascence of the English Drama', that is, the decade between 1885 and 1895, which embraced much of Pinero's best work, and most of Jones's himself; which saw Wilde's career as a dramatist in its entirety, and the start of Bernard Shaw's. Above all, perhaps (and certainly in terms of his influence on native dramatists), it was the decade of Henrik Ibsen. He was the guiding light of the 'new drama'; he was the prophet who showed what it was possible to achieve in dramatic form. Archer wrote in 1891 that Ibsen 'has been, and has deserved to be, one of the foremost literary topics of the past three years, and ... this is the first time for half a century (to keep well within the mark) that a serious literary interest has also been primarily a theatrical interest'. As the principal driving force behind the new intellectual drama, Ibsen stood out prominently as the playwright whose work showed 'an unexampled relevance to the spiritual problems of modern life'.[18]

Admittedly, in 1885 there were relatively few people who had actually read Ibsen and fewer still who had seen performances of his plays.[19] But, partly through his influence among a small body of talented dramatists and partly as a result of the atmosphere of genuine critical enquiry during the late 1880s and early 1890s, English play-wrights were seized with a new discovery: the revelation that it was the province of drama to dissect and minutely examine social and moral problems. In other words, drama had the right to study and engage itself with all aspects of human experience, however unpleasant, however opposed to orthodox values. That was the challenge which Ibsen's work helped to formulate. If English dramatists failed to grasp the full potential of the challenge, some portion of the blame is their own, through their inability to overcome both personal prejudices and the traditional limitations imposed by public opinion. But the censors, too, have their part in such a charge. Little was conceded to the new drama and plays continued to be judged on criteria which would have been more appropriate to the 1870s than the final fifteen years of the nineteenth century. Certainly, the licensing authorities had tried to take some account of the subtle changes in taste, and public opinion, browbeaten by a satiety of French comedy and farce, was inclined to take up rather more tolerant attitudes. Yet the revisions were minor. By the end of the century it was apparent that neither censorship in particular nor public opinion in general had made sufficient accommodation for the bolder forms of dramatic writing and the general treatment of subject-matter that had hitherto been classed as dubious, inappropriate, or otherwise unsuitable for public performance.

Ironically enough, one of the first victims of censorship during the post-1885 dramatic renaissance was Henry Arthur Jones himself. The Examiner described his play *Welcome Little Stranger* (1885) as 'founded on a nasty idea', the dialogue for which was 'suggestive and coarse'. In referring the MS. for the opinion of Spencer Ponsonby', Pigott explained that it was impossible to expurgate the dialogue because 'the whole is a succession of *double entendres*, and the question of licensing turns on the character of the piece *as a whole* — any passage detached from the context would appear perfectly harmless'. To Pigott's question, 'Is a piece of that sort fit to place before a mixed English audience?', the response was firmly negative.[20] In similar, if not more heated vein, Pigott achieved the suppression in the same year of an English adaptation of Alphonse Daudet's savagely realistic novel *Sapho*, the study of the moral and spiritual disintegration of a young provincial artist who forms a liaison with a Parisian model. The Examiner was so deeply convinced that this was a subject unfit for English ears that he wrote to Spencer Ponsonby declining absolutely to be responsible for the play and indicating that 'if I sign the Licence, it will be as Pilate signed the release of Barabbas, after washing my hands of it!'[21] Recourse to the opinions of a mythical 'mixed audience' was Pigott's most familiar line of defence.

The beginning of what Jones termed the 'Renascence of the English Drama' marks also the start of the long-continued campaign for the abolition of the Lord Chamberlain's censorship of the stage. The two major challenges to his authority were the intended performances of Shelley's *The Cenci* in 1886 and Ibsen's *Ghosts* in 1891, both of which succeeded in evading the official veto by means which guaranteed at least a limited exposure on the London stage to plays similarly prohibited, including Shaw's *Mrs Warren's Profession*. In theory, the idea of a private performance was sound enough — it seemed to provide an infallible route to the staging of all suppressed plays — but in practice the Lord Chamberlain's Office made it as awkward as it could for theatre managers to offer their theatres for productions of this nature.

The authorities' horrified reaction to the projected performance of *The Cenci* realised the fear expressed by Shelley himself on completion of the play in 1819, when he confided to Thomas Love Peacock his doubt whether 'any such a thing as incest in this shape however treated wd. be admitted on the stage'.[22] His uncertainties were echoed later in the century by those theatre managers (they were very few) who contemplated staging the tragedy. Macready, for one, recorded in his diary in 1847: 'Looked through *The Cenci* as a matter of form. The *idea* of acting such a monstrous crime, beautiful as the work is!'[23] But in 1886 a group of admirers of Shelley's work formed themselves into the Shelley Society under the chairmanship of Dr F. J. Furnivall (the Shakespearean scholar and bibliographer). One of the Society's prime objectives was a professional performance of *The Cenci* at a London theatre. Edward Pigott tried to scotch the idea from the start by suggesting to Spencer Ponsonby that 'timely notice' be given that the Lord Chamberlain had no intention of licensing the play. The Examiner, while recognising that *The Cenci* was 'a literary masterpiece', declared that 'all the genius in the world cannot make a play of which incest is the central theme, proper to be licensed for public representation'.[24] In the face of such stern official opposition, the Shelley Society (imitating the course taken by Sydney Grundy for *The Novel Reader* in 1882) concluded that a purely private performance open only to members of the Society was the sole expedient left. Before long the problem of finding a theatre for the purpose was resolved after the manager of the Grand, Islington, agreed to loan his premises for a single matinée performance on 7 May 1886. The news caused such a stir at St James's Palace that both Dr Furnivall and the manager were summoned for interview, at which they were warned in decidedly unfriendly terms that the performance had to remain strictly private and that on no account was there to be any publicity. As Pigott noted in an official memorandum of the conversation, part of Furnivall's justification for requesting the Lord Chamberlain's licence in the first place was that 'the story of the "Cenci" is open to doubt, as far as the actual incest is concerned', and that Byron's *Manfred* had already been licensed for public performance. 'Upon those somewhat contradictory or irrelevant allegations', the Examiner commented, 'it is enough to remark that all the genius of the greatest poets that have ever lived cannot make incest a subject fit for representation in a Christian country.'[25]

The performance of *The Cenci* took place before a large and distinguished audience (many of whom had become members of the Shelley Society just for the occasion) including Browning, George Meredith, and J. R. Lowell. Press reaction was predictably hostile.

Clement Scott in *The Daily Telegraph* (8 May 1886) fully endorsed the Lord Chamberlain's refusal to sanction Shelley's 'hideous tragedy'; a reviewer for *The Scotsman* (8 May) remarked in similarly hysterical terms that the play 'turns on an incident so horrible, so revolting, and so utterly obscene as hardly to bear telling', while Austin Brereton called it 'the most repulsive play that has been produced this century'.[26] The storm soon blew over and the affair was forgotten; but the performance established an important precedent. It was, as Michael Orme observes, 'in the nature of a discovery – a path to the presentation of censored plays'.[27]

Most obviously it was one of the main antecedents of J. T. Grein's Independent Theatre Society, formed in 1891 as a more permanent version of the Shelley Society. Grein's venture was conceived expressly for the performance of worthwhile plays which were either prohibited by the licensing authorities or else considered to be commercial risks. As an experiment in non-commercial theatre, Grein's Society was expressive of the new and adventurous spirit among contemporary dramatists and others who were tired of the limitations imposed by managers and official censorship. It was, too, an expression of rebellion. In 1891 there was no more rebellious play than Ibsen's *Ghosts*, which Grein bravely chose as his first production. The censor had already made clear the official position that under no circumstances was the play to be granted a licence from the Lord Chamberlain. Kate Santley of the Royalty Theatre, on being approached by Grein, readily gave permission for one private performance of *Ghosts* on 13 March. But in the meantime she had temporary misgivings about the venture when she learned from the newspapers that the Lord Chamberlain might find some way of showing his displeasure at this blatant evasion of his authority. Rather than risk her valuable licence, Miss Santley wrote at once to the Lord Chamberlain's Office for a statement of its official view. In reply, the authorities explained that they had no power to interfere so long as the performance remained absolutely private in character.[28] However, Grein's production stimulated so much public interest that he was besieged by more than three thousand applications for tickets, and some of the newspapers began to express doubts whether, in the circumstances, the performance was a private one at all. On the appointed day the press was amply represented at the Royalty Theatre and produced the anticipated avalanche of abuse in the review columns the next day. Reactions ranged from 'a morbid and sickening dissection of corrupt humanity' (Clement Scott), through 'a hideous nightmare', to 'a putrid drama the details of which cannot appear with any propriety in any column save those of a medical journal'.[29] As William Archer commented: 'The critical hatred of Ibsen and contempt for the Independent Theatre is perfectly genuine, perfectly sincere ... The Plain truth is that the theatrical journalism of the day is narrow-minded, *borné*, and if not illiterate, at any rate illiberal in its culture.'[30] And the Lord Chamberlain's Office could claim no more sophisticated or tolerant view than the press. When Spencer Ponsonby wrote his official memorandum of Grein's production he described *Ghosts* as a play 'which though thoroughly harmless in language is suggestive of an *unwholesome* state of things' and its author as 'a Danish writer who has attained a reputation of late as a Realistic Writer after the manner of Zola: his works however being Dramatic instead of Novelistic'.[31] The critical furore attending the performance of *Ghosts* once again lent support to the theory that the Lord Chamberlain's Office, in declining to licence unconventional plays, was pursuing a course required of it by the majority of the right-thinking public.

The storm had one further consequence which intimately affected the future policy of the Independent Theatre Society. When Grein, in order to satisfy the unexpected demand for tickets, tried to arrange another performance of Ibsen's play he found that Miss Santley (frightened by the adverse press reviews and anxious about her future relations with the Lord Chamberlain's Office) flatly refused to sub-lease her theatre.[32] Neither was anyone else willing to help. This fear of official reprisals — and the consequent impossibility of finding theatres for the performance of unlicensed plays — accounts for the fact that, *Ghosts* apart, none of the other twenty-eight plays staged by the Independent Theatre Society between 1891 and 1897 lacked official sanction.[33] While the record of the Society in presenting worthwhile, yet uncommercial, drama is quite impressive, its intended challenge to the restrictions imposed by the Lord Chamberlain's censorship was a manifest failure.

III

One recurrent theme that runs through much of the best and sometimes the most controversial drama of the 1890s is that of 'the woman with a past'. The idea was certainly not new and it has obvious connexions with the courtesan play imported from France. Arthur Pinero used it in *The Second Mrs Tanqueray* (1893), as did Oscar Wilde in *A Woman of No Importance* (1893), and Shaw (who represents the 'genre anti-type')[34] in *Mrs Warren's Profession* (1894, published 1898). Although only the last-named was actually prohibited by the Lord Chamberlain, the three plays provide instructive illustrations of the very different standards which the licensers applied to plays linked to some degree by the similarity of their underlying theme. The first two are markedly dissimilar, however, in their handling of what is essentially the same situation, in which the past threatens the domestic happiness of the present for Wilde's Mrs Arbuthnot and Pinero's Paula Tanqueray. Wilde's treatment of the former relationship between Lord Illingworth and Mrs Arbuthnot is studiedly delicate and shrouded in serio-comic Wildean epigrams. But Pinero's play has an altogether different tone. It sets out to examine seriously the consequences of Paula Tanqueray's improper past for her now happy marriage. Her dissolute youth is more than hinted at and the play represents, in its context of the early 1890s, a bold attempt for a native English dramatist at sexual explicitness. Curiously, however, not a line of it was cut by the censor, even though the audaciousness of the situation and some of the dialogue was fully recognised at the time by the theatrical profession. When Pinero offered his drama to John Hare at the Garrick, the latter observed 'we shall have to cut a lot of that out';[35] and after seeing the whole work in print Hare declined it flatly. It was offered instead to George Alexander, who agreed somewhat reluctantly to give the play a trial at the St James's Theatre. Cyril Maude, recalling Pinero's first reading of the script to the assembled company, wrote:

I remember we marvelled at Alexander ever having been able to get it past the Censor ... I was terrified at having to play the part of Cayley [Drummle] — a delightful part, though with an extraordinarily trying scene in the first act. I had to tell the whole of Paula's life and describe things which up until that time had rarely, if ever, been mentioned on the English stage.[36]

Pinero's *The Second Mrs Tanqueray* was courageous in conception and execution though the language remained at all times unobjectionable. Yet despite its radical character, there are elements in it which are solidly and unerringly Victorian. Paula's past does catch up with her and does jeopardise her respectable marriage. Even her step-daughter Ellean recognises in her the marks of the *demi-monde* and Paula finds that she cannot escape its taint. The tragic and inevitable conclusion of Paula Tanqueray's suicide acts out the Victorian axiom that the past must be paid for, even for the fallen woman who reforms. As the heroine plaintively observes in Act IV: 'I believe the future is only the past again, entered through another gate.'[37]

If the Examiner of Plays ever had any misgivings about licensing Pinero's play, there is no evidence of them in the official records. The reasons for the censor's non-intervention can thus be only a matter of conjecture; but clearly Pinero's already not inconsiderable reputation as a dramatist must have played its part in moulding the attitude of the authorities. They were reluctant to interfere in the work of one who by common consent had established himself in the first rank of late-Victorian drama and Pinero's undisputed skill in language, which was as unobjectionable as it was relevant to his difficult subject, must have clinched the grant of a licence.

With Bernard Shaw matters stood very differently. The similarity between *Mrs Warren's Profession,* his third play, completed in the following year, and Pinero's *The Second Mrs Tanqueray* lies solely in the common denominator of the past (and in Shaw's case still current) 'profession' of their respective heroines. Shaw's play works from quite opposite premises and comes to radically dissimilar conclusions. He described the play as 'cold bloodedly appalling . . . but not in the least. . . prurient', for Mrs Warren (proprietress of a string of continental brothels) has become a prostitute from economic necessity. As Shaw put it, 'I want to make an end, if I can, of the furtively lascivious Pharisaism of stage immorality, by a salutary dramatisation of the reality.'[38] Needless to say, unlike Paula Tanqueray, Mrs Warren does not resolve her predicament by committing suicide. On the basis of its subject-matter alone, Shaw was well aware of the dusty answer he was likely to receive from the censor and so did not even bother to submit the play for official examination. His only hope of public performance lay with the Independent Theatre Society, with whom he discussed the possibility at intervals over the next two years. But Shaw's plans were frustrated by Grein's inability to find a theatre manager willing to risk staging such a boldly controversial and unlicensed play. By 1896 Shaw was forced to acknowledge that 'there is no question of its immediate or remote production . . . although "Mrs Warren" is still talked of on both sides as eligible'.[39]

Mrs Warren's Profession did not come officially to the notice of the Lord Chamberlain until 1898 when, as a necessary protection for its publication in *Plays Pleasant and Unpleasant* in that year, Shaw applied for permission to mount a single copyright performance. As expected, the 1894 text proved totally unacceptable. To Shaw's suggested remedy of drastic expurgation' (amounting to the removal of the entire second act, thus 'leaving Mrs W's profession unspecified'), the Examiner responded by reminding him that it was his business, as author, to submit 'a licensable play', in which event George Redford would 'endeavour to forget that [he] ever read the original'.[40] Further negotiations ensued that resulted in Shaw's submission of an innocuous three-act version of *Mrs Warren*, which Redford then sanctioned for performance at the Victoria Hall, Bayswater. This was followed four years later by a private club production of the full text by the Stage Society (constructed on lines resembling Grein's venture) in January 1902. But it was another twenty-four years before the Lord Chamberlain of the day relaxed the official veto and licensed the original play.[41]

Society drama of the kind initiated by Arthur Pinero flourished apace during the mid and late 1890s, seeming to draw invigoration from the playwright's daring success of 1893. It was even possible for Henry Arthur Jones to claim by 1895 that audiences were becoming more sophisticated in taste and were far less likely to be shocked or repelled by the morally unconventional. He urged fellow dramatists to take advantage of the fact that 'in the midst of the vast heterogeneous, careless, indifferent mob of playgoers and amusement-seekers we have a smaller but not inconsiderable circle of cultivated and intelligent playgoers who are interested in drama as an art and as a study of life'.[42] Even so, the mainstream of public opinion was still the most articulate about, and easily incensed by, what was deemed to pass beyond the ordinary decencies of family life. Haddon Chambers's *John-a-Dreams* (1894) was a well-publicised victim of such views. In the *Times* annual review of the drama for 1894 (28 December), the play was described as one of those 'so-called society play[s] containing a heroine not only with a sordid past, but a questionable present and a doubtful future'. The trouble was that the heroine Kate Cloud (played by Mrs Patrick Campbell) did not even have the merit of paying for her past sins by committing suicide like more respectable heroines, such as Paula Tanqueray. In its original review of the production, *The Times* (8 December 1894) commented that 'in this case the Examiner of Plays must have been in the deepest slumber when he permitted the public glorification of harlotry as a fit subject of entertainment for our wives and daughters'.

The reception of Chambers' play seems to have startled the licensers into a more circumspect attitude to plays on sexual themes during the following year. Within a month of the controversy Edward Pigott had refused to licence William Heinemann's *The First Step* (1895), in which the two central characters, an aspiring playwright called Frank Donovan and his mistress Annie, are living together as husband and wife. (Shaw remarked that this fact alone must have been sufficient reason for the censor to ban the play, since it offended 'against Mr

Pigott's rule-of-thumb for determining whether a play is "moral" or not'.[43] But worse was to come, for in the second act Annie's sister Lizzie (a sheltered girl brought up in a Nonconformist household where the theatre is a forbidden entertainment) is taken, unchaperoned, to the play by Jack Durwen, a friend of Frank's to whom Frank is financially obligated. Frank spends the evening with his actress friend Mrs Courtree, who has commissioned him to write a play, and Annie remains at home alone. At four o'clock the following morning Lizzie and Jack have still not returned. Frank arrives drunk and unconcerned for Lizzie's fate, suggesting that the two are sheltering from the rain in Jack's rooms. Annie, finally coming to the realisation of what this means, confronts her lover with the horrified conclusion: 'You have sold her to him for his gold — you have bartered her away as if she had been your chattel!'[44] Given the awkward moral situation in the play, its suppression by the licensing authorities seems predictable enough. But the refusal of a licence deprived Heinemann's play (his first) of any chance of public performance — even by the Independent Theatre Society, which, having committed itself to staging the piece before news of the official veto emerged, was obliged to withdraw from the agreement on finding, as in previous cases, that no theatre manager was willing to risk staging an unlicensed play.[45]

The fate of *The First Step* does, however, provide an interesting foil to another important play of 1895, Pinero's *The Notorious Mrs Ebbsmith*, which, although turning on a very similar kind of situation, did receive the Lord Chamberlain's sanction. It was common knowledge, as William Archer remarked in *The Theatrical 'World'*, that *Mrs Ebbsmith* had 'escaped [the censor's] veto by the skin of her "pretty white teeth".'[46] Archer exaggerated, but the official records confirm that George Redford (then newly appointed Examiner on the death of Pigott) was certainly rather hesitant about the play and its controversial central situation in which Lucas Cleeve, a married man separated from his wife, and Agnes Ebbsmith, a widow, are living together as man and wife, scorning marriage even if it were possible. 'We have done with marriage,' Agnes exclaims, 'we distrust it. We are not now among those who regard marriage as indispensable to union. We have done with it.' In referring the case to Spencer Ponsonby, Redford explained that he was sending him the MS. of the play with 'certain passages' marked which he hoped would enable his superior 'to get at the pith of the piece without wading through the whole'. He went on: 'It is a "problem" play; one that as far as I can remember, has never been treated on the stage before, at any rate in the same way . . . It is diluted Ibsen, brought up to date, and applied to every day English life, with a picturesque setting in Venice.'[47] Redford was, however, full of praise for Pinero's treatment of the subject: it was 'most delicately handled, always with good taste, and discretion, and there is not a single word in the text that could be taken exception to'. His only misgiving was whether the 'motif' itself was licensable or not. But it turned out that Edward Pigott, shortly before his death, had verbally agreed with the manager of the Garrick Theatre to sanction the play and the Lord Chamberlain, feeling obliged to honour the commitment, directed that the provisional licence be sent.[48] It may be added that the licensing of such an advanced piece as *The Notorious Mrs Ebbsmith* owed much to Pinero's solidly respectable reputation as a playwright and that a name other than his (or possibly Henry Arthur Jones's) on the title page would have ensured that, as William Archer put it, 'this admirable work ... would have been consigned to the limbo of stillborn improprieties'.[49]

That reputation was sometimes the vital, deciding factor in doubtful cases is well illustrated in Robert Buchanan's *The New Don Quixote*, submitted for licensing for a projected copyright performance in December 1895. The author's literary and dramatic reputation was not high enough to intimidate the Lord Chamberlain's Office and the Examiner was free to judge the play irrespective of external pressures. Redford admitted his dislike of the play from the start. He objected to what he termed 'the baldly sexual tone of the piece' and to the prominence of the '"non-consummation" episode'. As he explained to Spencer Ponsonby 'I believe the situation has occurred in other plays — *The Ironmaster* for one but I never admit that argument, and Mr Robert Buchanan is not Mr Pinero'. He confessed himself unable to understand why there was any desire to produce the piece at all, since 'there's really no money in these sexual plays, and the public don't want them. This one is poor stuff, though it *is* dramatic, which is more than can be said for some of them.'[50]

Buchanan was outraged at the authorities' decision to refuse his play a licence and, bristling with injured pride, he wrote at great length to the Examiner, protesting at 'the imputation that I have written a play which is unfit for representation' and suggesting 'in all humility' that he had never once 'written one line which could offend or revolt a pure and open mind ... I am not ... a man trading in any public appetite for what is morbid and unwholesome', unlike some other plays licensed by the authorities including Pinero's *The Benefit of the Doubt* (1895). His own play, he argued, 'idealizes and ennobles human love in a way very unusual in modern drama ... [as] its whole argument, indeed, is to prove that human relationships demand the highest spiritual consecration'.[51] In his reply, George Redford reminded the disaffected author that the Examiner 'has no official cognizance of Authors as such, and I think you will agree that the difficult duties of his Post preclude the possibility of any "ex officio" correspondence or interview'. The result was an ever longer diatribe from Buchanan attacking an official attitude which he took to be more 'suggestive of the Dark Ages or the Star Chamber than of the nineteenth century' and cavilling at the Examiner's friendly hint that Lord Lathom might be favourably disposed to a revised version of the play. But, he continued, 'if that is so, may I enquire how any emendation is possible, when authors are completely ignorant of the nature of your objections?'[52]

To be fair to George Redford, in spite of his disclaiming all 'official cognizance of Authors as such', he was usually willing to give theatre managers advice on both textual matters and on staging. There is increasing evidence in the Lord Chamberlain's Day Books at the end of the century that the Examiner was anxious to cultivate a more personal approach by inviting managers to discuss points of dispute at interviews arranged in St James's Palace. In the case of *The Cuckoo* (licensed for the Avenue Theatre in 1899) − the play is by Charles Brookfield, Redford's successor as Examiner of Plays − the entry in the Day Book reads: 'Omit in Represent[ation] "the degrading three word Formula 'Saturday to Monday'" & other suggestive allusions agreed to be omitted, at an interview between Mr Hawtrey & the Examiner.' The MS. of the play preserves several passages marked in blue pencil and which were evidently discussed at the same time. The one referred to in the Day Book reads:

I don't know when I've felt so furious! Not with Hugh Farrant I'm sorry to say. With myself for not being furious with Hugh Farrant. He grossly insulted me. He suggested that I should go out of town. He even employed a low expression which should make any honest woman wince − the degrading three word formula 'Saturday to Monday'. And yet I never − genuinely − turned a hair. Thank goodness I know myself sufficiently well to *simulate* the greatest indignation to order him from my house never to enter it again.[53]

In other cases, a firmly phrased reminder sent to the manager was deemed more appropriate, as in the comedy *Coralie & Co. Ltd* (1901) when Redford warned the manager of the Strand Theatre that 'it must be clearly understood that "Ethel" does not take off her dress. The "business" is to be strictly kept to "measuring for" and not "trying on" and there must be no suggestion of impropriety in the "5 o'clock tea club"', or, in similar vein, the admonition in the licence for *The Lady Cyclist* (1897) that 'the business with men's bathing Drawers [is] to be omitted in Representation'.

By the end of the century the dilemma of the licensing authorities was complete. On the one hand, dramatists were engaged in writing ever more advanced plays turning on delicate moral and sexual situations (often hinting that the marriage contract was *passé* and taking as their heroines women whose views on life seemed by the standards of even ten years earlier to be decidedly improper, if not downright immoral) while, on the other, the press, such institutions as the National Vigilance Association, and the religious organisations inveighed bitterly against dramas which seemed to have plumbed the depths of moral degradation. In July 1899 the Queen's private secretary wrote to inform the Lord Chamberlain that Her Majesty was 'scandalised' by press reports of Isidore de Lara's opera *Messaline* playing in French at Covent Garden.[54] And in the same year the censors' ubiquitous touchstone of middle-class morality, Arthur Pinero, suffered an exceptional deluge of abuse for his latest play *The Gay Lord Quex*. The Lord Chamberlain received a number of letters (mostly based on hearsay) alleging its unfitness for the English stage. The chief secretary of the Church Army, for instance, wrote to say that *Quex* 'appears to me as likely to sap away that respect for matrimonial life which is the basis of English society',[55] and the Bishop of Wakefield (the same cleric who had publicly incinerated Hardy's novel *Jude the Obscure* in 1896), who, like the former correspondent, had not seen the play, branded it in the *Era* (15 April 1899) as 'the most immoral play that ever disgraced the stage of this country'. The Lord Chamberlain even had a letter from the self-appointed defender of middle-class values, Sydney Smith, M.P., who, on behalf of the many constituents who had complained to him on the topic, expressed his extreme disquiet at the 'suggestive and disgusting' scene in Act III when the curtain rises on 'the Bedroom actually with the Bedstead upon the stage'.[56] Rather surprisingly, the new Lord Chamberlain, Lord Hopetoun, replied in a way quite uncharacteristic of the usual placatory official style:

I am bound to say that I do not share the opinions you and your correspondents express. The Stage must always be a reflex of the age, and to banish from it altogether Plots which are founded upon lapses from the strictest line of morality would result in depriving us of the finest works of Shakespeare, Sheridan, and others.[57]

Such a sensible and moderate response illustrates how much the licensing authorities had conceded since the days of the ban, say, on Sydney Grundy's *The Novel Reader* in 1879.

But the moral dilemma of the censors remained very real. When (as with Pinero's *The Gay Lord Quex*) Redford did not interfere, the press

were almost unanimous in their condemnation of
of the Examiner. When he did interfere the reaction w
the same. Redford must have been especially disillus
of Frank Harris's *Mr & Mrs Daventry* (1900), over wl
considerable time and effort in expurgating what
obnoxious dialogue. The play was a little more tha
markable round of seduction and adultery. It conⱡⱡⱡⱡⱡⱡ ⱡ
theatrical second act, where Mrs Daventry overhears her husband making love to another woman, and a dénouement in which the repentant
husband, having made a vain plea for his wife to return to him, shoots
himself in a suite at the Palace Hotel, Monte Carlo. (Harris, incidentally,
had just bought the hotel and used the play as a free advertisement.)
The Times (26 October 1900) had no doubts about its reaction to the
play. In the first act, the reviewer declared, 'there is a certain joke about
the object of ladies dressing which is quite unquotable, although it is
put into the mouth of a lady'. (This is a reference to Lady Hallingdon's
comment that 'we don't dress for men; for them we — oh, I had nearly
said something awful and obvious. No I won't say what it was. You can
guess if you want to, but Hilda there [i.e. Mrs Daventry] does not like
the naked truth ...'[58] There were also remonstrances against the
'catastrophic sofa' scene in Act II, in which Mr Daventry makes love to
Lady Langham in the hearing of his wife. It was a more serious version
of the well-known 'screen scene' in Sheridan's *The School for Scandal*,
but *The Times* commented that, while it was 'enormously effective', it
was if not 'absolutely indecent ... as near to indecency as anything we
remember on the contemporary stage'.

The foundation of the play was a scenario written by Oscar Wilde as
far back as 1894 when he was working on *The Importance of Being
Earnest*. Later, after endless complications, the idea was bought by Frank
Harris, who worked it up into a full four-act play and submitted it to the
Examiner of Plays under the title *Her Second Chance*. Redford must have
been fairly impressed with the play because, contrary to usual practice,
he wrote to Harris setting out the conditions upon which the MS. could
be licensed:

I should be glad to hear from you that the situation in the 2nd Act will be
modified in representation and kept within the recognised limits of 'stage
business'. The words 'adultery with home comforts' must be omitted, and
allusions to his 'mistress' and 'kept woman' are needlessly offensive, and
should not be spoken on the stage.[59]

Harris agreed readily enough to the stipulations for the sofa scene,
assuring the Examiner that 'the play has been practically accepted by

rs Patrick Campbell and this in itself constitutes a guarantee'. The phrase 'adultery with home comforts' (which is Lady Hallingdon's gloss on 'the English vice' in Act I) was, at Harris's own suggestion, revised to 'the Eleventh Commandment' for performance; but he believed that the other two epithets were worth arguing for:

> You ... object, I think, to the word 'mistress'. This is used only once, by the angry wife in contempt and condemnation, and if I change, or paraphrase it, I fear that I may draw great attention to the fact that the word represents. Of course, if you tell me that the word 'mistress' is taboo, it shall be excised.
>
> You object also to the phrase 'kept woman' used by the angry husband in the fourth act. This expression has been introduced simply to show the coarse and vulgar character of Mr Daventry; and Mrs Daventry immediately characterises the expression as 'vile' and condemns it utterly. In my opinion, it would hurt the most important part of the play ... if I were to alter the expression. I have chosen purposely the mildest of the many expressions in English for the fact. 'Prostitute' would, of course, be more offensive; 'whore' quite inadmissible. I ask you then in some confidence, seeing that the word is immediately stigmatised as vile by the principal character of the play to allow me to keep it.[60]

From the evidence of the official correspondence, it seems most unlikely that, as he himself contended, Harris actually went to the Lord Chamberlain's Office to argue about the phrase 'adultery with home comforts'. Harris's story was that the Lord Chamberlain, though 'personally delighted' with it, nevertheless required its removal from the script of the acting version.[61] In spite of the press criticisms, *Mr & Mrs Daventry* (which was actually Wilde's original title for his scenario), enjoyed real popularity for a time. It ran for over a hundred performances at the Royalty Theatre — even the Prince of Wales came to see it — but when it was withdrawn on 23 February 1901 it was never afterwards revived.

The newspapers' reaction to this 'most daring and naturalistic production of the modern English stage', as the *Athenaeum* (3 November 1900) described it, shows an increasingly reactionary stance on the matter of stage morality. The press had always been unpredictable but at the turn of the century the insistent demand was for more restrictions on the dramatic treatment of sexual themes. Among the watch-dogs of the press, Clement Scott (who had by then severed his long connexion with *The Daily Telegraph*) was still in the vanguard of those arguing for a more rigid sense of the proprieties and, for the most part, the Lord Chamberlain's Office was more than willing to assist. Yet, on the other hand, the authorities could hardly afford to ignore the mounting campaign against the whole institution of dramatic censorship, fuelled by the censor's suppression of Maeterlinck's *Monna Vanna* (1902) and, more importantly, Edward Garnett's *The Breaking Point* and Harley Granville-Barker's *Waste*, both of which were prohibited in 1907.[62] Quite fortuitously, the proscription on the last-named play coincided with a deputation of dramatists and other interested parties to lobby the Home Secretary for the abolition, or at least the radical reform, of an institution described in a letter to *The Times* signed by seventy-one playwrights (29 October 1907) as 'autocratic in procedure, opposed to the spirit of the Constitution, contrary to common justice and common sense'.[63] While the issue of censorship floundered in the moral cross-currents of Edwardian society, George Redford's personal dilemma was resolved by his resignation from the Examinership of Plays with effect from January 1912;[64] but the general dilemma remained to tax the ingenuity and patience of censors, parliamentary committees, and playwrights alike for close on sixty years.

EPILOGUE

George Bernard Shaw, writing for the benefit of an American reader-ship in 1898, remarked that 'few things would surprise me more than to meet a representative Englishman who regarded my desire to abolish the Censor otherwise than he would regard the desire of a pick-pocket to abolish the police'.[1] And he was probably right. The movement for the abolition of governmental control over the drama was generated by a minority — a small body of so-called progressive dramatists, writers, and critics who recognised the justice of the claim that the theatre should enjoy the same freedom accorded to all the other arts. Shaw's 'representative Englishman', if he thought about the issue at all, was perfectly happy to endorse a paternalistic form of censorship which (in theory at least) guaranteed the audience an immunity from shock or outrage and which, furthermore, exercised a vital, protective role in upholding the far more intangible standards of decency, decorum, and respectability demanded of society as a whole.

That there was, until near the end of the century, little public interest in censorship is hardly surprising, since the licensers tried to work as unobtrusively as possible and were sheltered by the formality and bureaucracy that surrounds any government department, then or now. On those occasions when force of circumstance brought the issue into the public eye — during the sittings of the parliamentary commit-tees on the theatres or when some unhappy victim of the censor's blue pencil publicly abused the licensing authorities — the Lord Chamber-lain's Office tried, as far as it was able, to maintain a discreet, dignified, and enigmatic silence. What is surprising, however, is the apparent indifference of the majority of playwrights to such actions of the censor which affected their own interests. Until the last fifteen years of the nineteenth century those authors who protested at decisions which consigned their plays to obscurity, even before theatre audiences had had the opportunity to express their views, were very much the excep-tion. At least two reasons might be suggested for the dramatists' acquiescence. First, that there was a social (if not an artistic) stigma attached to the suppression of a play — the implication, in other words, that an author had written something which others of more wisdom and mature experience had pronounced unfit for public presentation — or, secondly, that the authors themselves recognised the fitness of the censor's decision. Certainly, authors like Mary Mitford were grateful for the Examiner's advice; so, too, were several witnesses at the 1866 Committee, among them Charles Reade. Only in the new and buoyant mood of the late 1880s and the 90s did dramatists, provoked by the increasingly anachronistic decisions of the licensers, begin to query the effect of censorship on their own sense of artistic integrity.

The question of whether dramatic censorship had any profoundly serious effect upon the drama of the nineteenth century is not easy to answer. It may hardly be doubted that the drama was restricted in many areas, sometimes in the subject-matter itself, sometimes in its treatment; but the degree of responsibility to be laid at the door of the censor is less clear, especially as opera and certain vigorous forms like the pantomime and burlesque enjoyed a fair degree of freedom. It was the authorities' habitual defence to claim that censorship was merely reflecting the wishes of the majority of the public, whose voice the Lord Chamberlain's Office listened to attentively throughout the century. In religion, political allusion, and morality the Victorians could always easily find to hand enough evidence to support and sustain the idea of an institution of censorship that could control the frightening power of the theatre to influence opinions, encourage imitation, or mould atti- tudes.[2] But for the most part its power was conceived only in negative terms and few Victorians of any note — Matthew Arnold, Henry Arthur Jones, and Bernard Shaw are the exceptions — seem seriously to have considered the theatre's potential as a civilising and cultural force. With sadly increasing frequency as the turn of the century approached, the censors were justly accused of using the instrument of censorship to reduce the drama to fatuousness when faced with the serious treatment of any subject of moment and consequence.[3] Indeed, the closer a play came to 'real life' the more likely it was that the censor would intervene.

The greatest writers of the nineteenth century (perhaps more than artists of any previous generation) were highly critical of and often at odds with their society. Yet as far as the drama is concerned, until the advent of Shaw, and to a lesser extent Pinero and Henry Arthur Jones, the best minds ignored the theatre in favour of the intellectually more respectable (and, incidentally, far more lucrative) medium of the novel. The theatre desperately needed new blood to revive its ancient claims to authority. But at the critical point in the last fifteen or twenty years of the century, when men of distinction were beginning to return to writing for the stage, the censorship ceased to be a mere irritant and minor frustration; it began to deny that freedom which playwrights needed in order to deal with the most serious issues of the day. Audiences might not have liked what they received from the pens of dramatists like Ibsen and Shaw, but at least the majority had the sophistication and maturity to sense the genuine quality of their convictions — and those of their followers, such as Brieux, Strindberg, Hauptmann, Granville-Barker, and Edward Garnett, all of whom fell victim to the *dicta* of the censor in the early years of the twentieth century. If there is any truth in the assertion that censorship succeeded in promoting only a safe, but spineless and intellectually barren drama (making the stage, as Henry Fielding warned at the beginning of the eighteenth century, 'as dull as a country pulpit'[4]), then the argument must start from the authorities' inability from the 1880s onwards to include the critical and adventurous artist within their terms of reference.

APPENDIX A

Lord Chamberlains and Examiners of Plays (with dates of office)*

Lord Chamberlains (1821–1905)

James Graham, 3rd Duke of Montrose	1821–7
William George Spencer Cavendish, 6th Duke of Devonshire	1827–8
Montrose returned to office	1828–30
George Child-Villiers, 5th Earl of Jersey	1830
Devonshire returned to office	1830–4
Jersey returned to office	1834–5
Richard Colley-Wellesley, 1st Marquess Wellesley	1835
Francis Nathaniel Conyngham, 2nd Marquess Conyngham	1835–9
Henry Paget, Earl of Uxbridge	1839–41
George John West, 5th Earl De La Warr	1841–6
Frederick Spencer, 4th Earl Spencer	1846–8
John Campbell, 2nd Marquess of Breadalbane	1848–52
Brownlow Cecil, 2nd Marquess of Exeter	1852
Breadalbane returned to office	1853–8
De La Warr returned to office	1858–9
John Robert Townshend, 3rd Viscount Sydney	1859–66
Orlando George Charles Bridgeman, 3rd Earl of Bradford	1866–8
Sydney returned to office	1868–74
Francis Hugh George Seymour, 5th Marquess of Hertford	1874–9
William Henry Edgecumbe, 4th Earl of Mount Edgecumbe	1879–80
Valentine Augustus Browne, 4th Earl of Kenmare	1880–5
Edward Bootle-Wilbraham, 1st Earl of Lathom	1885–6
Kenmare returned to office	1886
Lathom returned to office	1886–92
Charles Robert Carrington, 3rd Baron Carrington	1892–5
Lathom returned to office	1895–8
John Adrian Louis Hope, 7th Earl of Hopetoun	1898–1900
Edward Hyde Villiers, 9th Earl of Clarendon	1900–5

Examiners of Plays (1824–1912)

George Colman (1762–1836)	Jan. 1824–Oct. 1836
Charles Kemble (1775–1854)	Oct. 1836–Feb. 1840
John Mitchell Kemble (1807–57)	Feb. 1840–Mar. 1857

APPENDIX A

William Bodham Donne (1807—82) (also Acting
    Examiner Aug. 1849—Feb. 1856)   Mar. 1857—Aug. 1874
Edward Frederick Smyth Pigott (1824—95)   Aug. 1874—Feb. 1895
George Alexander Redford 184 [7?]—1916   Mar. 1895—Jan. 1912

*Compiled from the following sources: James E. Doyle, *The Official Baronage of England*, 3 vols. (London, 1889); G[eorge] E[dward] C[okayne], *The Complete Peerage*, ed. Vicary Gibbs *et al.*, 13 vols. in 14 (London, 1910—59); *Lodge's Peerage, Baronetage, Knightage & Companionage of the British Empire for 1908*, ed. Sir Arthur E. Vicars, 77th edn, rev. and enlarged (London [1908]); and *DNB*. The appointments for the Examiners of Plays are to be found, respectively, in L.C. 3:70, fol. 176; L.C. 3:71, fol. 150; L.C. 5:237, fol. 138; L.C. 5:238, fol. 228; and L.C. 5:240, fol.153.

APPENDIX B

Fees received for licensing plays, 1840–50. Amounts are in pounds and shillings.

	1840	1841	1842	1843	1844	1845	1846	1847	1848	1849	1850
January	£11	£3	£12	£16.10	£32.5	£52	£23	£30	£37	£34	£29
February	14	8	19	17	31.5	29.5	34	33	14	20	32
March	13	4	12	26	37	45	28	43	27	26	35
April	9	28	24	19.10	24	29	48.5	35.10	44	34	37
May	9	5	28	13.15	31.5	43	36	31	36	22	20.5
June	20	15	17	6	21	53	21	18	38	11	22.5
July	9	14	5	12	12	17	15	11	14	–	13
August	4	10	12	5	22	24.5	19	11	13	–	10.5
September	14	10	12	15	26	27	23	15	13	12	26
October	10	11	16	34.15	28	31	31	24	18	29	27
November	13	10	10	38	41	28	19	30	21	27	24.5
December	7	10	25	52	36	50	35.5	47.5	45	39	23
Total £	133	128	192	255.10s	341.15s	428.10s	332.10s	328.15s	320	[254]	[299]

Note: From August 1849 onwards the figures are Donne's; Kemble had gone abroad by then.
Source: The Fee Book belonging to John Mitchell Kemble (L.C. 7 : 19)

APPENDIX C

The Lord Chamberlain's Form of Licence for Plays

The following is reproduced from a play licence granted in 1901 (L.C. 1:752). A similar form was in use for much of the nineteenth century, though the instructions on the reverse date from the 1870s. See also the licence form prefacing the Lord Chamberlain's Day Book, vol. VII (Add. MS. 53,708).

It having been represented to Me by the Examiner of All Theatrical Entertainments that a [Manuscript entitled]

does not in its general tendency contain any thing immoral or otherwise improper for the Stage I The Lord Chamberlain of His Majesty's Household do by virtue of my Office and in pursuance of the Act of Parliament in that case provided Allow the Performance of the said [Manuscript] at your [Theatre] with the exception of all Words and Passages which are specified by the Examiner in the endorsement of this License and without any further variations whatsoever

Given under my hand

this day of

Lord Chamberlain

The Manager of the

On the reverse of the form there is space for recording any censored passages or special instructions, together with the following printed memorandum:

The particular attention of the Management is called to the following Regulations, which refer to all Stage Plays licensed by the Lord Chamberlain. The strict observance of these Regulations is to be considered as the condition upon which the License is signed.

Notice of the change of title of a piece to be given to the Examiner of Plays.

No profanity or impropriety of language to be permitted on the Stage.

No indecency of dress, dance, or gesture to be permitted on the Stage.

No offensive personalities or representations of living persons to be permitted on the Stage, nor anything calculated to produce riot or breach of the peace.

NOTES

Introduction

1 Frank Fowell and Frank Palmer, *Censorship in England* (London, 1913), and Richard Findlater, *Banned! A Review of Theatrical Censorship in Britain* (London, 1967).

2 Add. MSS. 42,856—43,038 (plays submitted 1824—51); and 52,929—53,701 (plays submitted 1852—99).

3 The Public Record Office collection of nineteenth-century theatrical MSS. is described in full in the bibliography.

4 *British Museum. Catalogue of Additions to the Manuscripts. Plays Submitted to the Lord Chamberlain 1824—1851: Additional Manuscripts 42865—43038* (London, 1964).

5 Add. MSS. 53,702—8 comprise seven volumes covering the period from 1824 to 1903. Details of plays licensed are recorded under titles in alphabetical order year by year.

6 Samuel Johnson, 'Prologue Spoken by Mr Garrick at the Opening of the Theatre in Drury-Lane, 1747'.

1 Licensing and the law

1 1832 *Report*, q. 955.

2 See Virginia Crocheron Gildersleeve, *Government Regulation of the Elizabethan Drama* (New York, 1908), esp. pp. 4—88; and, in summary, E. K. Chambers, *The Elizabethan Stage* (Oxford, 1923), I, 269—307.

3 William Beeston of Drury Lane was unlucky enough to be committed to the Marshalsea prison in 1640 for allowing performance of an unlicensed play at his theatre (Gerald Eades Bentley, *The Jacobean and Caroline Stage*, I, Oxford, 1941, pp. 332—4). See also *The Dramatic Records of Sir Henry Herbert: Master of the Revels, 1623—1673*, ed. Joseph Quincy Adams (New York, 1917).

4 Preface to *The Satires of Decimus Junius Juvenalis* in *The Poems of John Dryden*, ed. James Kinsley (Oxford, 1958), II, 606. Cf. Nicoll, II, 279—84 for summary of early eighteenth-century documents on play licensing.

5 See P. J. Crean, 'The Stage Licensing Act of 1737', *Modern Philology*, XXXV (1938), 239—55.

6 *The Statutes at Large*, ed. Danby Pickering, XVII (Cambridge, 1765), 141. The penalty for infringement was £50 and annulment of the theatre's licence, if any.

7 [Elizabeth] Inchbald (ed.), *The British Theatre* (London, 1808), XII,

remarks in her preface to *Venice Preserv'd* that it was acted almost every year 'except when an order from the Lord Chamberlain forbids its representation lest some of the speeches of Pierre should be applied, by the ignorant part of the audience, to certain men, or assemblies, in the English state'. *King Lear* was prohibited during the period of George III's insanity (L. W. Conolly, *The Censorship of English Drama 1737–1824*, San Marino, Calif., 1976, p. 126).

8 The topic is treated fully in Watson Nicholson, *The Struggle for a Free Stage in London* (New York, 1966). Cf. also Ernest Bradlee Watson, *Sheridan to Robertson: A Study of the Early Nineteenth-Century London Stage* (Cambridge, Mass., 1926), pp. 20–57.

9 Watson, *Sheridan to Robertson*, p. 27.

10 1832 *Report*, qq. 18, 34, 36.

11 *Statutes at Large*, ed. Pickering, XVII, 142. The Lord Chamberlain was also empowered to licence theatres 'in such places where his Majesty, his heirs or successors, shall in their royal persons reside, and during such residence only'. By implication, the licensing of theatres elsewhere was prohibited. But see below, n. 13.

12 The licensing arrangements of these theatres are usefully summarised in Michael R. Booth, *et al.*, *The Revels History of Drama in English (Volume VI 1750–1880)* (London, 1975), pp. 40–3. See also below, p. 20.

13 Nicholson, *The Struggle for a Free Stage*, pp. 125–6. These Acts attempted to regularise the status of theatres like Sadler's Wells, which had grown up contrary to the interpretation of the 1737 Act. Further legislation was needed in 1788 (28 Geo. III. c. 30) to permit the licensing of provincial theatres by local magistrates. See Sybil Rosenfeld, *Strolling Players & Drama in the Provinces 1660–1765* (Cambridge, 1939), pp. 2, 5–9; and Cecil Price, *Theatre in the Age of Garrick* (Oxford, 1973), pp. 175–6, for evidence of the continuity of theatrical activity in the provinces in defiance of the law.

14 1832 *Report*, q. 37. A similar point was made about the Olympic (*ibid.*, q. 38), but Mash explained that this theatre lay 'within the liberty of Westminster'.

15 Nicoll, IV, 137, quotes from an exchange of letters on the topic in 1824 between the Duke of Montrose and Colman (in Add. MS. 42,865, fols. 431–45).

16 Joseph Donohue, 'Burletta and the early nineteenth century theatre', *Nineteenth Century Theatre Research*, I (1973), 35, 41. Cf. discussion of the form in Donohue's *Theatre in the Age of Kean* (Oxford, 1975), pp. 46–50.

17 1832 *Report*, q. 384. On the other hand, burlettas were subject to censorship if submitted for examination. In the Adelphi Theatre's *The Opening Night! A Personal Prelude; or, Piece and no Piece* (1825), Colman scored out in red ink the following reference to the patent controversy, where Littlevalue, a theatrical critic, having tried unsuccessfully to obtain a private box for somewhat dubious purposes at a minor theatre in return for good press notices, exclaims angrily: 'Hum! I can make nothing of you I see — so I shall leave you — You'll soon be ruin'd and then perhaps I may be called on — There's a great deal too many Theatres — You should all be put down. We only want the Royals — I've fifty thousand in one of them' (Add. MS. 42,873, fol. 104).

18 1832 *Report*, q. 2982. Cf. Colman's note (29 Oct. 1824) on [J. T. G. Rod-well's] *The Young Widow; or, the Lesson for Lovers*, a one-act burletta for the Adelphi: 'This piece contains but One Song, & a Duet, with a few mar-ginal Directions for "Musick" to be played, in the Melodramatical way, at intervals of the Dialogue; – if this be a *Burletta*, I have nothing to say against it's [sic] representation, after having expunged some improper expressions' (Add. MS. 42,869, fol. 25).

19 1832 *Report*, qq. 1631–3. Christopher Murray, *Robert William Elliston: Manager* (London, 1975), p. 133, remarks that Jerrold's tragedy was 'the first such full-length play to be staged at a minor theatre'.

20 See below, pp. 40–1, 42.

21 Donohue, 'Burletta and the early nineteenth century theatre', p. 30. Use of the term did not die with the Theatre Act of 1843. The Day Books record occasional licensing of burlettas as late as 1860 (cf. *No. 49*, for St James's Theatre, 29 Feb.).

22 For the background to the 1832 Committee, see Dewey Ganzel, 'Patent wrongs and patent theatres: drama and the law in the early nineteenth century', *PMLA*, LXXVI (1961), 384–96. For the last years of the mono-poly, see Nicholson, *The Struggle for a Free Stage*, pp. 389–420. (The one immediate result of the deliberations of the 1832 Committee was the passing of a bill on dramatic copyright in 1833, which did much to im-prove the status of playwrights.)

23 Conolly, *The Censorship of English Drama*, pp. 17–18.

24 The full Act is printed in *The Statutes of the United Kingdom of Great Britain and Ireland* (London, 1843), pp. 428–34.

25 The Lord Chamberlain's jurisdiction as theatre licenser was enlarged to include 'all theatres (not being Patent Theatres) within the Parliamentary Boundaries of the Cities of *London* and *Westminster*, and of the Boroughs of *Finsbury*, and *Marylebone*, the *Tower Hamlets*, *Lambeth*, and *Southwark*'. His powers of censorship, however, were explicitly stated to apply to all plays 'intended to be produced for hire at any Theatre in *Great Britain*'. On the difficulties of maintaining his authority as censor outside London, see below, pp. 15–6, 83–4, 176 n.5.

26 See Conolly, *The Censorship of English Drama*, p. 4. Colman's widow, at the suggestion of the Examiner's executor, was paid £100 by the Lord Chamberlain's Office for making over to it all the MSS. in her possession (L.C. 1:19, letters 1593–4, 19, 28 Nov. 1836).

27 1832 *Report*, qq. 976, 982.

28 *Ibid.*, p. 4. But William Donne still believed the appointment was for life (1866 *Report*, q. 2042). Four of the seven nineteenth-century Examiners (Larpent, Colman, John Kemble, and Pigott) died in office.

29 [John G. Lockhart], *Theodore Hook: A Sketch*, 3rd edn (London, 1852), p. 87.

30 Conolly, *The Censorship of English Drama*, p. 30.

31 1832 *Report*, q. 883. Colman was interrogated at length on the subject (*ibid.*, qq. 869–80, 890–1, and 910–30). He disclosed (q. 981) that his income from fees in 1830 was 222 guineas.

32 *Ibid.*, qq. 350, 707–707*, 877, 920, and appendix 11, p. 248.

33 *Report of the Commissioners appointed to inquire into the Fees, Gratuities,*

Requisites, and Emoluments of the Several Public Officers on the Civil List Establishment, in *British Sessional Papers* (1837), XXXIV, pt. 1, p. 201.

34 L.C. 1:45, fol. 163, 13 Jan. 1837.

35 Catharine B. Johnson (ed.), *William Bodham Donne and his Friends* (London, 1905), p. 225.

36 Alfred Bunn, *The Stage: Both Before and Behind the Curtain, From Observations Taken on the Spot'* (London, 1840), II, 195. See also Richard Brinsley Peake, *Memoirs of the Colman Family* (London, [1841]), II, 439.

37 1853 *Report,* q. 8150.

38 1866 *Report,* q. 2253.

39 1832 *Report,* q. 865. See also below, pp. 23—4.

40 Letter to J. E. Reade (1 Sept. 1867) in private collection of Mary Barham Johnson. By 1870 Donne was able to comment on the great improvements in standards: 'When I began acting as the Devil's archdeacon — for are not Theatres *his* ideas of a Church — in 1857, 20 Theatres then occupied me far more time, and required besides curses, far more ink and paper than 35 do now' (Johnson, ed., *William Bodham Donne,* p. 276).

41 In 1894, Edward Pigott asked to be excused because of ill-health and his feeling of superfluousness (L.C. 1:617, 23 Aug. 1894).

42 MSS. reports for 1883—4, 1887, 1894, and 1900 in L.C. 1:418, 435, 490, 617, and 731 respectively. Cf. figures quoted by Frank Fowell and Frank Palmer, *Censorship in England* (London, 1913), p. 353.

43 1866 *Report,* q. 2068.

44 1832 *Report,* q. 400.

45 See L.C. 7:7, 4 Dec. 1846. Records were kept noting omissions on the part of managers in sending the playbills. See also below, p. 174n 20.

46 Series of letters L.C. 1:47, fol. 169, 16 Feb. 1843; L.C. 1:25, letter 2261, 16 Feb.; L.C. 1:47, fol. 172, 21 Feb. See also *The Diaries of William Charles Macready, 1833—1851,* ed. William Toynbee (London, 1912), II, 196.

47 L.C. 1:113, 23 June 1862; 9 Oct. 1862.

48 L.C. 1:263, 3 Apr. 1872. The play (an adaptation of Trollope's novel *Ralph the Heir*) was subsequently licensed; but there was much press criticism of its alleged indecency and Charles Reade successfully sued the *Morning Post* for libel (see John Hollingshead, *Gaiety Chronicles,* London, 1898, pp. 211—16).

The Hon. Spencer Brabazon Ponsonby-Fane (1824—1915) was Comptroller of the Lord Chamberlain's Office from 1857 to 1901. (He assumed the additional surname of Fane by royal licence in 1875; but for the sake of clarity I refer to him throughout as Spencer Ponsonby.)

49 See below, p. 176 n.45.

50 The printed circular (n.d.) is in L.C. 1:546.

51 In L.C. 1:582. The play concerned was entitled *Deeming; or, Doomed at Last.* Pigott gleaned his initial information from the *Era* (11 June 1892).

52 L.C. 1:232, 26 Mar. 1870.

53 There is a small collection of letters (mostly 1875—9) testifying to the esteem in which E. F. S. Pigott was held by the theatre managers in the Henry E. Huntington Library, San Marino, California.

54 1832 *Report,* q. 868.

2 The censors

1 Frank Fowell and Frank Palmer, *Censorship in England* (London, 1913),
p. 184, refuse to discuss personalities after Colman on the grounds that
they are 'less interesting'. Richard Findlater, *Banned! A Review of Theatrical
Censorship in Britain* (London, 1967), ignores the Kembles altogether and
deduces from selective evidence that William Donne was little short of
an incompetent idiot (pp. 65—7).

2 See appendix A for a detailed list (with dates) of all the holders of the
office between 1821 and 1905.

3 James Graham, 3rd Duke (1775—1836), an ambitious politician who rose
to great favour under George III. N. W. Wraxall, *The Historical and
Posthumous Memoirs of Sir Nathaniel William Wraxall 1772—1784*, ed.
Henry B. Wheatley (London, 1884), III, 385, comments that, while
Montrose 'possessed no distinguished talents, he displayed various
qualities calculated to compensate for the want of great ability; particularly the prudence, sagacity, and attention to his own interests so
characteristic of the Caledonian people'. For biographical information
on all nineteenth-century Lord Chamberlains I have relied on G [eorge]
E [dward] C [okayne], *The Complete Peerage*, ed. Vicary Gibbs *et al.*, (13
vols. in 14, London, 1910—59) and, where appropriate, *DNB*.

4 Richard Brinsley Peake, *Memoirs of the Colman Family* (London, [1841]),
II, 447—9.

5 *1832 Report*, qq. 898—9.

6 Peake, *Memoirs*, II, 444.

7 William George Spencer Cavendish, 6th Duke (1790—1858). Aside from
his work as Lord Chamberlain, he is probably best remembered for the
extensive alterations and additions (including a splendid private theatre)
carried out at the family seat, Chatsworth House, Derbyshire.

8 Alfred Bunn, *The Stage: Both Before and Behind the Curtain, From 'Observations Taken on the Spot'* (London, 1840), I, 51.

9 Peake, *Memoirs*, II, 447.

10 Performed 16 May 1851. John Forster, *The Life of Charles Dickens*, ed. A. J.
Hoppé (London, 1969), II, 69, commented that the episode was 'one of the
many instances that adorned a life which alone perhaps in England was
genuinely and completely that of the Grand Seigneur. Well-read and very
accomplished, he had the pleasing manners which proceed from a kind
nature; splendid in his mode of living beyond any other English noble,
his magnificence, by the ease and elegance that accompanied it, was
relieved from all offence of ostentation.'

11 Francis Nathaniel Conyngham, 2nd Marquess (1797—1876).

12 Bunn, *The Stage*, I, 44.

13 Henry Paget, Earl of Uxbridge (later 2nd Marquess of Anglesey) (1797—
1869).

14 *The Diaries of William Charles Macready, 1833—1851*, ed. William Toynbee
(London, 1912), II, 3—4. When Uxbridge removed the restriction on the
opening of the patent houses on Wednesdays and Fridays in Lent,
Macready remarked sourly: 'This *boon* from persons in brief authority is
something like the gifts of Ajax and Hector' (*ibid.*, II, 44—5).

15 *The Croker Papers. The Correspondence and Diaries of the late Right Honourable John Wilson Croker, L.L.D., F.R.S., Secretary to the Admiralty. From 1809 to 1830.* ed. Louis J. Jennings, 2nd edn (London, 1885), I, 173.

16 See Roger Fulford, *The Prince Consort* (London, 1949), pp. 60—1, 72.

17 See below, p. 47.

18 John Campbell, 2nd Marquess (1796—1862).

19 1892 *Report*, q. 4982.

20 John Robert Townshend, 3rd Viscount (1805—90). Created Earl Sydney of Scadbury on his retirement as Lord Chamberlain (27 Feb. 1874).

21 Letter dated 7 July 1866 in private collection of Miss Mary Barham Johnson.

22 Catharine B. Johnson (ed.), *William Bodham Donne and his Friends* (London, 1905), p. 295.

23 L.C. 1 : 507, to Spencer Ponsonby, 2 July 1888.

24 *Areopagitica,* in *Complete Prose Works of John Milton,* II, ed. Ernest Sirluck (New Haven and London, 1959), p. 530. The first separate republication of this work was in 1738, with a preface by James Thomson, when the the Stage Licensing Act provoked fears that the renewal of press censorship was imminent.

25 The standard biography is Jeremy F. Bagster-Collins, *George Colman the Younger, 1762—1836* (New York, 1946). See chapters 12 and 13. Cf. also *DNB* and Peake's *Memoirs,* II, 429—50, the record of a conversation with his friend S. J. Arnold about Colman's work as Examiner.

26 1832 *Report*, q. 860.

27 Findlater, *Theatrical Censorship,* p. 58. Cf. Fowell and Palmer, *Censorship in England*, pp. 164—83.

28 1832 *Report*, qq. 852, 859, 903—4.

29 Peake, *Memoirs*, II, 436.

30 *Ibid.,* II, 405.

31 *Byron: A Self-Portrait, Letters and Diaries 1798 to 1824,* ed. Peter Quennell (London, 1950), II, 647—8.

32 Theodore Hook, 'Recollections of the late George Colman', *Bentley's Miscellany,* I (1837), 11. This article is a spirited defence of Colman's record as Examiner.

33 *Diaries,* ed. Toynbee, I, 353. Christopher North [John Wilson], in a vitriolic attack on Colman's *Random Records,* described him as a 'superannuated buffoon' (*Blackwood's Magazine,* XXVIII, 1830, p. 363).

34 *Diaries,* ed. Toynbee, I, 353.

35 Quoted in Bagster-Collins, *George Colman,* p. 301n. (Charles attended the Jesuit College at Douai.) For more favourable reactions to the appointment, see Jane Williamson, *Charles Kemble, Man of the Theatre* (Lincoln, Nebr., 1970), p. 219. This, the only modern biography of Kemble, has virtually nothing to say of his career as Examiner of Plays.

36 Bunn, *The Stage*, II, 151.

37 Until the death of his brother John Philip Kemble, Charles's career as an actor suffered by comparison. But during the late 1820s and 30s he received acclaim for his interpretations of Shakespearean roles, for instance, Faulconbridge, Mercutio, and Hamlet, the last of which William Bodham Donne believed was his 'highest achievement as an actor' (Donne,

Essays on the Drama, London, 1858, p. 175). Kemble's last years were devoted to a series of public readings from Shakespeare.

38 Percy Fitzgerald, *The Kembles. An Account of the Kemble Family, including the Lives of Mrs Siddons, and her brother, John Philip Kemble* (London, [1871?]), II, 389. See also 1866 *Report*, qq. 2224, 2226.

39 1866 *Report*, q. 2227.

40 Letters dated 17 Aug. and 26 Sept. 1837 in private collection of Miss Mary Barham Johnson.

41 L.C. 1:22, fol. 1958, 16 Jan. 1840.

42 *Diaries*, ed. Toynbee, II, 37.

43 There is no full-length biography of Kemble. But see [William Bodham Donne], 'John Mitchell Kemble', *Fraser's Magazine*, LV (1857), 612—18, and Frances M. Brookfield, *The Cambridge 'Apostles'* (London, 1906), pp. 159—87.

44 On Kemble's editorship (1836—44), which shifted the emphasis of the magazine to a more contemporary literary interest, see Walter E. Houghton (ed.), *The Wellesley Index to Victorian Periodicals 1824—1900*, III (Toronto, 1979), 67—75. (William Donne was a frequent contributor to the *Review*.)

45 Fragment dated 13 June 1849 in private collection of Miss Mary Barham Johnson.

46 Letter of 5 Aug. 1849, *ibid*.

47 Letter of 26 Sept. 1849, *ibid*.

48 Letter of 29 Apr. 1850, *ibid*.

49 L.C. 1:52, fols. 12—13, 11 Dec. 1851. It was rumoured that Kemble was about to be sacked. Fitzgerald wrote to Donne (1 Jan. 1852): 'I hear ... that, unless Kemble returns to his Duties, he will probably be dispossessed of his place; — and you *may* have an offer of it.' He urged Donne to accept if given the opportunity: 'If *any one* ever cd. suppose that you had been securing to yrself K's nest while pretending to keep it warm for him, you have oceans of evidence to the Contrary: beside that of all other friends, you have Kemble's own family: — and, as I believe, you would have *his own*: which wd. certainly settle the question' (Neilson Campbell Hannay, ed., *A Fitzgerald Friendship, Being Hitherto Unpublished Letters from Edward Fitzgerald to William Bodham Donne*, London, 1932, p. 45).

50 L.C. 1:51, 23 Mar. 1857.

51 There is no full-length biography of Donne. But see Johnson (ed.), *William Bodham Donne*, for a large selection of his correspondence; *DNB* (mistaken in the assertion that Donne remained Examiner until his death); and references in *Diary, Reminiscences, and Correspondence of Henry Crabb Robinson, Barrister-at-Law, F.S.A.*, sel. and ed. Thomas Sadler, 2nd edn (London, 1869), III, *passim*.

52 Writing to Richard Trench in June 1837, Donne declared: 'I think much more respectfully of the XXXIX than when I absconded — and would sign them even if they were forty' (Johnson, ed., *William Bodham Donne*, p. 33).

53 [Hallam Tennyson], *Alfred Lord Tennyson. A Memoir. By his Son* (London, 1897), I, 500—1.

54 See list of Donne's articles in Johnson (ed.), *William Bodham Donne*, pp. 340—3, now supplemented by Houghton (ed.), *The Wellesley Index*.

55 Johnson (ed.), *William Bodham Donne*, p. 316.
56 Donne, *Essays*, p. 142.
57 1866 *Report*, qq. 2456–9.
58 Donne, *Essays*, p. 120.
59 James F. Stottlar, 'A Victorian stage censor: the theory and practice of William Bodham Donne', *Victorian Studies*, XIII (Mar. 1970), 282. Donne also gave a series of lectures at the Royal Institution in Jan. and Feb. 1872 (see *The Letters of Edward Fitzgerald to Fanny Kemble 1871–1883*, ed. William Aldis Wright, 2nd edn, London, 1902, p. 10n).
60 Johnson (ed.), *William Bodham Donne*, p. 233. The burden of this 'most unlooked-for responsibility and care' was eased by Donne's engagement of George Ellis (Charles Kean's former acting manager) to supervise the proceedings. See also Charles H. Shattuck, 'A Victorian stage manager: George Cressall Ellis', *Theatre Notebook*, XXII (1968), 108. Programmes in the Enthoven Collection, Victoria and Albert Museum, identify Ellis as 'Stage Manager' for the Christmas theatricals.
61 Johnson (ed.), *William Bodham Donne*, p. 298. There was also an appreciative letter from the Queen and an unexpectedly handsome pension of £350 per annum (*ibid.*, p. 299).
62 Unless otherwise indicated, the following sketch of Pigott's career up to 1874 relies on Frederick Boase, *Modern English Biography* (London, 1965 [reprint of 1892–1921 edn.]), II, 1531. There is also a brief biography in *The Times* (1 Aug. 1874). Pigott is not entered in *DNB*.
63 William Archer, 'George Henry Lewes and the stage', *Fortnightly Review* N.S., LIX (1896), 222. E. E. Kellett, 'The press', in *Early Victorian England*, ed. G. M. Young (Oxford, 1934), II, 58, refers to Pigott as founder of the *Leader*.
64 See Gordon S. Haight (ed.), *The George Eliot Letters* (London and New Haven, 1954–6), IV, 414 n. 2.
65 *Ibid.*, III, 456 n. 9; VI, 219.
66 *The Autobiography and Letters of Mrs O. W. Oliphant*, ed. Mrs Harry Coghill (Edinburgh and London, 1899), pp. 132, 135–6.
67 George Bernard Shaw, *Our Theatres in the Nineties* (London, 1932), I, 49.
68 Clement Scott, *The Drama of Yesterday & Today* (London, 1899), II, 480. Other temperate views appear in *The Theatre*, N.S. (Apr. 1895), pp. 193–6 and (curiously enough) in William Archer, *The Theatrical 'World' of 1895* (London, 1896), pp. 66–73, who commented that, while Pigott lived in 'difficult times' and 'troubles thickened around him as the years went on ... he came through it all with a certain mute dignity which one could not but respect'.
69 1892 *Report*, q. 5183. (From a statement originally written in 1883.)
70 *Ibid.*, q. 5228.
71 L.C. 1:638, Redford to Lord Chamberlain's Office, 28 Feb. 1895; 1 Mar. 1895.
72 L.C. 5:242. (This whole volume is devoted entirely to matters relating to the appointment of Pigott's successor.)
73 *Who Was Who 1916–1928*, 2nd edn (London, 1947).
74 See Hansard, *Parliamentary Debates*, 4th ser., LXXXIII (1900), 738–9.
75 Asked to explain, Redford replied: 'Simply bringing to bear an official

point of view and keeping up a standard. It is really impossible to define what the principle may be. There are no principles that can be defined. I follow precedent. I was under Mr Pigott for a great many years − that is to say, as a personal friend − and I obtained an insight into the duties then' (1909 *Report*, q. 194).

76 John Palmer, *The Censor and the Theatres* (London, 1912), p. 73. Ironically, on his resignation from the Examinership of Plays in 1912, Redford became chief examiner on the newly created British Board of Film Censors.

3 Political drama and the establishment

1 *The Dramatic Records of Sir Henry Herbert: Master of the Revels, 1623−1673*, ed. Joseph Quincy Adams (New York, 1917), p. 19.

2 For a detailed treatment of this subject, see L. W. Conolly, *The Censorship of English Drama 1737−1824* (San Marino, Calif., 1976), pp. 83−112, 126−36.

3 1832 *Report*, q. 968.

4 See below, p. 45.

5 [Robert Southey], 'State of the French drama', *Quarterly Review*, LI (1834), 212. In support of his point Southey cited Victor Hugo's *Le Roi s'amuse* (afterwards prohibited for a time in France), in which a line was taken to refer to the supposed bastardy of Louis *Egalité* (executed 1783), father of Louis Philippe: 'that line, it is confessed, *branded as with a red-hot iron,* the domestic character of a whole family, and might have thrown a great city, perhaps a whole nation, into bloody conflict!'

6 1832 *Report*, q. 393. Cf. also Thomas Morton's evidence (*ibid.,* q. 4413).

7 *Ibid.,* q. 967.

8 [John Genest], *Some Account of the English Stage, from the Restoration in 1660 to 1830* (Bath, 1832), X, 244.

9 Martin Archer Shee, *Alasco: A Tragedy in Five Acts ... Excluded from the Stage, by the Authority of the Lord Chamberlain* (London, 1824), p. lii. See also Martin Archer Shee, *The Life of Sir Martin Archer Shee ... By his Son* (London, 1860), I, 365−95.

10 Shee, *Alasco*, pp. 3−4; 27−8; 76.

11 Richard Brinsley Peake, *Memoirs of the Colman Family* (London, [1841]), II, 400. (Peake erroneously attributes authorship of *Alasco* to Richard Sheil.)

12 T. Tickler [William Maginn], 'Pike, prose, and poetry', *Blackwood's Magazine*, XV (1824), 595.

13 Shee, *Alasco*, p. xviii.

14 Richard M. Fletcher, *English Romantic Drama 1795−1843: A Critical History* (New York, 1966), p. 145.

15 See Conolly, *Censorship of English Drama*, pp. 109−10.

16 *The Letters of Mary Russell Mitford*, sel. with introd. by R. Brimley Johnson (London, 1925), p. 178. The original preface to the play was reprinted in *The Dramatic Works of M. R. Mitford* (London, 1854) because, as Miss Mitford explained, it gave 'a curious view of a state of things now happily passed away' (*Dramatic Works*, I, xxx).

17 Add. MS. 42, 873, fol. 408, Colman to Montrose, 29 Sept. 1825. Before

dispatch of the MS. to the Lord Chamberlain, Colman copied on the verso of fol. 480 an extract from *Biographia Dramatica* (1812) regarding W. Havard's *King Charles the 1st* (1737), performed at the theatre in Lincoln's Inn Fields, part of which reads: '"Lord Chesterfield, in his Speech on the Licensing Act (of which His Lordship was a violent opponent) mentioning this Play, says 'the catastrophe was too recent, too melancholy, & of too solemn a nature to be heard of anywhere but in a pulpit'."' Colman commented: 'It is to be remembered that the above Play was acted before The Lord Chamberlain's control over Drama was established by Act of Parliament.'

18 Add. MS. 42,873, fols. 410, 411.

19 *Ibid.*, fol. 413.

20 See Edward Hyde, *The History of the Rebellion and Civil War in England by Edward Earl of Clarendon*, new edn. (London, 1843), II, 741—2.

21 Mitford, *Dramatic Works*, I, 244. In its review of the production at the Victoria (Coburg) Theatre, *The Times* (3 July 1834) commented that the play contained 'nothing ... to offend the feelings of the most strenuous supporter of the monarchical principle'.

22 1832 *Report*, q. 972.

23 Add. MS. 42, 875, fol. 82.

24 Add. MS. 42,894, fols. 350, 355. The excisions were noted in a separate reminder Colman sent to the manager of Drury Lane, 17 Feb. 1829 (Folger MS. Y. d. 483 [14]).

25 1832 *Report*, q. 3945. He reminded the Committee (*ibid.*, q. 3946) of the case of James Kenney's *Masaniello* (from Scribe's *La Muette de Portici*) which, following a request from William IV in 1830 for a command performance, occasioned the printing of handbills urging the masses to assemble in Drury Lane Theatre 'to teach [the King], through the story of Massaniello [sic] the Fisherman, the danger to his throne if he disobeyed the wish of his people, and the King was advised to change the play in consequence of that'.

26 See preface in Alfred Bunn, *The Minister and the Mercer* (London, 1834).

27 Alfred Bunn, *The Stage: Both Before and Behind the Curtain, From 'Observations Taken on the Spot'* (London, 1840), I, 150.

28 See preface to *The Dramatic Works of Sir Edward Lytton Bulwer, Bart., Now First Collected* (London, 1841), p. v. See also Charles H. Shattuck (ed.), *Bulwer and Macready: A Chronicle of the Early Victorian Theatre* (Urbana, Ill., 1958), p. 7, who comments that Bulwer Lytton, encouraged by the models of Victor Hugo and the elder Dumas, began 'to regard the theatre as available for the infusion of republican ideas'.

29 *The Diaries of William Charles Macready, 1833—1851*, ed. William Toynbee (London, 1912), I, 445. Bulwer Lytton's authorship was kept secret until 24 Feb., three nights after Macready's speech.

30 George Rowell, *The Victorian Theatre 1792—1914: A Survey*, 2nd edn (Cambridge, 1978), p. 51. In the preface to *The Lady of Lyons* (*Dramatic Works*, pp. 187—8) Bulwer Lytton described Claude Melnotte his hero as 'a type of that restless, brilliant, and evanescent generation that sprung up from the ashes of the terrible [French] Revolution' and asserted how difficult it was to avoid all political allusions to the present times, since

there 'is scarcely a single play, the scene of which is laid in Rome, in Greece, in Switzerland, wherein political allusions and political declamations are not carefully elaborated as the most striking and telling parts of the performance'.

31 *Diaries*, ed. Toynbee, II, 41–2. On the general circumstances of the production, see Alan S. Downer, *The Eminent Tragedian: William Charles Macready* (Cambridge, Mass., 1966), pp. 195–6.

32 *Diaries*, ed. Toynbee, II, 42.

33 Add. MS. 42, 954, fol. 37. The cut begins at 'We must search out ...'

34 For example: 'To save a nation we must not be nice / About the means ...' (fol. 39), Darnley's jaundiced reference to 'the vision of the matrimonial crown', the queen's reminder to him that he is king, and her husband's rejoinder: 'Yes, yes; you call me king / As slaves are called by mighty Caesar's name / To mark their wretchedness more bitterly. / I thank you for the boon' (fol. 43, verso). See also Sally Vernon, '*Mary Stuart*, Queen Victoria, and the censor', *Nineteenth Century Theatre Research*, VI (1978), 37–8.

35 James Haynes, *Mary Stuart: An Historical Tragedy, Now Performing at the Theatre Royal, Drury Lane*, 3rd edn (London, 1840), p. 10. This speech is heavily obliterated in the MS. (fol. 31).

36 Cf. contemporary satire (quoted in Roger Fulford, *The Prince Consort*, London, 1949, pp. 45–6): 'He [Albert] comes the bride-groom of Victoria's choice, / The nominee of Lehzen's vulgar voice; / He comes to take "for better or worse" / England's fat Queen and England's fatter purse.'

37 See Vernon, '*Mary Stuart*, Queen Victoria, and the censor', p. 39.

38 Quoted in William Archer, 'The censorship of the stage', in *About the Theatre. Essays and Studies* (London, 1886), p. 122.

39 First performed 1 May 1837 at Covent Garden. One reviewer objected very strongly to the degrading treatment of Charles in the play and declared that if public taste did not 'execute justice on Mr Browning for this atrocious caricature, [then] Mr Charles Kemble, as a good and loyal censor, is really bound to interfere, and rescue royalty from such misrepresentation' ([Herman Merivale], 'Browning's "Strafford; a Tragedy"', *Edinburgh Review*, LXV, 1837, p. 143).

40 [W. J. Fox], 'Bulwer's tragedies', *Westminster Review*, LIII (1837), 270.

41 [Emma Robinson], *Richelieu in Love; or, The Youth of Charles I. An historical comedy. In five acts. As accepted at the Theatre Royal, Haymarket, and prohibited by the authority of the Lord Chamberlain. With a preface explanatory* (London, 1844), pp. xi-xii.

42 [Emma Robinson], *The Prohibited Comedy. Richelieu in Love; or, The Youth of Charles I. An historical comedy. In Three acts. By the Author of 'Whitefriars' &c. As Performed at the Theatre Royal, Haymarket, October 30th, 1852* (London, 1852). The licensed text is in Add. MS. 43,026, fols. 168–278.

43 Add. MSS. 42,972, fols. 608–32 (refusal noted on fol. 608); and 42,977, fols. 636–91 (entered in Kemble's fee book on 30 Aug. 1844 with a note of the return of licensing fee, 5 Sept.).

44 *All the Year Round*, N.S., XII (1874), 392. The writer asserted that the ban followed the precedent established by John Larpent, who 'regarded it as his chief duty to protect the court against all possibility of attack from the

stage', clinging to 'the old superstition that the British drama had only a right to exist as the pastime of royalty'.

45 L.C. 1:58, Donne to Ponsonby, 6 Feb. 1858. There is a note against the entry for the play in the Day Book (24 Feb. 1852): 'Mr Mitchell [of the St James's Theatre] promises never to perform it again – official Letter 2929 March 24 / '52.' The same kind of reasoning lay behind the ban in 1851 on *The Queen and Mortimer the Royal Favourite; or, Evil to him who Evil Thinks* (Add. MS. 43,037, fols. 846–92).

46 L.C. 1:58, 6 Feb. 1858. The play was performed at the Marylebone Theatre 7 Feb. 1858 (Nicoll, V, 747).

47 L.C. 1:84, 26 Oct. 1860.

48 The text is readily available in Michael R. Booth (ed.), *English Plays of the Nineteenth Century: Dramas 1800–1850*, I (Oxford, 1969), 201–33. He comments that the play's 'radical social consciousness is advanced even for socially aware melodrama, and its unrelenting severity and power of serious dramatic expression also place it well ahead of its time' (*ibid.*, p. 204).

49 David Mayer III, *Harlequin in his Element: The English Pantomime, 1806–1836* (Cambridge, Mass., 1969), p. 256. Mayer asserts that such politically allusive scripts were exceptional since Colman struck out 'even minor impertinences ... and no theatre managers were encouraged to discover a permissiveness today which might turn to licence tomorrow' (*ibid.*, p. 239).

50 *The Extravaganzas of J. R. Planché, Esq., (Somerset Herald) 1825–1871*, ed. T. F. Dillon Cook and Stephen Tucker (London, 1879), III, 311. Cf. also *Fortunio and his Seven Gifted Servants* (1843), which includes allusions to 'Tariff beef' and the 'Corn Question' (*ibid.*, II, 204, 205).

51 George Davidge of the Coburg Theatre was questioned about this piece at the 1832 Committee. He explained that it was 'played as it has been for the last 50 years, without the alteration of a single line' and that the advertisement (drafted while he was out of town) had been stopped immediately on his return, following 'a polite communication from Mr Roe, the magistrate of Bow-Street' (1832 *Report*, qq. 1253–4, 1258). At the same inquiry, Davidge disclosed that during the run of George Macfarren's *George III, the Father of his People* (30 Aug. to 9 Oct. 1824) the Coburg 'was visited by the different branches of the Government and they could not see anything obnoxious; but at the next licensing day the magistrates, who held discretionary power, told me that they thought such representations injudicious, if not improper, representing sacred characters and the highest personages in the realm' (*ibid.*, q. 1249). Apart from the King and the Prince of Wales, the spectacle included representations of Charles James Fox, William Wilberforce, and Sheridan (see *The Times*, 31 Aug., 7 Sept. 1824).

52 Add. MS. 42,956, fols. 742–55 and fols. 756–75. Printed in *Duncombe's British Theatre. 1828–1852*, LXII.

53 *Oxberry's Dramatic Biography*, VI (London, 1826), 130–1. Performed (after modification) as *The Guerilla Chief* at the English Opera House, 6 July 1826 (Nicoll, IV, 469).

54 L.C. 1:47, fol. 143, William Martins (Comptroller of the Lord Chamberlain's Office) to Theatre Royal, Liverpool, 18 Oct. 1840.

55 Add. MS. 43,000, fols. 475—529. Pitt's authorship is acknowledged on the title page. (Nicoll has no reference to this play.)

56 Bram Stoker, *Personal Reminiscences of Henry Irving* (London, 1906), II, 133—4.

57 But a magistrate for the county of Middlesex did complain about a production of the latter in 1868, because it contained scenes (set in Ireland during the rebellion) and introduced 'circumstances', together with 'a Song called "The Wearing of the Green", which I take the liberty of submitting for your consideration, as highly improper subjects, for dramatic representation at the present time' (L.C. 1:200, Francis Morley to Lord Chamberlain, 25 Jan. 1868). *Arrah-na-Pogue; or, the Wicklow Wedding* was first performed in England in 1865.

58 The original version is Add. MS. 43,010, fols. 870—8; the revised text Add. MS. 43,012, fols. 102—14. The play was readvertised in *The Times* and elsewhere as *Pas de Fascination; or, Catching a Governor.* Cf. Nicoll, IV, 275.

59 L.C. 7:8, unsigned, undated report. For an account of the disturbances see *The Times* (13 June 1848). Macready, after visiting the theatre to see for himself, observed that he had never witnessed 'anything more offensive, brutal, stupid and disgusting' (*Diaries*, ed. Toynbee, II, 395). He sent a letter of protest to *The Times*, printed on 15 June 1848.

60 Samuel Johnson, *A Dictionary of the English Language in which the Words are Deduced from their Originals*, 8th edn, corr. and rev. (London, 1799).

61 Add. MS. 43,009, fol. 831.

62 *Ibid.*, fol. 831, verso.

63 L.C. 1:49, fol. 66, 8 Mar. 1848. The withdrawal of the play is noted in Kemble's fee book (3 Mar. 1848).

64 Add. MS. 43,009, fol. 878.

65 Add. MS. 43,012, fol. 556.

66 Cf. the suppression of *The Storming of Comorn; or, the Hungarian Patriot* (1851), in which a comic Irish tinker Pat O'Pipkin, replying to a question from his new-found Hungarian girlfriend about his quitting Ireland, remarks: 'How did I find my way? Why ye see I was inclined to *pat . . . riotism* [sic] and as they wouldn't let us kick up a shindy in ould Ireland, I thought I might as well come & lend a hand in countries where they're not so particular' (Add. MS. 43,032, fol. 990). The refusal to licence is noted on fol. 981.

4 The opposition to Newgate drama

1 See Leon Radzinowicz, *A History of English Criminal Law and its Administration from 1750*, I (London, 1948), 166—205.

2 First published 1773. The best nineteenth-century edition (ed. Andrew Knapp and W. Baldwin, 4 vols., London, 1824–6) offers 'interesting memoirs of the most notorious characters who have been convicted of outrages on the laws of England since the commencement of the eighteenth century, with . . . last exclamations of sufferers'.

3 John Thurmond, *Harlequin Jack Sheppard*; and *The Prison Breaker; or, the Adventures of John Sheppard* (Nicoll, II, 360, 244, 381). For a full bibliography, see Horace Bleackley, *Jack Sheppard . . . With an Epilogue on*

Jack Sheppard in Literature and Drama (Edinburgh and London, 1933).

4   William. H. McBurney (ed.), *The London Merchant* (London, 1965), pp. xii—xiii.

5   William Eben Schultz, *Gay's 'Beggar's Opera': Its Content, History & Influence* (New York, 1967, reissue of 1923 edn), p. 282.

6   James Boswell, *Life of Johnson*, ed. George Birkbeck Hill, rev. L. F. Powell (Oxford, 1934), II, 367. Cf. also Schultz, *Gay's 'Beggar's Opera'*, pp. 226—65.

7   *1832 Report*, q. 966.

8   Add. MS. 42,865, fols. 405—30. His trial aroused enormous interest and his execution at Newgate (Nov. 1824) was witnessed by over 100,000 people (*DNB*).

9   Edward Fitzball, *Thirty-Five Years of a Dramatic Author's Life* (London, 1859), II, 403. An earlier performance in 1823, while the case was *sub-judice*, was stopped by court injunction (Keith Hollingsworth, *The Newgate Novel, 1830—1847*, Detroit, 1963, p. 36). On Thurtell's extraordinary literary notoriety, see *ibid.*, pp. 35—40.

10 Hollingsworth, *The Newgate Novel*, p. 139. Most of them date from late Oct. 1839.

11 *The Letters and Private Papers of William Makepeace Thackeray*, ed. Gordon N. Ray, I (London, 1945), 395. (Letter dated 1—2 Dec. 1839.)

12 His execution attracted about 40,000 spectators, including Dickens, Thackeray, and Charles Kean (who had been 'drawn to this terrible exhibition by the example of his father, the more celebrated Edmund Kean, who had witnessed the execution of Thistlewood "with a view", as he himself said, "to his professional studies"'.) (A. Griffiths, *The Chronicles of Newgate*, London, 1884, II, 283). Thackeray has a personal account of the execution in 'Going to see a man hanged', *Fraser's Magazine*, XXII (1840), 150—8.

13 *1866 Report*, q. 2416.

14 *The Diaries of William Charles Macready, 1833—1851*, ed. William Toynbee (London, 1912), I, 475. But Dickens adapted it for his public readings in 1868.

15 Add. MSS. 42,945, fols. 683—707 and 42,950, fols. 12—35.

16 Kathleen Tillotson (ed.), *Oliver Twist* (Oxford, 1966), p. xxi. Appendix F (*ibid.*, p. 399) has a useful bibliography of Newgate criticism at this juncture.

17 Philip Collins, *Dickens and Crime* (London, 1962), p. 265.

18 *Fraser's Magazine*, XXI (1940), 211. Cf. also *ibid.*, p. 228 (attributed to Thackeray), a warning of the dangers implicit in the model of Jack Sheppard 'metamorphosed from a vulgar ruffian into a melodramatic hero'.

19 Preface to *Oliver Twist* (1841 edn) and retained for future edns. [John Genest], *Some Account of the English Stage from the Restoration in 1660 to 1830* (Bath, 1832), IX, 125, comments that, as a concession to the early nineteenth-century emphasis on a high moral tone, *The Beggar's Opera* was invariably performed in a managerially expurgated and moralised form.

20 F. Renard Cooper, *Nothing Extenuate: the Life of Frederick Fox Cooper* (London, 1964), pp. 101—2. See also the exchange of letters between Fox

and the Lord Chamberlain on the subject, *ibid.*, pp. 231–42. A circular early in 1846 required all theatres to submit playbills for the weekly inspection of the Lord Chamberlain.

21 L.C. 7:7, 23 May, 24 July 1848.

22 Quoted in Bleackley, *Jack Sheppard*, p. 108. The playbill implies that the piece had been newly expurgated for the occasion.

23 L.C. 1:50, fol. 127, 17 July 1852. Similar letter to the Bower Saloon (*ibid.*, fol. 126, 16 July 1852).

24 S. M. Ellis, *William Harrison Ainsworth and his Friends* (London, 1911), I, 363.

25 Nicoll, IV, 401, 363, 247. Rede's play is not listed.

26 Day Book (Add. MS. 53,702, fol. 226, 23 Aug. 1844). Kemble's letter to Lord De La Warr (15 Aug.) informing him that he had 'directed the Managers to suspend their preparations until they receive further directions from your Lordship' is *ibid.*, fol. 227. Another play of similar type, *The Great Metropolis; or, Life's Shadows* (Add. MS. 42,977, fols. 795–978) was probably also refused a licence since it appears in Kemble's fee book (5 Sept. 1844) with a marginal note to the effect that the licence fee had been refunded.

27 1866 *Report*, appendix no. 1 (K), also noted in Day Book (Add. MS. 53,703, fol. 372). The 'swell mobsmen' were 'gentlemen' pick-pockets, who travelled around the country to fairs, large cities, or worked on the Dover packets. See [H. W. Holland], 'Professional thieves', *Cornhill Magazine*, VI, (1862), 650.

28 Day Book (Add. MS. 53,703, fol. 314, 13 Oct. 1853). Michael R. Booth, 'East End melodrama', *Theatre Survey*, XVII (1976), 60–1, comments on the generally less restrained examples of melodrama to be found outside London's West End.

29 Add. MS. 52,948 (69 fols.). Licence sent 28 June 1854.

30 L.C. 1:53, fol. 40, 22 June 1854.

31 Add. MS. 52,948 (39 fols.). Licence sent 28 June 1854.

32 Donne referred to this letter (dated 24 Sept. 1855) in L.C. 1:200, 1 Apr. 1868, but the original is missing from the official records.

33 L.C. 1:58, letters exchanged 20–26 May 1858. For Jeremiah Avershaw (or Abershaw), a notorious highwayman executed in 1795 for shooting a peace officer, see *The Newgate Calendar*, ed. Knapp and Baldwin, III, 241–3.

34 L.C. 1:70, Donne to Ponsonby, 30 Apr. 1859.

35 *Ibid.*, [Apr. 1859], 16 Apr. 1859.

36 L.C. 1:83, 2 Jan. 1860. On his own initiative Donne stopped *Oliver Twist* at the Effingham Saloon in 1860. 'I think', he explained to Ponsonby, 'the old-standing prohibition will bear me out, as Oliver Twist is, in my opinion, even less tolerable than Jack Sheppard' (*ibid.*, 11 June 1860).

37 See H. Chance Newton, *Crime and the Drama; or Dark Deeds Dramatised* (London, 1927), pp. 76–83, 99, and *passim*, for examples of this practice.

38 1866 *Report*, appendix no. 1 (K). There are detailed reports of the trial and the circumstances surrounding the murder in *The Times*, 13, 15, 16, 19–24, 26 July 1861.

39 L.C. 1:98 [7 Aug. 1861], [10 Aug. 1861]. The play (by Nelson Lee, jun.)

was also performed under the title *The Money Lender; or, the Life of a Vagrant* (Nicoll, V. 720, 802).

40 L.C. 1:112; 19 Aug., 20 Aug. 1862.
41 L.C. 1:200, letters exchanged between 26 Mar. and 19 Apr. 1868.
42 Nicoll, V, 510. Another version was licensed for the Garrick Theatre in the same month (*ibid.*, V, 728).
43 L.C. 1:200, 14 May 1868.
44 The Lord Chamberlain's agreement is noted on the reverse of the same letter.
45 See Bleackley, *Jack Sheppard*, p. 100 n. 5. The play went on provincial tour with the (presumably unlicensed) title *Little Jack Sheppard*. But Jack Sheppard was always considered a much less emotive topic in the provinces than in London. There is evidence that the play was produced there without interference from the Lord Chamberlain during its various prohibitions in London (see L.C. 1:311, 23 Jan. 1876).
46 L.C. 1:263, MSS. summary, 4 Jan. 1872.
47 The 'Mint' was a sanctuary in South London for thieves and prostitutes.
48 L.C. 1:277, 28 Feb. 1873.
49 *Ibid.*, 10 Mar. 1873. Donne, submitting the letter to Webster for his superior's approval, commented: 'I think he must be mad, or think me so, if he expects me to recommend for license this *alias* of Jack Sheppard.'
50 *Ibid.*, 24 Mar. 1873. First performed 22 Mar. 1873 (Nicoll, V, 754, erroneously, gives 18 Mar.).
51 *Dick's Standard Plays* (London, [1874-1907]), no. 506.
52 See Bleackley, *Jack Sheppard*, pp. 114-23.

5 Early challenges to Victorian morality

1 See Maurice J. Quinlan, *Victorian Prelude: A History of English Manners 1700-1830* (New York, 1941), p. 269; and Ashley H. Thorndike, *English Comedy* (New York, 1929), p. 513.
2 *1832 Report*, q. 3188.
3 Ian Watt, *The Rise of the Novel: Studies in Defoe, Richardson and Fielding*, 5th imp. (London, 1967), p. 199. Cf. Charles Reade's evidence, *1866 Report*, q. 6743.
4 See Kathleen Tillotson, *Novels of the Eighteen-Forties* (Oxford, 1954), p. 66.
5 Walter Bagehot, *The Collected Works*, ed. Norman St John-Stevas, II (London, 1965), 98. (From an article on Dickens first printed in the *National Review*, 1858.)
6 [Elizabeth] Inchbald (ed.), *The British Theatre*, VIII (London, 1808).
7 *1832 Report*, q. 3736. See Barry N. Olshen, 'The Beaux Stratagem of the nineteenth century stage', *Theatre Notebook*, XXVIII (1974), 70-80.
8 *The Age* (12 Dec. 1831). Cf. the same newspaper's comments on a performance of Vanbrugh's *The Provok'd Husband* at Covent Garden (30 May 1830).
9 *1832 Report*, q. 851.

10 *Ibid.*, q. 178. (Moncrieff also reported that Colman had cut out the phrase 'goblin damned' on the grounds of blasphemy.)

11 Add. MS. 42,865, fol. 309. Also excised was the line 'An apple munching Eve was the ruin of Adam' (fol. 310). Planché was directed to remove from his musical drama *The Frozen River* (1828) a song about 'young Pauline', who lost her footing while skating with her lover: 'No doubt 'twas a warning to give her — / For the very next spring, / Pray don't mention the thing, / When dancing one night / In the Grove by moonlight, / Alas poor Pauline! / You may guess what I mean! / You've more to fear from a fall on the grass / Than a slip on the Frozen River' (Add. MS. 42,869, fol. 149).

12 Quoted in Jeremy F. Bagster-Collins, *George Colman the Younger, 1762—1836* (New York, 1946), p. 303.

13 A comedy *Keep Your Temper; or, Know Whom You Marry* (Add. MS. 42,895, fols. 110—66) was 'withdrawn' in 1829 but this was probably for technical reasons. Note on fol. 110 reads: 'Allowed. 5th April 1829. Licensed for Drury Lane Theatre — though not accepted there.'

14 Add. MS. 42,875, fols. 81—5 (letters tipped in with play text).

15 Scribe's play is noted in Kemble's fee book (Dec. 1845). On Alfieri's tragedy, suppressed contrary to John Kemble's advice, see letters for June 1856 tipped into Day Book (Add. MS. 53,703, fols. 181—3). Kemble suggested that, while the play dealt with incest (a topic 'which may naturally be considered repulsive and shocking to the universal feeling'), the setting was remote from ordinary experience and there were precedents like *Oedipus Tyrannus* and Racine's *Phèdre* in its favour. But Lord Breadalbane declined to licence it, believing he could not do so 'without endangering the morals of the Country'.

16 [Robert Southey], 'State of the French drama', *Quarterly Review*, LI (1834), 210—11. One play cited, the elder Dumas' *La Tour de Nesle* (1833), the story of Margaret of Burgundy (*fl.* 1344) as an adulteress, was prohibited by William Donne in 1852. The Day Book (6 Feb.) notes that the MS. was sent back to the St James's Theatre 'at once as wholly unfit for Representation, and was not even submitted to the Lord Chamberlain'.

17 *Dramatic Essays: John Forster, George Henry Lewes. Reprinted from the 'Examiner' and the 'Leader'*, ed. William Archer and Robert W. Lowe (London, 1896), pp. 241—2.

18 Catharine B. Johnson (ed.), *William Bodham Donne and his Friends* (London, 1905), p. 197. See Alfred Loewenberg, *Annals of Opera, 1597—1940*, 2nd edn (Geneva, 1955), I, 907. In contrast to his experience in his native Italy, where he was a frequent victim of censorship (mainly of a political nature), Verdi had few difficulties with the censor in England. But see below, p. 103 n. 26.

19 1866 *Report*, q. 2284. Donne was further questioned on this point (*ibid.*, qq. 2299—303).

20 L.C. 1:70, 26 Mar., 24 Mar. 1859.

21 1866 *Report*, q. 233.

22 Donne, in recommending the refusal of an English adaptation entitled *Camille* (by the American actress Matilda Heron), remarked to Spencer Ponsonby that 'the Lord Chamberlain's veto on the French prose version

in March 1859, applies to every English version of the same story, notwithstanding that in the Provinces an English Play of that name is occasionally performed' (L.C. 1:83, 11 June 1860).

23 L.C. 1:113, 1 Aug., 4 Aug., [5] Aug. 1862. Donne pointed out that the same unlicensed version had been published in *Lacy's Acting Edition*.

24 1866 *Report*, appendix no. 1 (K), where it is described as 'unsuited to the English stage' and in consequence 'withdrawn without examination'.

25 L.C. 1:83, 22 Nov. 1860. Donne feared that the title was 'awkward', since 'many who will see the Papers and the Bills may not know the import of the French word'.

26 1866 *Report*, q. 2236.

27 *Ibid.*, q. 389.

28 W. R. Greg, *Literary and Social Judgments* (London, 1868), p. 178.

29 The plays that were refused licences were *Les Intimes* (described by Donne as 'precisely the sort of piece that instructs young gentlemen in the art and mystery of making love to their neighbours' wives') (L.C. 1:185, 8 July 1867); *L'Amour; ou, qu'est-ce que c'est que ça?* (*ibid.*, originally prohibited in 1860); *Les Coullisses de la Vie* and Augier's *Maître Guérin* (*ibid.*, 9 July 1867). The last-named was later licensed for the St James's (3 Apr. 1868) on condition that the hero and heroine were made cousins by marriage and not aunt and nephew, so that 'the projected marriage in a later Act will then be without objection'.

30 L.C. 1:185, 8 June, 18 June 1868.

31 L.C. 1:200, 14 Mar., 23 Mar. 1868. The season at the St James's occasioned much comment that year (see *Pall Mall Gazette*, 10 June 1868). One particularly contentious item was Offenbach's *La Grande Duchesse de Gérolstein*, with Mlle Schneider (notorious for her suggestive winks and gestures) in the lead. Donne was sent to the dress rehearsal but found nothing untoward, despite the fact that, as he reported to Lord Bradford, 'I sat in the front row of the stalls and took my strongest glasses with me' (L.C. 1:201, 20 June 1868).

32 The letters relating to the controversy are in L.C. 1:221, 25 Aug. to 10 Sept. 1869. In the following year Donne made various cuts in a burlesque, *Miss Formosa*, rendering it 'now a mere caricature of the [Boucicault] original and in my opinion stupid and passable' (L.C. 1:232, 31 May 1870).

33 L.C. 1:246, 24 Mar. 1871. The plays included George Sand's *L'Autre*, Sardou's *Séraphine*, Augier's *Le Mariage d'Olympe*, and Dumas' *Le Bâtard*. None seems to have been refused a licence but they all must have undergone the usual deodorising process.

34 L.C. 1:246, 5 Apr. 1871.

35 *Ibid.*, 23 June 1871. The excisions for *Fleur du Thé* are not recorded in the Day Book; but cf. later entry (6 Oct. 1875) for the same piece, when the cuts imposed cover two pages.

36 L.C. 1:247, 13 July 1871.

37 L.C. 1:263, 3 July 1872. Of *Le Timbrale* Donne observed that, while there was nothing in it which might fairly be described as immoral, there was much that was suggestive of things not mentioned in respectable society and he feared that if the piece were licensed 'there might be some

clearance of the stalls at the St James's Theatre, even before the carriages are ready' (L.C. 1:263, 29 Apr. 1872).

38 L.C. 1:276, 21 Oct., 1873. For comment on Valnay and Pitron's activities at the Princess Theatre, see *Athenaeum* (12 Apr. 1873).

39 In L.C. 1:285.

40 *Ibid.*, 27 Apr. 1874. In a note to the theatre, Donne begged leave to express his surprise 'that a Drama so indecent and unfit for the stage should have been sent for examination'.

41 *Ibid.*, 1 June, 13 June 1874.

42 The same bill advertises the ban on *La Jolie Parfumeuse*. This was later performed in an expurgated version by H. J. Byron at the Alhambra, 18 May 1874 (Loewenberg, *Annals of Opera*, I, 1031), a music hall and thus outside the Lord Chamberlain's jurisdiction.

43 L.C. 1:285, 13 June 1874.

6 Religion and the stage

1 See James Fullarton Arnott and John William Robinson, *English Theatrical Literature 1559—1900: A Bibliography* (London, 1970), pp. 37—73, and L. W. Conolly and J. P. Wearing, *English Drama and Theatre, 1800—1900: A Guide to Information Sources* (Detroit, 1978), pp. 1—3. (Both incorporate useful annotations.)

2 Maurice J. Quinlan, *Victorian Prelude: A History of English Manners 1700—1830* (New York, 1941), p. 207; Matthew Arnold, 'The French Play in London', *Nineteenth Century*, VI (1879), 239.

3 [T. H. Lister], 'Mr Sheridan Knowles's *Wife of Mantua* — state and prospects of the drama', *Edinburgh Review*, LVII (1833), 296. The second part of Lister's article was prompted by the publication of the 1832 *Report* and its evidence of prostitution in the theatres. This is also discussed in Dewey Ganzel, 'Patent wrongs and patent theatres: drama and the law in the early nineteenth century', *PMLA*, LXXVI (1961), 391.

4 1832 *Report*, qq. 852, 857; 1866 *Report*, q. 2049; 1909 *Report*, q. 2519 (quoted by Laurence Housman from a letter of Redford's indicating the impossibility of licensing Housman's play *Bethlehem*).

5 1832 *Report*, q. 967.

6 Quoted in Jeremy F. Bagster-Collins, *George Colman the Younger, 1762—1836* (New York, 1946), p. 295 (from holograph letter dated 30 Dec. 1826 inserted in Richard Brinsley Peake's *Memoirs of the Colman Family*, Brander Matthews Dramatic Museum, Columbia University).

7 Holograph letter dated 6 Jan. 1829, Folger MS. Y. d. 483 (12). The licensed text is Add. MS. 42,894, fols. 1—45. Performed at Drury Lane Jan. 1829 (Nicoll, IV, 416).

8 Holograph note dated 14 Feb. 1829, Folger MS. Y. d. 483 (13). The play is set in England during the period following the Third Crusade.

9 Add. MS. 42,887, fol. 330. The play is by T. C. Grattan. George Raymond, *Memoirs of R. W. Elliston* (London, 1844—5), II, 401, confirms the Lord Chamberlain's support of the author.

10 See Nicoll, IV, 512. But Larpent had licensed *The Prodigal* for Drury Lane in 1816 (*ibid.*).

11 Thomas Wade, *The Jew of Arragon; or, the Hebrew Queen. A Tragedy in Five Acts* (London, 1830). Apart from the larger excisions Wade's play suffered, the author also complained that 'the revered name of the Deity, wherever it occurs, was erased by the great religious and moral pen of the licenser, and altogether abjured in stage utterance'. See also Murray Roston, *Biblical Drama in England from the Middle Ages to the Present Day* (London, 1968), p. 229.

12 Charles H. Shattuck, 'E. L. Bulwer and Victorian censorship', *Quarterly Journal of Speech*, XXXIV (1948), 66.

13 Quoted *ibid.*, p. 68. The reviewer was demanding, in effect, no more than Thomas Bowdler had of Shakespeare: 'My earnest wish is to render his plays unsullied by any scene, by any speech, or, if possible, by any word that can give pain to the most chaste, or offence to the most religious of his readers' (preface to 1st edn, reprinted in *The Family Shakespeare. In One Volume*, 7th edn, London, 1839, p. vii).

14 Alfred Bunn, *The Stage: Both Before and Behind the Curtain, From 'Observations Taken on the Spot'* (London, 1840), II, 176.

15 Shattuck, 'E. L. Bulwer and Victorian censorship', p. 69.

16 See Day Book entries for *The Voice from the Sea; or, The King's Casket* (10 Feb. 1859); *My Cook and Housekeeper* (3 Mar. 1854); and *The Hebrew Tribe of Rome; or, the Greek Hero and the Jewish Maid* (21 Jan. 1852).

17 Donne's entry in the Day Book for Tom Taylor's *'Twixt Axe and Crown; or, Lady Elizabeth* (19 Jan.) reads: 'Act II stage direction at opening of scene I omit Ivory crucifix: substitute a plain cross for the crucifix – as the latter gives offence to many spectators.' Cf. John Brougham's *The Actress of Padua* (entered 3 Apr. 1855).

18 1866 *Report*, q. 4060.

19 Refusals noted in Kemble's fee book, 13 Mar., 4 Apr. 1847.

20 See *British Museum Catalogue ... Plays Submitted to the Lord Chamberlain 1824–1851: Additional Manuscripts 42865–43038* (London, 1964), p. 11.

21 'I saw no reason why a religious drama of that kind should not be re-presented, nor do I, provided it is not doctrinal' (1866 *Report*, q. 2463).

22 See Day Book entry for 24 Jan. 1852.

23 Letter dated 30 Aug. 1855, in Day Book (Add. MS. 53,703, fol. 151).

24 Roston, *Biblical Drama*, p. 230. The Pavilion's minor-theatre status explains Roston's mystification that this play slipped 'through an apparently impenetrable net' of religious censorship.

25 Add. MS. 52,955. The entry for the licensed version in the Day Book (14 Sept. 1855) warns that 'the manager is hereby directed to adhere strictly to the last and amended version of the MS. herewith recommended for license'.

26 Alfred Loewenberg, *Annals of Opera, 1597–1940*, 2nd edn (Geneva, 1955), I, 657, 819. The exiled Hebrews were transformed into exiled Babylonians. Benjamin Lumley, *Reminiscences of the Opera* (London, 1864), p. 146, declared that the practice was necessitated by 'that repugnance which is prevalent in the English mind against any dramatic subject referring however remotely to biblical history'.

27 Catharine B. Johnson (ed.), *William Bodham Donne and his Friends* (London, 1905), pp. 224–5.

28 L.C. 1 :58, 26 May 1858. In the same letter Donne referred to his licensing of *Polyeucte* and *The Prodigal Son*, remarking that while the former 'passed unnoticed' the latter 'excited a good deal of comment'. But, he went on, 'I had the satisfaction of hearing it admitted by the late Bishop of London, who had remonstrated against the *Prodigal* at first, that the story, being a generic one, was a fit theme for theatrical representation.'

29 L.C. 1 :58, 2 June 1858.

30 Add. MS. 42,969, fols. 524–71.

31 Edward Fitzball, *Thirty-Five Years of a Dramatic Author's Life* (London, 1859), II, 54, 55.

32 See Loewenberg, *Annals of Opera*, I, 777.

33 See entry in Kemble's fee book, 2 June 1845, when the libretto was referred to Lord De La Warr.

34 Add. MS. 43,020, fols. 385–438.

35 Add. MS. 43,032, fol. 1106. The *dramatis personae* parallels almost exactly that for *Azael the Prodigal*.

36 L.C. 1 :50, fol. 7, 28 Feb. 1851.

37 Fitzball, *Thirty-Five Years*, II, 275. Cf. Benjamin Lumley's comment on the production in Italian at Her Majesty's Theatre: 'A certain curiosity was occasioned by the fact that the subject was founded on the well-known parable of Holy Writ, and might thus be deemed objectionable to English feeling. It may be said at once that every fear was dissipated' (*Reminiscences*, p. 311).

38 L.C. 1 :50, fol. 60, 6 Nov. 1851.

39 'The Church Congress on the drama', *The Theatre*, N.S., I (1878), 255–9.

40 Quoted in Marjorie Thompson, 'Henry Arthur Jones and Wilson Barrett: some correspondence, 1879–1904', *Theatre Notebook*, XI (1956–7), 42, 43.

41 L.C. 1 :277, 9 July 1873. Some scriptural quotation does appear to have crept into the production because the *Illustrated London News* (24 May 1873) declared in its review that 'the citation of Gospel texts on the stage is . . . repulsive'.

42 L.C. 1 :417, 19 Feb. 1883. The Examiner was alerted to the case by a letter from a member of the public.

43 L.C. 1 :547, 2 Nov. 1890. See also *The Times* (26 Sept., 13 Oct. 1890). The rumour restarted in 1891 (see L.C. 1 :564, April).

44 L.C. 1 :751, 14 Nov. 1901; L.C. 1 :752, 20 Nov. 1901.

45 L.C. 1 :399, 14 Aug., 24 Aug. 1882. The *Times* reviewer (25 July 1882), though not unduly hostile, did remark that in the working of the plot 'the extreme limits of good taste are reached; some may think they are overstepped'.

46 Walter Jerrold, *Douglas Jerrold: Dramatist and Wit* (London [1914]), I, 187.

47 Arthur Pinero, 'The theatre in transition', in *Fifty Years. Memories and Contrasts. A Composite Picture of the Period 1882–1932 by Twenty-Seven Contributors to 'The Times'* (London, 1932), p. 73. Pinero believed that George Redford (whom he mistakenly calls 'Mr Redwood') 'took a slightly less rigid view of the proprieties', but he was presumably writing from his own less-than-representative experience. In *The Notorious Mrs Ebbsmith* (1895), Pinero, flying in the face of all the official 'rules' about not producing the Bible on stage, was permitted to show Agnes Ebbsmith

throwing it into the fire in protest against its false teaching. Admittedly, Pinero never calls the book a Bible in either the stage directions or the dialogue, but the fact is strongly implied and all the reviewers took it to be the Bible.

48 Gerald Weales, *Religion in Modern English Drama* (London, 1961), p. 4.

49 Doris Arthur Jones, *The Life and Letters of Henry Arthur Jones* (London, 1930), pp. 89–90. Cf. Jones's first reply to his critics (a letter to the *Daily News*, 29 Sept. 1884), quoted *ibid.*, p. 90.

50 Henry Arthur Jones, *Saints and Sinners. A New and Original Drama of Modern English Middle-Class Life in Five Acts* (London, 1891), p. xxi.

51 Henry Arthur Jones, *The Renascence of the English Drama* (London, 1895), pp. 28–9, 37–8.

52 L.C. 1:657, 2 Jan. 1896.

53 *Ibid.*, 17 Jan. 1896.

54 Bernard Shaw, *Our Theatres in the Nineties* (London, 1932), II, 23.

55 L.C. 1:730, 13 Nov. 1900.

56 L.C. 1:582, 27 June 1892.

57 *The Letters of Oscar Wilde*, ed. Rupert Hart-Davis (London, 1962), pp. 316, 318.

58 Quoted *ibid.*, p. 317 n. 1. See also reviews of *Salomé* after publication in 1893, in *Oscar Wilde: The Critical Heritage*, ed. Karl Beckson (London, 1970), pp. 135–42.

59 Jones, *Renascence of the English Drama*, p. 120.

60 Martin Meisel, *Shaw and the Nineteenth-Century Theater* (Princeton, 1963), p. 337. Archer's opinion of the play (quoted *ibid.*, p. 338) is distinguished by his disgust at 'the hideous vulgarity of the whole thing'.

61 Shaw, *Our Theatres in the Nineties*, III, 45–6.

62 L.C. 1:675, 26 Nov. 1897. The former, by the Rev. Henry Cresswell, was performed early in the following year in the Great Hall at Church House, Westminster, where it evaded the Lord Chamberlain's jurisdiction 'by not taking money at the doors' (Shaw, *Our Theatres in the Nineties*, III, 295).

63 L.C. 1:657, 26 Aug. 1896.

64 Robert Speaight, *William Poel and the Elizabethan Revival* (London, 1954), p. 162. Poel later changed his mind about religious plays: 'I have come to see that their tendency is dangerous. Religion can never be acted' (*ibid.*, p. 166). Cf. Una Ellis-Fermor, *The Frontiers of Drama*, 2nd edn (London, 1964), p. 4, who comments that the history of religious drama 'is a long record of failures or partial success', since the religious experience 'is incompatible with the essential mood of drama'.

65 Roston, *Biblical Drama*, p. 243, cites Owen Lally's *Jezebel* (Comedy Theatre, Mar. 1912) as the first specifically biblical play to be licensed by the Lord Chamberlain in the twentieth century.

7 Political and personal satire

1 James Sutherland, *English Satire* (Cambridge, 1958), p. 133.

2 See Nicoll, V, 13–14, and sources there cited. Of the disturbance when the Bancrofts tried to abolish the pit at the Haymarket in 1880, George

Rowell, *The Victorian Theatre 1792—1914: A Survey*, 2nd edn (Cambridge, 1978), p. 4, remarks that 'the spirit of the O [ld] P [rice] Rioters died hard'.

3 William Bodham Donne, *Essays on the Drama* (London, 1858), p. 4 (from an article, 'Athenian Comedy', *Westminster Review*, 1856). John Larpent's severity towards personal allusion had done much to exclude personal satire from the nineteenth-century stage. See L. W. Conolly, *The Censorship of English Drama 1737—1824* (San Marino, Calif., 1976), pp. 113—36.

4 L.C. 1:47, letter book K, fol. 54, 5 Jan., 7 Jan 1848. A reference to Charles Kean himself ('Tell me of something that will make me sad. / See Kean play Hamlet that will do it. / Oh! . . . that remedy's much too severe / My nerves would never stand the shock I fear!') was cut from a burlesque *William Tell* (Strand Theatre, Apr. 1857).

5 In a burlesque of Hugo's *Ruy Blas*. Edwardes announced the threat in his advertisements (unidentified newspaper cutting, 27 Sept. 1889 in L.C. 1:527). Irving's complaint (26 Sept. 1889) is in L.C. 1:526.

6 *The Letters of Oscar Wilde*, ed. Rupert Hart-Davis (London, 1962), p. 316.

7 L.C. 1:564, 6 Oct. 1891. See Frank Fowell and Frank Palmer, *Censorship in England* (London, 1913), p. 199. They explain that Churchill was caricatured as 'Randy-Pandy' and that, on interference from the Lord Chamberlain, this was changed to 'Jack-a-Dandy'.

8 J. R. Planché, *The Recollections and Reflections of J. R. Planché: A Professional Autobiography* (London, 1872), II, 109—10.

9 The tax stamp on the boxes included the singularly appropriate motto 'Ex luce lucellum'; See R. C. K. Ensor, *England 1870—1914* (Oxford, 1936), p. 20.

10 See Donne to J. W. Blakesley, 18 Jan. 1872, quoted in Catharine B. Johnson (ed.), *William Bodham Donne and his Friends* (London, 1905), p. 278.

11 As Donne pointed out, the practice was not new. See his evidence on this topic, 1866 *Report*, qq. 2260—77, and Spencer Ponsonby's evidence, *ibid.*, q. 170.

12 The problem was such that in later years memoranda were sent out with the licences for pantomimes stressing that managers ought 'to omit in representation any personalities, or other topical allusions, which may be calculated to give offence to any portion of a mixed audience, and thereby to provoke ill-feeling and disorder' (printed notice, preceding the text of the Lord Chamberlain's Day Book, Add. MS. 53,706).

13 L.C. 1:263, 14 Nov. 1872. Restrictions on the sale of intoxicating liquor provoked much discussion, controversy, and even rioting between 1871 and 1874 (see Ensor, *England 1870—1914*, pp. 20—1). In F. W. Green and Robert Soutar's burlesque *Lothair* (1873) one of the cuts reads: 'we were obliged to get rid of Bruce [the Home Secretary]: he is gone to our house of Lords, & his first Act will be to make us close at 11 every night'.

14 Martin Meisel, 'Political extravaganza: a phase of the nineteenth-century British theater', *Theatre Survey*, III (1962), 19.

15 Henry Barton Baker, *A History of the London Stage*, 2nd edn (London, 1904), p. 502. See Elwood P. Lawrence, '"The Happy Land": W. S. Gilbert as Political Satirist', *Victorian Studies*, XV (1971—2), 161—83.

16 F. Latour Tomline [W. S. Gilbert] and Gilbert A'Beckett, *The Happy Land:*

A Burlesque Version of 'The Wicked World' ... *First Performed at the Royal Court Theatre, March 3rd, 1873. Prohibited by the Lord Chamberlain, March 7th* (London, 1873), p. 18. The speech is Ayrton's. Many years later Gilbert made the possibly disingenuous claim that 'my maturer judgment [now] teaches me that the Lord Chamberlain's interference was absolutely justified' (1909 *Report*, q. 3453).

17 Meisel, 'Political extravaganza', pp. 19—20.

18 L.C. 1:277, 6 Mar. 1873.

19 As reported in *The Times* (8 Mar. 1873).

20 L.C. 1:277, memo 7 Mar.; Spencer Ponsonby to Miss Litton, 7 Mar.; memo 8 Mar. 1873. (The revised version was licensed 7 Mar. 1873.)

21 The excisions do not in fact appear in capital letters, though they are indicated in the published text. (Lord Sydney visited the theatre on 5 Mar.) Lawrence, ' "The Happy Land" ', pp. 175—8, discusses the 'short-lived but vigorous debate' on censorship and the stage conducted in the press as a result of official interference in the play.

22 L.C. 1:276, 13 Oct. 1873.

23 L.C. 1:277, telegram 15 Oct. 1873.

24 *Ibid.*, 15 Sept [error for Oct.] 1873.

25 Quoted in William Davenport Adams, *A Book of Burlesque: Sketches of English Stage Travestie and Parody* (London, 1891), p. 161.

26 L.C. 1:276, 1 Nov., 1873.

27 *Ibid.*, 4 Nov. 1873.

28 L.C. 1:285, 2 Feb. 1873.

29 Martin Meisel, *Shaw and the Nineteenth-Century Theater* (Princeton, 1963), p. 90.

30 1866 *Report*, qq. 4061, 4064.

31 L.C. 1:127, 25 May 1863. The ticket-of-leave system enabled a prisoner of good behaviour who had served two-thirds of his sentence to be paroled.

32 L.C. 1:232, 10 May 1870.

33 *Ibid.*, 24 June 1870. Reade's *The Wandering Heir* (1875), suggested by the celebrated affair of the Wapping butcher Arthur Orton who claimed he was the long-lost Sir Roger Tichbourne, was also untouched by the censor; yet during the early 1870s all references to the Claimant and his counsel Dr Kenealy were systematically excised from all licensed MSS. The anon. *The Great Tichbourne Case* was prohibited (L.C. 1:263, 21 May, 19 June 1872).

34 The speeches here and below are quoted from the licensed text (Add. MS. 53,048), differing in minor detail from the copyist entries in the Day Book.

35 L.C. 1:166, 20 Feb. 1866.

36 L.C. 1:285, 2 Feb. 1874.

37 Shirley Brooks described to the 1866 Committee how his adaptation of Disraeli's *Coningsby* had been suppressed in the late 1840s, since in Lord De La Warr's view it was 'a kind of *quasi*-political piece ... exhibiting a sort of contrast between the manufacturing people and the lower classes' (1866 *Report*, q. 4480).

38 L.C. 1:153, 15 Aug., 16 Aug. 1865. Donne took the unusual step of explaining the reasons for the play's prohibition to the theatre manager

concerned, as he was 'a very respectable man and I thought it might *adoucir* his disappointment' (*ibid.*, 22 Aug. 1865).

39 L.C. 1:233, 6 Sept. 1870. According to Donne the play had been previously licensed (cf. Nicoll, V, 693).

40 L.C. 1:233, 8 Sept., 19 Sept. 1870.

41 L.C. 1:246, 10 Jan. 1871.

42 L.C. 1:692, 1 Feb. 1898.

43 L.C. 1:730, 6 July 1900. Originally licensed for the Grand Theatre, Cardiff (Dec. 1896). The Turkish Ambassador had earlier complained of the impersonation of the Sultan in *Don Juan* (1893), after which the caricature was stopped on the Lord Chamberlain's instructions (L.C. 1:601, 3 Nov., 10 Nov., 1893).

44 Hansard, *Parliamentary Debates*, 4th ser., XCVII (1901), 92–3.

45 Fowell and Palmer, *Censorship in England*, p. 208.

46 Meisel, *Shaw and the Nineteenth-Century Theater*, p. 397, remarks that Gilbert's *Utopia Limited; or, the Flowers of Progress* (1893) is 'the most thoroughly political of his later pieces', and points out its close associations with *The Happy Land*. In the opera the Lord Chamberlain appears as Lord Dramaleigh, who is 'to cleanse our Court from moral stain / And purify our Stage'. Another character enquires: 'Are you aware that the Lord Chamberlain, who has his own views as to the best means of elevating the national drama, has declined to license any play that is not in blank verse and three hundred years old — as in England?' (W. S. Gilbert, *Original Comic Operas*, 2nd ser., London, n.d., pp. 27, 40).

8 Moral decorum and the advanced drama

1 Catharine B. Johnson (ed.), *William Bodham Donne and his Friends* (London, 1905), p. 295.

2 See Barry Duncan, *The St James's Theatre: Its Strange & Complete History, 1835–1957* (London, 1964), pp. 162–6.

3 L.C. 1:297, 17 Jan. 1875.

4 *Ibid.*, 3 Jan. 1875.

5 L.C. 1:168, 25 June 1866.

6 Quoted in *The Dramatic Works of James Albery*, ed. Wyndham Albery (London, 1939), II, 205.

7 L.C. 1:325, 7 Apr. 1877.

8 That is, *L'Ingénue* (Gaiety), *Baby* (Strand), *The Double Ladder* (Duke's), and *La Bonne aux Camélias* (Gaiety) (L.C. 1:342, annual report for 1877, 7 June 1878).

9 L.C. 1:357, 14 Feb. 1879.

10 Arthur Matthison, *A False Step* (London, [1879]), p. 3. A reprint of letter printed in *The Times* (2 Oct. 1879).

11 'A false step towards discrediting the censorship', *The Theatre*, N.S., I (1879), 261, 262.

12 L.C. 1:358, 8 May 1879.

13 *Ibid.*, 10 May 1879.

14 1892 *Report*, q. 5199.

15 L.C. 1:401, memo, n.d.

16 L.C. 1:400, memo, Oct. 1882. Pigott informed Spencer Ponsonby (5 Oct.) that the licence had been signed but that he intended visiting the theatre for the first performance.

17 1909 *Report*, qq. 665—6.

18 William Archer, 'The free stage and the new drama', *Fortnightly Review*, L (1891), 664—5. See also the same author's *The Old Drama and the New. An Essay in Re-Valuation* (London, 1923), pp. 306—9.

19 See C. R. Decker, 'Ibsen's literary reputation and Victorian taste', *Studies in Philology*, XXXII (1935), 632—45. (Archer eventually translated all Ibsen's plays.)

20 L.C. 1:453, 14 Oct. 1885. See John Russell Taylor, *The Rise and Fall of the Well-Made Play* (London, 1967), p. 39, who suggests the play was banned because 'it opened with a mysterious scene of comings and goings along a corridor which ended with a nurse coming in and announcing "It is a fine boy".'

21 L.C. 1:453, 29 Dec. 1885. Daudet's novel was still omitted from Mudies's Select Library list as late as 1904. See Donald Thomas, *A Long Time Burning: The History of Literary Censorship in England* (London, 1969), p. 255.

22 *The Letters of Percy Bysshe Shelley*, ed. Frederick L. Jones (Oxford, 1964), II, 102.

23 *The Diaries of William Charles Macready, 1833—1851*, ed. William Toynbee (London, 1912), II, 361.

24 L.C. 1:453, 29 Dec. 1885.

25 L.C. 1:469, 1 May 1886.

26 *The Theatre*, N.S. VII (1886), 530.

27 Michael Orme [Mrs J. T. Grein], *J. T. Grein, The Story of a Pioneer, 1862—1935. By his Wife* (London, 1936), p. 74. (A private performance effectively evaded the Lord Chamberlain's authority, which could operate only where plays were acted 'for hire, gain or reward' — Theatre Act 1843, clause XV.)

28 L.C. 1:564, 7 Mar. 1891. The Lord Chamberlain's unwillingness to grant *Ghosts* a licence is discussed in N. Schoonderwoerd, *J. T. Grein, Ambassador of the Theatre, 1862—1935* (Assen, Neth., 1963) p. 108.

29 Quoted in Orme, *J. T. Grein*, p. 87. See also George Bernard Shaw, 'The quintessence of Ibsenism', *Major Critical Essays* (London, 1932), pp. 70—2

30 Archer, 'The free stage and the new drama', p. 671.

31 L.C. 1:565, 14 Mar. 1891.

32 L.C. 1:564, 20 Mar. 1891. The next major production of the play was again by the Independent Theatre Society but it was delayed until 1897 (Schoonderwoerd, *J. T. Grein, Ambassador of the Theatre*, p. 116).

33 For a list of productions by the Society, see Schoonderwoerd, *J. T. Grein, Ambassador of the Theatre*, pp. 115—16.

34 Martin Meisel, *Shaw and the Nineteenth-Century Theater* (Princeton, 1963), p. 141.

35 Sir Arthur Pinero, 'The theatre in transition', in *Fifty Years. Memories and Contrasts. A Composite Picture of the Period 1882—1932 by Twenty-Seven Contributors to 'The Times'* (London, 1932), p. 72.

36 Cyril Maude, *Behind the Scenes with Cyril Maude* (London, 1927), p. 86.

37 Arthur W. Pinero, *The Second Mrs Tanqueray. A Play in Four Acts* (London, 1895), p. 188.

38   *Collected Letters 1874—1897*, ed. Dan H. Laurence (London, 1965), p. 566.
     Martin Meisel, *Shaw and the Nineteenth-Century Theater*, pp. 146—68,
     discusses the different approaches of Shaw and Pinero to the courtesan
     theme.

39   *Collected Letters 1874—1897*, ed. Laurence, p. 632.

40   *Collected Letters 1898—1910*, ed. Dan H. Laurence (London, 1972), pp. 13,
     14. On the difficulties attached to the Stage Society's production in 1902,
     see *ibid.*, pp. 240—3.

41   First full professional performance 3 Mar. 1926. See Shaw's note for
     this event in *The Bodley Head Bernard Shaw. Collected Plays with their Pre-
     faces*, ed. Dan H. Laurence (London, 1970), I, 365—7.

42   Henry Arthur Jones, *The Renascence of the English Drama* (London, 1895),
     p. 127.

43   George Bernard Shaw, *Our Theatres in the Nineties* (London, 1932), I, 23.

44   William Heinemann, *The First Step. A Dramatic Moment* (London, 1895),
     p. 71.

45   Schoonderwoerd, *J. T. Grein, Ambassador of the Theatre*, p. 126 n. 5.

46   William Archer, *The Theatrical 'World' of 1895* (London, 1896), p. 76.

47   Arthur W. Pinero, *The Notorious Mrs Ebbsmith. A Drama in Four Acts*
     (London, 1895), p. 38.

48   L.C. 1:638, 9 Mar. 1895. Redford's markings are preserved on the licensed
     text (Add. MS. 53,570). In response to a query from William Archer,
     Pinero confirmed that *'Mrs Ebbsmith* suffered no mutilation at the
     Chamberlain's office [but] *I* made a few cuts at rehearsal' (*The Col-
     lected Letters of Sir Arthur Pinero*, ed. J. P. Wearing, Minneapolis, 1974,
     p. 166).

49   Archer, *The Theatrical 'World' of 1895*, p. 76.

50   L.C. 1:639, 4 Dec. 1895.

51   *Ibid.*, 12 Dec. 1895. Redford informed Buchanan that the ban had been
     elicited on the independent advice of Spencer Ponsonby and Lord
     Lathom; but while the latter supported Redford's reply in substance he
     agreed with Spencer Ponsonby that the Examiner 'might have left our
     names out' (*ibid.*, 15 Dec. 1895).

52   *Ibid.*, 13 Dec., 15 Dec. 1895. Arthur Bourchier, the theatre manager
     concerned, wrote to *The Observer* (22 Dec. 1895), after the affair had
     been made public, to acknowledge that Redford had 'most courteously
     explained and pointed out the official objection to the play in question'.

53   Add. MS. 53,679. The speech occurs in Act I. In Act II Redford marked
     another passage: ' [*Guinevere* (with her mouth full)] "Everything's ex-
     cellent! We might be at the Savoy." [*Farrant*] "Only at the Savoy they
     turn you out at half-past twelve, whereas here we could -----."'

54   L.C. 1:712, 15 July 1899. Redford's reply to the criticism was that *Mes-
     saline* was no more immoral than *La Traviata, Don Giovanni*, or *Carmen*:
     'As you are aware', he wrote to Spencer Ponsonby, 'there has always been
     considerable latitude allowed to French plays, and operas in Foreign
     Languages' (*ibid.*, 18 June [error for July] 1899).

55   L.C. 1:711, 19 Apr. 1899.

56   *Ibid.*, 5 May 1899.

57   *Ibid.*, 10 May 1899. Cf. J. T. Grein, *Dramatic Criticism* (London, 1899), I,
     264, where he commented that the play 'is — though very daring — very

vulgar'. Samuel Smith eventually initiated a debate in the House of Commons on 'the growing tendency to produce immoral plays'. Two plays only were mentioned by name during the whole debate: *Zaza* (Garrick Theatre Apr. 1900), which Redford went to see after adverse comments in the press, and afterwards directed the manager to cut the line 'Do they *have* women in America?' (L.C. 1:730, 23 Apr. 1900); and *The Gay Lord Quex*, described in the debate as 'by far the ablest of these corrupting plays' (Hansard, *Parliamentary Debates*, 4th ser., LXXXIII, 1900, p. 278).

58 Frank Harris, *Mr & Mrs Daventry. A Play in Four Acts*, ed. H. Montgomery Hyde (London, 1956), p. 54.

59 L.C. 1:731, 27 Aug. 1900.

60 *Ibid.*, 29 Aug. 1900.

61 Harris, *Mr & Mrs Daventry*, ed. Hyde, introd., p. 32.

62 See John Galsworthy's ironic pamphlet *A Justification of the Censorship of Plays* (London, 1909) and the evidence supplied by the 1909 *Report*.

63 Granville-Barker's *Waste* was performed privately by the Stage Society 24 Nov. 1907 to much public outrage, since it mentioned the taboo subject of abortion. Pinero commented on the unlucky coincidence of the production with the imminent deputation: 'A week ago we had the Press pretty well with us; to-day it is thanking God for His mercy in bestowing a Censor on us' (*Collected Letters of Sir Arthur Pinero*, ed. Wearing, p. 209).

64 The news of Redford's resignation came in December 1911 and was greeted with relief by the dramatic profession. Pinero reported privately to William Archer that the Examiner had decided to quit as he was 'unable to comply with the conditions imposed upon him for next year' (*ibid.*, p. 236).

Epilogue

1 George Bernard Shaw, 'The censorship of the stage', *North American Review*, CLXIX (1899), 257.

2 Of the four parliamentary reports on theatres and theatre licensing in the nineteenth century, only the 1832 *Report* questioned the principle of censorship. In 1866 and 1892 there were even recommendations for its extension: 'We consider "that the censorship of plays has worked satisfactorily, and that it is not desirable that it should be discontinued; on the contrary, that it should be extended as far as practicable to the performances in music-halls and other places of public entertainment" (Report, Committee of 1866)' (1892 *Report*, p. vii).

3 During the 1866 Committee's proceedings the following exchange took place between Spencer Ponsonby and his questioner on the problem of whether, if censorship were abolished, the result would be more immoral plays: 'Yes. I think that you would have plays of the same kind as they have in France. [Mr Locke:] And now you have them in England, with the objectionable parts struck out, and something more stupid put in; is not that so? [Spencer Ponsonby;] That is a matter of opinion' (1866 *Report*, qq. 391—2).

4 See Lord Richly's speech (II, v), *The Modern Husband* (1732).

BIBLIOGRAPHY

Manuscript sources

British Library, Bloomsbury, London WC1

Day Books indexing the Lord Chamberlain's Plays (1824–1903), 7 vols., Add. MSS. 53,702–8

Plays submitted to the Lord Chamberlain (1824–51), Add. MSS. 42,865–43,038

Plays submitted to the Lord Chamberlain (1852–99), Add. MSS. 52,929–53,701

Public Record Office, Chancery Lane, London, WC2

Appointments (1824, 1836, 1840, 1857, 1874, 1895) L.C. 3:69; 3:70–1; 5:237–8; 5:240

Fee Book for Play Licenses (1837–49) (J. M. Kemble) L.C. 7:19

General Letters (Theatres) (1858–1901) L.C. 1:58–752

Lord Chamberlain's Letter Books (1833–58) L.C. 1:45–51

Original Letters (1836–57) L.C. 1:19–35

Semi-official Letter Books (1851–6) L.C. 1:52–3

Warrants of Several Sorts (1834–66) L.C. 5:249–51

Weekly Account of Bills, Posters, etc. (1861–70) L.C. 7:20–3

Folger Shakespeare Library, Washington, D.C., U.S.A.

Theatrical MSS. and letters Y. c. 426 (1–2); Y. d. 483 (8–13)

Henry E. Huntington Library, San Marino, California, U.S.A.

Letters of Edward Pigott

Victoria and Albert Museum, South Kensington, London SW3

Bills, posters, programmes, Gabrielle Enthoven Collection

Mary Barham Johnson (private) collection

Letters of John Mitchell Kemble and William Bodham Donne

Printed sources: select list

Adams, Joseph Quincy (ed.). *The Dramatic Records of Sir Henry Herbert: Master of the Revels, 1623–1673.* New York: Cornell University Press, 1917.

Archer, William. *About the Theatre. Essays and Studies.* London, 1886.

'The free stage and the new drama,' *Fortnightly Review*, L(1891), 663–72.

The Old Drama and the New. An Essay in Re-Valuation. London: William Heinemann, 1923.

The Theatrical 'World' for 1893. London [1894].

The Theatrical 'World' of 1894. London, 1895.

The Theatrical 'World' of 1895. London, 1896.

Bagster-Collins, Jeremy F. *George Colman the Younger, 1762–1836*. Morningside Heights, New York: King's Crown Press, 1946.

Baker, Henry Barton. *A History of the London Stage*. 2nd edn, London: George Routledge, 1904.

Bleackley, Horace. *Jack Sheppard ... With an Epilogue on Jack Sheppard in Literature and Drama, a Bibliography, a Note on Jonathan Wild, and a Memoir of Horace Bleackley by S. M. Ellis*. Edinburgh and London: William Hodge, 1933.

Booth, Michael R. (ed.), *English Plays of the Nineteenth Century*. 5 vols. Oxford: Clarendon Press, 1969–76.

   et al. The Revels History of Drama in English (Volume VI 1750–1880). London: Methuen & Co Ltd, 1975.

British Museum. Catalogue of Additions to the Manuscripts. Plays Submitted to the Lord Chamberlain 1824–1851: Additional Manuscripts 42865–43038. London, 1964.

Buckstone, John Baldwin. *Jack Sheppard. A Drama In Four Acts* (Webster's Acting National Drama, VII). [London, 1840].

   The Stone Jug. Dicks' Standard Plays, (London, [1874–1907]), no. 506.

Bunn, Alfred. *The Stage: Both Before and Behind the Curtain, From 'Observations Taken on the Spot'*. 3 vols. London, 1840.

Conolly, L. W. *The Censorship of English Drama 1737–1824*. San Marino, Calif.: Huntington Library, 1976.

Crean, P. J. 'The Stage Licensing Act of 1737', *Modern Philology*, XXXV (1938), 239–55.

Decker, C. R. 'Ibsen's literary reputation and Victorian taste', *Studies in Philology*, XXXII (1935), 632–45.

Donne, William Bodham. *Essays on the Drama*. London, 1858.

Donohue, Joseph. 'Burletta and the early nineteenth century theatre', *Nineteenth Century Theatre Research*, I (1973), 29–51.

   Theatre in the Age of Kean. Oxford: Basil Blackwell, 1975.

Downer, Alan S. *The Eminent Tragedian: William Charles Macready*. Cambridge, Mass. and London: Harvard University Press, 1966.

Duncan, Barry. *The St James's Theatre: Its Strange and Complete History, 1835–1957*. London: Barrie & Rockcliff, 1964.

'The Examiner of Plays', *All the Year Round*, N.S. XII (1874), 391–6.

'The Examinership of Plays', *The Theatre*, N.S. (April 1895), pp. 193–6.

Filon, Augustin. *The English Stage; Being an Account of the Victorian Drama*, trans. Frederic Whyte. London, 1897.

Findlater, Richard. *Banned! A Review of Theatrical Censorship in Britain*. London: Macgibbon & Kee, 1967.

Fitzball, Edward. *Thirty-Five Years of a Dramatic Author's Life*. 2 vols. London, 1859.

Fitzgerald, Percy. *The Kembles. An Account of the Kemble Family, including the lives of Mrs Siddons, and her brother, John Philip Kemble.* 2 vols. London, [1871].

A New History of the English Stage From the Restoration to the Liberty of the Theatres. 2 vols. London. 1882.

Fletcher, Richard M. *English Romantic Drama 1795—1843: A Critical History.* New York: Exposition Press, 1966.

Fowell, Frank, and Frank Palmer. *Censorship in England.* London: Frank Palmer, 1913.

Ganzel, Dewey. 'Patent wrongs and patent theatres: drama and the law in the early nineteenth century', *PMLA,* LXXVI (1961), 384—96.

Garnett, Edward. *The Breaking Point. A Censured Play, with a Preface and a Letter to the Censor.* London: Duckworth, 1907.

[Genest, John]. *Some Account of the English Stage, from the Restoration in 1660 to 1830.* 10 vols. Bath, 1832.

Gilbert, William Schwenk. See Tomline, F. Latour.

Gildersleeve, Virginia Crocheron. *Government Regulation of the Elizabethan Drama.* New York: Columbia University Press, 1908.

Grein, J. T. *Dramatic Criticism.* 5 vols. London, 1899—1903.

Haynes, James. *Mary Stuart: An Historical Tragedy, Now Performing at the Theatre Royal, Drury Lane.* 3rd edn. London, 1840.

Heinemann, William. *The First Step. A Dramatic Moment.* London, 1895.

Herbert, Sir Henry. *The Dramatic Records of Sir Henry Herbert, Master of the Revels, 1623—1673,* see Joseph Quincy Adams (ed.).

Hollingsworth, Keith. *The Newgate Novel, 1830—1847.* Detroit; Wayne State University Press, 1963.

Hook, Theodore. 'Recollections of the late George Colman', *Bentley's Miscellany,* I (1837), 7—16.

Johnson, Catharine B. (ed.), *William Bodham Donne and his Friends.* London: Methuen & Co., 1905.

Jones, Doris Arthur. *The Life and Letters of Henry Arthur Jones.* London: Victor Gollancz, 1930.

Jones, Henry Arthur. *The Renascence of the English Drama.* London, 1895.

Laurence, Dan H. (ed.). *Collected Letters 1874—1897.* London: Max Reinhardt, 1965.

Collected Letters 1898—1910. London: Max Reinhardt, 1972.

Law, William. *The Absolute Unlawfulness of the Stage Entertainment Fully Demonstrated.* London, 1726.

Lawrence, Elwood P. '"The Happy Land": W. S. Gilbert as political satirist', *Victorian Studies,* XV (1971—2), 161—83.

[Lister, T. H.]. 'Mr Sheridan Knowles's *Wife of Mantua* —state and prospects of the drama', *Edinburgh Review,* LVII (1833), 281—312.

Loewenberg, Alfred. *Annals of Opera, 1597—1940.* 2nd edn, rev. & corr., Geneva: Societas Bibliographica, 1955.

Lumley, Benjamin. *Reminiscences of the Opera.* London, 1864.

Macready, William Charles. *The Diaries of William Charles Macready, 1833—1851,* see Toynbee, William (ed.).

Matthison, Arthur. *A False Step.* London [1879].

Mayer, David, III. *Harlequin in his Element: The English Pantomime, 1806—1836.* Cambridge, Mass: Harvard University Press, 1969.

Meisel, Martin, 'Political extravaganza: a phase of the nineteenth-century British theater,' *Theatre Survey*, III (1962), 19—31.

Shaw and the Nineteenth-Century Theater. Princeton: Princeton University Press, 1963.

Morley, Henry. *Journal of a London Playgoer from 1851 to 1866*. London, 1891.

Newton, H. Chance. *Crime and the Drama; or, Dark Deeds Dramatised*. London: Stanley Paul, 1927.

Nicholson, Watson. *The Struggle for a Free Stage in London*. New York: Benjamin Blom, 1966 (reissue of Boston, 1906 edn).

Nicoll, Allardyce. *A History of English Drama, 1660—1900*. 6 vols. Cambridge: Cambridge University Press, 1965—7.

Olshen, Barry N. '*The Beaux Stratagem* of the nineteenth century stage', *Theatre Notebook*, XXVIII (1974), 70—80.

Palmer, John. *The Censor and the Theatres:* London: Fisher Unwin, 1912.

Peake, Richard Brinsley. *Memoirs of the Colman Family; including their Correspondence with the Most Distinguished Personages of their Time*. 2 vols in 1. London, [1841].

Pinero, Arthur Wing. *The Collected Letters of Sir Arthur Pinero*, see J. P. Wearing (ed.).

Planché, James Robinson. *The Recollections and Reflections of J. R. Planché: A Professional Autobiography*. 2 vols. London, 1872.

Price, Cecil. *Theatre in the Age of Garrick*. Oxford: Basil Blackwell, 1973.

Report from the Joint Select Committee of the House of Lords and the House of Commons on the Stage Plays (Censorship), in British Sessional Papers (1909), VIII, 459—905.

Report from the Select Committee on Dramatic Literature: With Minutes of Evidence, in *British Sessional Papers* (1831—2), VII, 1—252.

Report from the Select Committee on Public Houses & c; together with the Proceedings of the Committee, Minutes of Evidence, Appendix and Index, in *British Sessional Papers* (1852—3), XXXVII, 1—788.

Report from the Select Committee on Theatres and Places of Entertainment: together with the Proceedings of the Committee, Minutes of Evidence, and Index, in *British Sessional Papers* (1892), XVIII, 1—592.

Report from the Select Committee on Theatrical Licenses and Regulations; together with the Proceedings of the Committee, Minutes of Evidence, and Appendix, in *British Sessional Papers* (1866), XVI, 1—420.

[Robinson, Emma]. *The Prohibited Comedy. Richelieu in Love; or, The Youth of Charles I. An historical comedy. In Three Acts. By the Author of 'Whitefriars' &c. As Performed at the Theatre Royal, Haymarket, October 30th, 1852*. London, 1852.

Richelieu in Love; or, The Youth of Charles I. An historical comedy. In five acts. As accepted at the Theatre Royal, Haymarket, and prohibited by authority of the Lord Chamberlain. With a preface explanatory. London, 1844.

Roston, Murray. *Biblical Drama in England from the Middle Ages to the Present Day*. London: Faber & Faber, 1968.

Rowell, George. *The Victorian Theatre 1792—1914: A Survey*. 2nd edn. Cambridge: Cambridge University Press, 1978.

Schoonderwoerd, N. *J. T. Grein, Ambassador of the Theatre, 1862—1935*. Assen, Netherlands: Van Gorcum & Co., 1963.

Schultz, William Eben. *Gay's 'Beggar's Opera': Its Content, History & Influence.* New York: Russell & Russell, 1967 (reissue New Haven, 1923 edn).

Scott, Clement. *The Drama of Yesterday and Today.* 2 vols. London, 1899.

Shattuck, Charles H. 'E. L. Bulwer and Victorian censorship', *Quarterly Journal of Speech,* XXXIV (1948), 65—72.

(ed.), *Bulwer and Macready: A Chronicle of the Early Victorian Theatre.* Urbana, Illinois: University of Illinois Press, 1958.

Shaw, George Bernard. 'The censorship of the stage', *North American Review,* CLXIX (1899), 251—62.

Major Critical Essays. London: Constable, 1932.

Our Theatres in the Nineties. 3 vols. London: Constable, 1932.

Collected Letters 1874—1897, see Dan H. Laurence (ed.).

Collected Letters 1898—1910. See Dan H. Laurence (ed.).

Shee, Martin Archer. *Alasco: A Tragedy in Five Acts ... Excluded from the Stage, by Authority of the Lord Chamberlain.* London, 1824.

[Southey, Robert]. State and prospects of the French drama, *Quarterly Review,* LI (1834), 177—212.

Stephens, John Russell. 'William Bodham Donne: some aspects of his later career as Examiner of Plays', *Theatre Notebook,* XXV (1970—1), 25—32.

'*Jack Sheppard* and the licensers: the case against Newgate plays', *Nineteenth Century Theatre Research,* I (1973), 1—13.

Stottlar, James F. 'A Victorian stage censor: the theory and practice of William Bodham Donne', *Victorian Studies,* XIII (Mar. 1970), 253—82.

Thomas, Donald. *A Long Time Burning: The History of Literary Censorship in England.* London: Routledge & Kegan Paul, 1969.

Tomline, F. Latour [W. S. Gilbert] and Gilbert A'Beckett, *The Happy Land: A Burlesque Version of 'The Wicked World' ... First Performed at the Royal Court Theatre, March 3rd, 1873. Prohibited by the Lord Chamberlain, March 7th.* London, 1873.

Toynbee, William (ed.). *The Diaries of William Charles Macready, 1833—1851.* 2 vols. London: Chapman and Hall, 1912.

Vernon, Sally. '*Mary Stuart,* Queen Victoria, and the censor', *Nineteenth Century Theatre Research,* VI (1978), 35—40.

Wade, Thomas. *The Jew of Arragon; or, The Hebrew Queen. A Tragedy in Five Acts.* London, 1830.

Watson, Ernest Bradlee. *Sheridan to Robertson: A Study of the Early Nineteenth-Century London Stage.* Cambridge, Mass.: Harvard University Press, 1926.

Wearing, J. P. (ed.). *The Collected Letters of Sir Arthur Pinero.* Minneapolis: University of Minnesota Press, 1974.

INDEX

195

Scribe, Eugène: *Bertrand et Raton*, 44;
La Famille Riqueborg, 81; *La Muette
de Portici*, 170 n. 25; *Rodolphe*, 80
Second Mrs Tanqueray, The (Pinero),
143–5
Secret Passion, The, 51–2
Secrets of the Harem, 130–1
Séraphine (Sardou), 178 n. 33
Seven Champions of Christendom, The
(Planché), 53
Seymour, Francis Hugh George, 5th
Marquess of Hertford (Lord Cham-
berlain), 21, 136; acts against
indecent dresses, 133–4; appoint-
ment of, 21, 157; moral strictness
of, 22; prohibits can-can, 135;
refuses *Lords and Labourers*, 127
Shakespeare, William, 6, 41, 166 n. 37;
King Lear prohibited, 162 n. 7
Shaw, George Bernard, 1, 36, 113, 139,
140, 146–7, 156; *Mrs Warren's Pro-
fession*, 145–6; and the courtesan
play, 143–4; his wish to abolish
censorship, 154–5; on Pigott, 33–4;
on religious bigotry, 111
Shee, Martin Archer: *Alasco*, 18, 39–41,
115
Sheil, Richard Lalor, 169 n. 11
Shelley, Percy Bysshe: *The Cenci*, 140–2
Shelley Society, 138, 141–2
Sheridan, Richard Brinsley, 25, 115,
172 n. 51; *The School for Scandal*,
30, 136, 151
Shilly-Shally (Reade), 15
Sign of the Cross, The (Barrett), 113
Smith, Edward Tyrrell (manager), 128–9
Smith, Sydney, M.P., 150, 187 n. 57
Smollett, Tobias, 62
Sophocles: *Oedipus Tyrannus*, 177 n. 15
Soutar, Robert: (with Green) *Lothair*,
183 n. 13
Southey, Robert, 30; advocates control
of the stage, 37–8; attacks French
drama, 38, 81–2
Spedding, James, 29
Spencer, Earl, *see* Spencer, Frederick
Spencer, Frederick, 4th Earl Spencer
(Lord Chamberlain), 15, 157
Spencer, Herbert, 32
Stage Licensing Act (1737), 10, 11, 37,
166 n. 24; provisions of, 5–6, 7
Stage Society, 146
Standard Theatre, 72
Stanhope, Philip Dormer, 4th Earl of
Chesterfield, 1, 170 n. 17

Stewart, Mrs Duncan, 33
Still Waters Run Deep (Taylor), 30
Stirling, Edward: *Guido Fawkes*, 55;
Oliver Twist, 65
Stone Jug, The (Webster), 75–6
Storming of Comorn, The, 173 n. 66
Stout Gentleman, The, 80
Strafford (Browning), 48, 171 n. 39
Strand Theatre, 7, 13, 20, 100, 149, 183
n. 8
Strindberg, August, 156
Sullivan, Sir Arthur, *see Patience; Utopia
Limited*
Sultan, Turkish, 131
Supplice d'une Femme, Le (Dumas), 85,
137
Surrey Theatre, 7, 8, 65 , 66, 83, 128,
129; as refuge for suppressed play,
40–1; outspoken play at, 52
Swell Mobsman, The, 69
Sydney, Viscount, *see* Townshend, John
Robert

Talfourd, Sir Thomas Noon: *Ion*, 41
Talleyrand, Prince: caricatured, 44
Taylor, Thomas Prochis: *George
Barrington*, 67
Taylor, Tom 32, 124, 126; *Still Waters Run
Deep*, 30; *The Ticket-of-Leave Man*,
125; *'Twixt Axe and Crown*, 180 n. 17
Temple, Henry John, 3rd Viscount
Palmerston: pantomime reference
to, 116
Tennyson, Lord Alfred, 27, 29
Terry Tyrone (Pitt), 56
Thackeray, William Makepeace, 66, 79,
174 n. 12; on *Jack Sheppard*, 63–6
Theatre Act, *see* Theatre Regulation Act
Theatre Regulation Act (1843), 6, 7,
163 n. 21; provisions of, 9–11, 13
theatres: licensing of (in London), 6–8;
licensing of (in provinces), 162 n.
13; licensing irregularities in, 13,
15–16, 176 n. 45, 177 n. 22;
prostitution at, 92–3; safety
inspections of, 13–14, 21; violent
behaviour at, 37–8, 44, 54, 57, 115,
182 n. 2; *see also under* individual
theatres; minor theatres; patent
monopoly
Thieves' House, The (Atkyns), 69
Thirty Years of a Gambler's Life, 72
Thomas à Beckett (Jerrold), 8
Thomson, James, 166 n. 24
Thornhill, Sir James, 63

in BCh³

R0147208314   HUM   822.
                      809
       39.50   ST4

STEPHENS, JOHN RUSSELL
      CENSORSHIP OF
ENGLISH DRAMA 1824 1901

R0147208314   HUM   822.   8/02
                      809
                      ST4

HOUSTON PUBLIC LIBRARY

CENTRAL LIBRARY
500 MCKINNEY